Communications Writing and Design

Communications Writing and Design

The Integrated Manual for Marketing, Advertising, and Public Relations

John DiMarco, Ph.D.

WILEY Blackwell

This edition first published 2017
© 2017 John DiMarco

All rights reserved. No part of this publication may be reproduced, stored in a retrieval system, or transmitted, in any form or by any means, electronic, mechanical, photocopying, recording or otherwise, except as permitted by law. Advice on how to obtain permission to reuse material from this title is available at http://www.wiley.com/go/permissions.

The right of John DiMarco to be identified as the authors of the editorial material in this work has been asserted in accordance with law.

Registered Offices
John Wiley & Sons, Inc., 111 River Street, Hoboken, NJ 07030, USA

Editorial Office
1606 Golden Aspen Drive, Suites 103 and 104, Ames, Iowa 50010, USA

For details of our global editorial offices, customer services, and more information about Wiley products visit us at www.wiley.com.

Wiley also publishes its books in a variety of electronic formats and by print-on-demand. Some content that appears in standard print versions of this book may not be available in other formats.

Limit of Liability/Disclaimer of Warranty
While the publisher and authors have used their best efforts in preparing this book, they make no representations or warranties with respect to the accuracy or completeness of the contents of this book and specifically disclaim any implied warranties of merchantability or fitness for a particular purpose. It is sold on the understanding that the publisher is not engaged in rendering professional services and neither the publisher nor the author shall be liable for damages arising herefrom. If professional advice or other expert assistance is required, the services of a competent professional should be sought.

Library of Congress Cataloging-in-Publication Data

Hardback ISBN: 9781119118909
Paperback ISBN: 9781119118879

Cover Design: Wiley
Cover Images: (From Left to Right and Top to Bottom) © angellodeco/Shutterstock; © ESB Professional/Shutterstock; © Bosca78/Gettyimages; © alterfalter/Shutterstock; © Scanrail1/Shutterstock; © z_amir/Fotolia; © Brothers Good/Shutterstock; © B & T Media Group Inc./Shutterstock; © VLADGRIN/Gettyimages; Martin Bond/Alamy Stock Photo; © Rawpixel.com/Shutterstock; © VLADGRIN/Gettyimages; catalog, courtesy of author; © aleksandarvelasevic/Gettyimages; © Niloo/Shutterstock; © Artnis/Shutterstock; (Background) © jeremykramerdesign/Gettyimages

Set in 10/12pt WarnockPro by Aptara Inc., New Delhi, India

Printed in the United States of America

10 9 8 7 6 5 4 3 2 1

Contents

Acknowledgements *vii*
Foreword *ix*
Preface *xi*

1 The Connectivity between Research, Writing, and Design *1*

2 Writing Technical, Persuasive, and News Communication *9*

3 Communication Design *45*

4 Creative Research Methods *83*

5 Design Tools *103*

6 Marketing Projects *123*

7 Advertising Projects *145*

8 Public Relations Projects *163*

9 Social Media for Marketing, Advertising, and Public Relations *191*

Index *199*

Acknowledgements

My sincere love and thanks go to my family, Kim, David, and Jack, who are everything to me.

My sincere gratitude goes out to my mentor and dear friend, professor and New York Times Best Selling Author Dr. Frank Brady. Frank took time to review my ideas and proposals and graciously wrote the opening foreword. His kind, thoughtful encouragement and advice have been instrumental in my growth as a scholar and author over the past decade.

My colleagues and students at St. John's University are dear to me. They motivate me to tirelessly pursue knowledge, truth, and understanding.

My sincere appreciation goes out to the team at Wiley for collaborating with me on another academic work. A hearty thank you must go to my editor at Wiley, Haze Humbert, and the editorial team of Maddie Koufogazos, Kari Capone, and Dhanashree Phadate for being so very patient, gracious, and supportive during the project and the peer review. They really helped me construct my ideas into a valuable learning product that will benefit students and professionals in the creative industries.

I am blessed and grateful to present the work of my students, as well as the most celebrated, thoughtful, and iconic designers in the world in this textbook. The firms that contributed major work for this project include Pentagram, TurnStyle, and Milton Glaser, Inc. As well, other colleagues, archivists, and students provided their assistance along with photographs and designs. I am very thankful to the people who put their heart, soul, and creativity into these projects as I try to give them further breath as educational examples.

Thank you to all who contributed…

Claire Banks
Michael Bierut
Michael Calandra
Diana Colapietro
Kristen Crawford
Elise Cruz
Michael Gericke
Milton Glaser
Luke Hayman
Angus Hyland
Nick Heller
Natasha Jen
Megan Monfiston
Paula Scher
DJ Stout
Lisa Strausfeld
Brian Wallace
Steven Watson
Artianna Wynder

Foreword

Although it might sound like hyperbole, this book is truly meant for all writers and designers: professionals and beginners, academics and students, journalists and copywriters, marketing and advertising creators, speechwriters and public relations specialists, authors and essayists.

Red Smith, the Socrates of sportswriters who wrote a daily column for decades, was once asked whether writing was difficult. "Why, no," he said laconically. "You simply sit down at a typewriter, open your veins and bleed." The point is that if you find writing easy, you are probably doing it wrong. If you study or even dip into Dr. DiMarco's book, you will find it enormously helpful as it will ease any problems you may have in putting pen or computer to paper or screen.

John DiMarco knows how difficult writing can be: he has had spent decades solving problems as a writer and designer for corporations and for his own businesses and projects, and has incorporated everything he has learned and experienced into Communications Writing and Design. His methods have been successful not only among professionals but also in academe where he has taught students who aspire to be writers and designers, and to thousands of others at conferences and seminars.

You will find in this book such discussions as the elements of style, the grace of rhetoric, the details of how to create a press release. You'll learn how to construct and design copy for an advertisement, the keys to how to structure an annual report, the composition of fact sheets and media backgrounders, in addition to a myriad of other strategies and techniques that professional corporate copywriters need to know. DiMarco populates the book with real life examples, and includes fully illustrated solutions that you can apply to your own work. His explanation of research and conceptualization alone is worth the price of admission.

This is a book – a complete manual really – that belongs next to your computer and creative team. Over the years, I guarantee you will be earmarking it, highlighting passages, and writing in its margins all the things you will have learned. Plan to wear it out from constant and inevitable use.

Dr. Frank Brady

Preface

Objectives

In communications, writing and design educates, informs, persuades, and entertains audiences. With an increased need for content across disciplines, creative, perceptive students and industry professionals in marketing, advertising, and public relations prompted the creation of this book. The main goal is to help readers learn by fostering a valuable, directed approach to building knowledge and skills through theory, technique, and practice, using an array of industry-standard projects in the integrated communications fields of marketing, advertising, and public relations.

Marketing, advertising, and public relations rely on persuasive, technical, and news writing coupled with graphic design to create content. Today's most valued communications generalists must become writers who design, and designers who write, with a keen eye for aesthetics and a strong hand for prose, all in the pursuit of content creation.

After reading this book and following the exercises, you should be able to:

– Understand basic and important aspects of graphic design and persuasive writing.
– Evaluate vital aspects of design thinking and visual composition.
– Apply writing and design problem solving techniques.
– Synthesize visual design and written communication better during creative situations.
– Create successful communication pieces across marketing, advertising, and public relations.

Method

Taking a primer and project based approach; the book prescribes memorable problem-solving frameworks that teach both writing and design to students and professionals. Sourcing over one hundred references and images, this book serves as a beautifully useful deskside tool for the new or continuing marcom professional.

The main features of the book are:

- Chapter learning objectives – Rooted in the domains of Blooms' Revised Taxonomy (aka Bloom's Digital Taxonomy)
- Mnemonic Learning (BANGPP, GACMIST, GROWN, WWCCRR) – Helps you remember how
- Small relevant chunks – Gives referenced snippets of theory and applied knowledge that can be absorbed quickly

- Exploded Visual examples – Over 100 professionally written and designed project samples satiate your appetite for beautiful, unique images that are captioned with analysis of text, images, and design principles.
- Real Life Projects and Application – Illustrates solutions that can be used right away in your own work.
- Playbook style approach – Offers a quick reference resource and reference for future knowledge cravings.
- Chapter references – Provides a path for further exploration and learning with over 70 references to critical works.
- Chapter exercises and creative assignments – Reinforces learning with objectives-driven assignments
- Instructor website – provides a restricted access instructor exam bank with chapter slide decks and exams for easy adoption into courses.
- Student website – provides chapter slides and e-learning videos that help teach project design and development inside and outside of the classroom.

1

The Connectivity between Research, Writing, and Design

By limiting and filtering the visible, structure enables it to be transcribed into language.
Michel Foucault 1994

Chapter objectives
After completing this chapter, you should be able to: • understand differences and connections between a text, a document, and a work. • analyze how research and writing unites with design. • evaluate signs to determine their value on communication. • create a semiotic sign system to communicate an idea.

1.1 The anatomy of a text, a document, and a work

Let us begin by establishing a simple view of how research, writing, and design collide in creating communication for mass audiences by relating the collective analytical thoughts of sociologists, linguists, writers, designers, information scientists, and philosophers.

French researcher, sociologist, and author Roland Barthes (Barthes and Miller 1975, 64) called text "tissue", which he explains as "a product, a ready-made veil, behind which lies, more or less hidden meaning (truth)" and he purports that "text is made, is worked out in a perpetual interweaving". The perpetual interweaving of text in modern mass communication represents the endless, interdependent relationship between research, writing, and design. In the information science world, three main items represent the things we research, write and design; they are a text, a document, and "a work". The text is the sets of words that create writing. The document is the physical container where the text is recorded, and "a work" is the set of ideas embedded "into a document using text with the intention of being communicated to a receiver" (Smiraglia 2001, 3–4). In advertising, for example, we see this in writing lines of copy (text), that then go into individual advertisements (document), which then go into a campaign (a work). In book publishing, the lines of words become the text, while the text becomes the documents in the form of chapters and sidebars, and the chapters, front matter and indexes become the work in the form of a completed book that communicates a set of ideas.

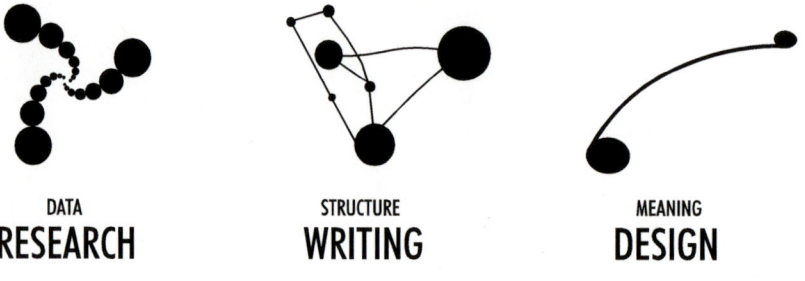

Figure 1.1 From Complex to simple. Text, document, and work are the result of research, writing, and design. Illustration by John DiMarco.

1.2 Research

Research offers methods to perform inquiry and observation that yield questions, data, and theories. It becomes the starting point for making meaning about something and spawns a desire to define a problem, get ideas, and then ultimately create form (Lupton and Phillips 2011). Research can be formal (structured and systematic) or informal (loose and divergent) and scholarly, building knowledge for knowledge's sake, or corporate, building knowledge for commerce's sake. Regardless of the type of research we use, once we can make meaning and build data, then we can begin to represent our ideas in written form. Research offers more than just data gathering on a formal level. It ignites inspiration of new concepts or magnifies clarification of what we think we know, especially when ideas swirl around inside our heads. In communication design, research generates data (text) and data becomes food for generating content (document), thus designed into a final communication product (a work) for advertising, marketing, and public relations.

Figure 1.2 Data drives campaigns. The "Truth" campaign uses hard data in the form of statistics to persuade young adults to stop smoking. The website and ads encourage millennials to be the generation that disavows smoking by showing a statistical trend leaning to success and feasibility, thus empowering them as group to be seen as making a historical contribution to society. www.truth.com.

Data in action

Data generated by research and can be qualitative, which means that it is narrow, patterned, thematic, and represented by words or images. Alternatively, data can be quantitative, which is broad, statistical, generalized, and represented by numbers. Data is critical in public relations, advertising, and marketing as it drives business decisions and vital to creating targeted, persuasive content and messages. In these disciplines, the secondary research, survey methods, interviews, and the focus group become sources of hard data, which require numbers (quantitative), and patterned themes (qualitative) interpreted into meaning for communications. One example is the anti-smoking ads put out in the "TRUTH" campaign, which hammers the quantitative notion that only 7% of young adults smoke, and that this generation could be the one that can ensure that tobacco smoking disappears among that group.

1.3 Writing

When we write, whether it is an essay or advertisement copy, we are designing within a system. Writing uses either an ideographic system or a phonetic system (de Saussure et al. 2005). The ideographic writing system uses symbols. An example of this type of system is Chinese. The phonetic writing system is based on sounds, which occur in words built from letters in an alphabet that represent those sounds, such as with English. Both systems richly communicate ideas, generate stories, and persuade people.

The two writing systems differ in their basis. Ideographic systems such as Chinese rely sole on marks, whereas the phonetic system utilizes sounds.

Linguistic value

Graphic design authors Lupton and Miller (2008, 53) highlight Structuralism scholar Ferdinand de Saussure's principle of linguistic value as "the identity of a sign rests not in the sign itself, but on its relation to other signs in the system." They cite the example of the sound *cow*. Saussure recognized that there is no link between sound and concepts, meaning that the signifier (the sound) does not adhere to the signified (the mental concept). The sign alone is empty; there is no natural meaning when we say cow in relationship to the image of a cow. Saussure distinguishes when we say the word *cow*, the sound only becomes recognizable within a system of the same words, like now, bow, chow,

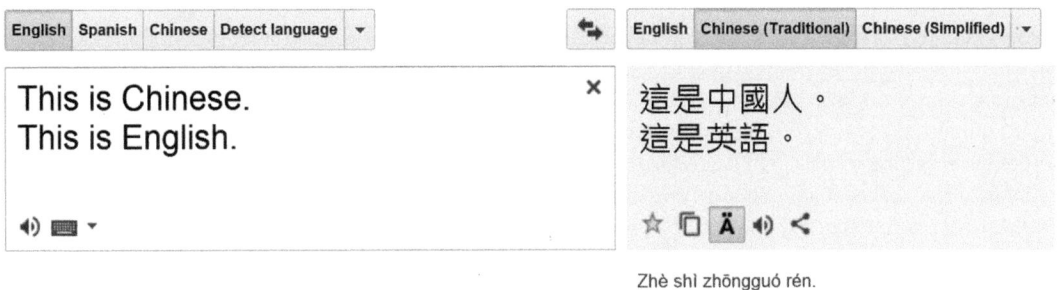

Figure 1.3 Writing systems and symbols. Screenshot from Google Translate.

Figure 1.4 Linguistic value moves across image, text, and sound.

and so on. Alternatively, the concept becomes recognizable as opposition to other concepts within a system. *Cow* has meaning when it is opposite horse, chicken, and moose. The clear summary of this is when Saussure states (p. 118) "In the language itself, there are only differences," which leads us to see writing, typography, and design with the connected ideas of research as structural components in yielding meaning.

Understanding the concept of linguistic value provides an important takeaway for creative professionals. Lupton and Miller's essay on the modernist view of letters touts typography "as the endless manipulation of abstract elements." So now, we know that characters have no meaning unless seen within the relationship to other characters across the alphabet, and words are abstract, gaining linguistic value when they are the system of the sentence. Using this same path of reason, when we write or design, we are assembling text and/or images to create linguistic value in the form of oppositions on a page or screen. These oppositions create meaningful content.

1.4 Design

Graphic communication and design thinking provide visual and applied methods to solving problems across education, persuasion, entertainment, and information domains (DiMarco 2010). In marketing, advertising, and public relations, the persuasion industries, we design "works," which are initiated by "projects" on the job, in order to solve problems that contribute to things like sales figures, reputation, employees, customers, vendors, the government, charities, social causes, and other issues that need a voice. The relationship between type and image has ancient roots, but truly came to develop, as the natural world was classified and recorded in the late seventeenth century.

Form as meaning

Medieval manuscripts present rich detail and vivid connections between writing and design, showing great innovation between artists and designers in combining letters with images (Meggs 1989). In addition, the connection between research, writing, and design has a strong foundation in the classification of natural history. We see this described by Foucault (1994) as he explained the extension of the object in recording of nature. The recording of natural things systematically, was put forth as a way to move into the classical age, beyond the late 1600s in which descriptions were expressed in words by experiences, rather than by "undertaking meticulous examination of things and then of transcribing what it has gathered in smooth, neutralized, faithful words" (Foucault 1994, 131). The new approach was considering the proper object, image elements, and order, with consideration to the meaning it conveys in a language. Meaning can be affected by four variables: "the form of the elements, the

Figure 1.5 The use of design to illustrate biology goes back to the origins of science. This modern day example shows how beautiful and meaningful the connection between text and image can be. Design by D.J. Stout, Pentagram. Reproduced with kind permission of Pentagram.

quantity of the elements, the way they are distributed in space, and the relative magnitude of each element" (Foucault 1994, 134), each contributing to critical visual understanding, whether it is text, image, or both together. Design began to matter more in the realm of communicating complex ideas such as describing biology, both textually and visually, to record the most accurate account of that structure at that time, making classification more meaningful. This approach forged salient content creation in the arts and sciences and guided graphic communication in commercial, industrial, and technical disciplines.

Icon, index, symbol

Semiotics is an analytical tool used by linguists, anthropologists, and communication theorists in the study of signs and interpretation of information. The principles of semiotics, founded by Charles S. Pierce, has fueled intellectual directions in psychology, anthropology, literature, and art (Lupton 2011), which has led to a way to design meaning systems and touch points for brands. Understanding the three kinds of sign: icon (represents something), index (points to something), and symbol (abstracts something) is important to writers and designers because we use them to create meaningful works that span scholarly and commercial projects. Icons are clear representations of things, indexes are related things and point to them, and words are abstract because they do not have a real meaning unless we make that connection through opposition via context, so icons become the most literal of all signs due to the fact that we can make meaning immediately.

Figure 1.6 Marrying text and image requires great care and can illicit precise meaning as we see with the Franklin Mills logotype and brandmark created by legendary graphic designer Milton Glaser. The image of a kite, with a lightning bolt nested inside, together offer an icon representing exploration and innovation. The graphic provides an index, pointing to Benjamin Franklin, cleverly connecting to our elementary history and science lessons with the geography of the iconic shopping mall. The final element, the logotype symbol is words, which lose abstraction when added to mark.

1.5 Summary

The inter-dependence between research, writing, and design gives us a creative holy trinity that generates text, documents, and works. Theoretically, this content becomes successful by initiating relationships between content and viewer knowledge. As writers and designers, we must understand how people make sense of text as tissue, the interpretation of sign, linguistic value, and the alliance between type and image. Keeping these ideas relevant to our process and output creates better connectivity between content, context, and meaning.

1.6 Chapter exercises

1 Sign designs

Taking things and representing them in multiple signs (icon, index, and symbol) is the job of the marketing, advertising, and public relations professional. Build your conceptual thinking skills by using semiotics as a guide in creating a series of rough drawings or computer illustrations that make meaningful icons and indexes for the abstract symbols (words) below. Use any methods you wish: pencil sketches and drawing, cutouts from magazines and collage, photos elements, or any other media you wish to explore. Combine words to expand the designs (flower child or bee man, for examples). Discuss these designs within your team or class to gain feedback on the effectiveness of the concepts. Then try creating your own word list to apply the technique further.

- flower
- bee
- car
- phone
- bird
- elephant
- man
- woman
- child

2 Putting research, writing, and design in action
Use research, writing, and design to put data in action by developing a simple, three sign infographic on one of the topics below. You should perform research on government, academic, or non-profit websites to gain meaningful statistics on your topic, which you will use for the assignment. Then, write a one-line description that clearly states what the statistic is about and who is affected by what it represents. Next, find an image that explicitly makes meaning of who is affected in an iconic way (represents it) and an image that makes meaning in an indexical way (points to it). Place the numbers and images together to create an infographic (a work) within any software program that allows you place text and images on a page. Look at other infographics online to get inspiration. Print or post and discuss with others in your group or class.

– hunger
– homelessness
– poverty
– income inequality
– climate change

Chapter references

Barthes, Roland, and Richard, Miller. 1975. *Pleasure of the Text*. New York: Hill and Wang.
De Saussure, F., Charles, Bally, Albert, Sechehaye, Albert, Riedlinger, and Roy, Harris. 2005. *Course in General Linguistics*. London: Duckworth.
Foucault, Michel. 1994. *The Order of Things*. New York: Vintage Books.
Lupton, Ellen, and Abbott, J. Miller. 2008. *Design Writing Research: Writing on Graphic Design*. London: Phaidon.
Lupton, Ellen, and Jennifer Cole Phillips. 2011. *Graphic Design Thinking: Beyond Brainstorming*. Baltimore: MD Institute College of Art.
Meggs, Philip B. 1989. *Type and Image: The Language of Graphic Design*. New York: Van Nost.
Schenker, Marc. 2010. "Trump Campaign Rebrands after Web Reacts." Webdesigner Depot. http://www.webdesignerdepot.com/2016/07/trump-campaign-rebrands-after-web-reacts/ (accessed November 12, 2016).
Smiraglia, Richard P. 2001. *The Nature of "a Work": Implications for the Organization of Knowledge*. Lanham, MD: Scarecrow Press.

2

Writing Technical, Persuasive, and News Communication

You'll never make your mark as a writer unless you develop a respect for words and a curiosity about their shades of meaning that is almost obsessive.

Zinsser 2006

Chapter objectives

After completing this chapter, you should be able to:

- apply research strategies to writing.
- identify and define how news writing, persuasive copywriting, and technical writing drive marketing communications.
- apply newswriting, technical writing, and persuasive copywriting techniques to print and web projects.
- analyze how marketing communications writing connects to design.
- remember syntax-critical grammar rules.
- create simple writing pieces exhibiting technical, persuasive, and news focus.

2.1 Writing for "Marcom" touchpoints

Non-fiction writing is a tool used throughout the creative process from note taking, to thumb nailing, to reporting, and to designing. The persuasion, style, and arrangement of words that fill an array of designs in marketing, advertising, and public relations create communication for commerce and cause. Writing shepherds creativity into form. In "Marcom " or "IMC," which is short for integrated marketing communications, we write persuasively and use digital design to make a final communication product that is generally labeled by industry folks as: "work," "piece," "vehicle," "media," "project," "design," "spot," "campaign," "publication," 'output,' "deliverable," or "production." Each "Marcom" product becomes a touchpoint for the brand, which according to Wheeler (2009, 3) is "an opportunity to increase awareness and build customer loyalty." Touchpoints are scattered across marketing, advertising, public relations, and sales promotion in many forms from the simplest email to the most elaborate campaign. Planning and problem solving lead to new creative projects that brand the organization by providing navigation in understanding products, reassurance that the consumer has made the right choice, and engagement through images, language, and meaning (Wheeler 2009).

Communications Writing and Design: The Integrated Manual for Marketing, Advertising, and Public Relations,
First Edition. John DiMarco.
© 2017 John DiMarco. Published 2017 by John Wiley & Sons, Ltd.

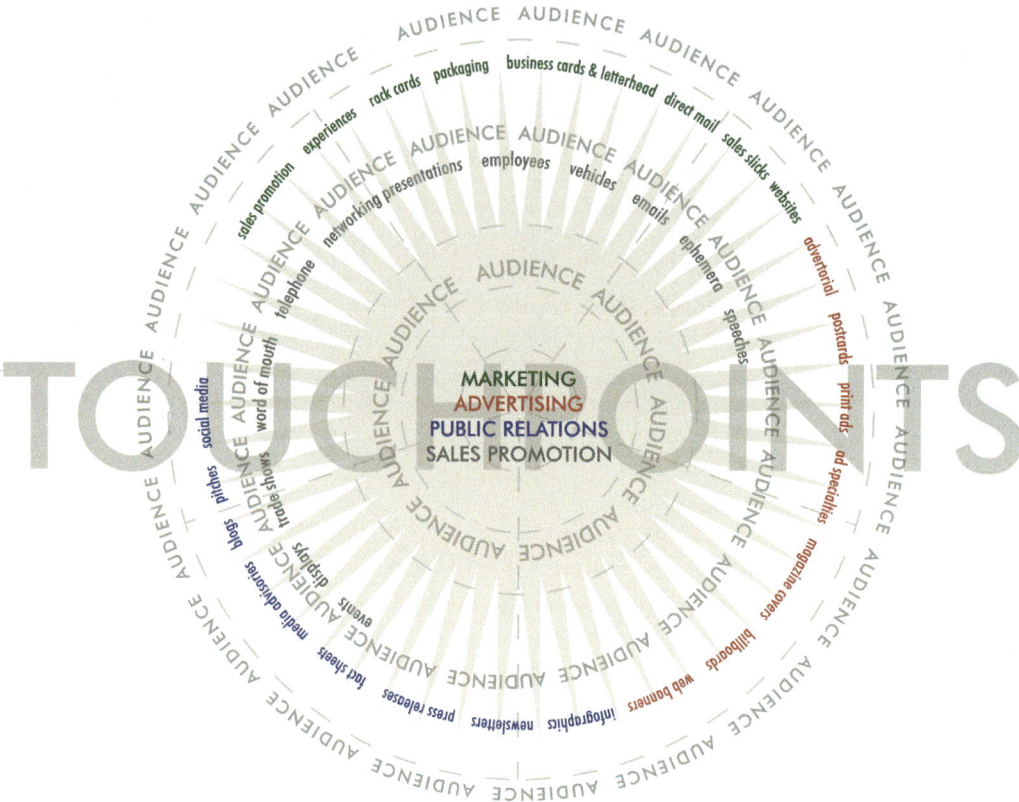

Figure 2.1 Integrated communications touchpoints use technical, persuasive, and news writing.

These components solicit and ignite manipulation of the mind by using persuasion principles to create unwavering brand loyalty and bring people to action. Persuasive writing makes things happen and is truly about "finding the most natural way to communicate" (Shaw 2012, 11).

2.2 Effecting persuasion

Persuasive writing is a challenge because ultimately, measurement comes from the actions of the reader. Persuasion gets someone to do something or think something because of what was said, done, or shown in a delivered message. Rhetoric, the art of communication, creates a seduction using words and images that alter persuasion (Lupton 2011). According to Aristotle's work, *Rhetoric*, from 350 B.C.E., the three means of effecting persuasion are first "to reason logically"; second "to understand human character and goodness in their various forms"; third, "to understand emotions-that is to name them and describe them, to know their causes and the way in which they are excited."

Modern-day communication theorists Pettyand Cacioppo (1986) offer the Elaboration Likelihood Model of persuasion that offers the idea that people process information on a boundary of effort based on their need for cognition, which is "thinking time." Some people spend lots of time making decisions and "elaborate" on the decision based on information quality and quantity. These

Identification of ideas, events, opinions, and points of view directly relating to target groups and audiences.	**Trust** from sources that have perceived familiarity, such as celebrities, physicians, lawyers, and athletes.	**Clarity** of message that is clear, simple, and short fits into a "sound-bite" package for mass dissemination.	**Action** must be suggested early and conveniently initiated so gratification can be obtained fast and frequently.

effecting persuasion

Callout 2A Identification, trust, clarity, and action are strategies for effecting persuasion (adapted from Bivins (2011)). Design by Luke Hayman, Pentagram. Reproduced with kind permission of Pentagram.

Figure 2.2 Identification, trust, clarity, and action are evident in this advertisement for the Public Theater. Design by Paula Scher. Reproduced with kind permission of Pentagram.

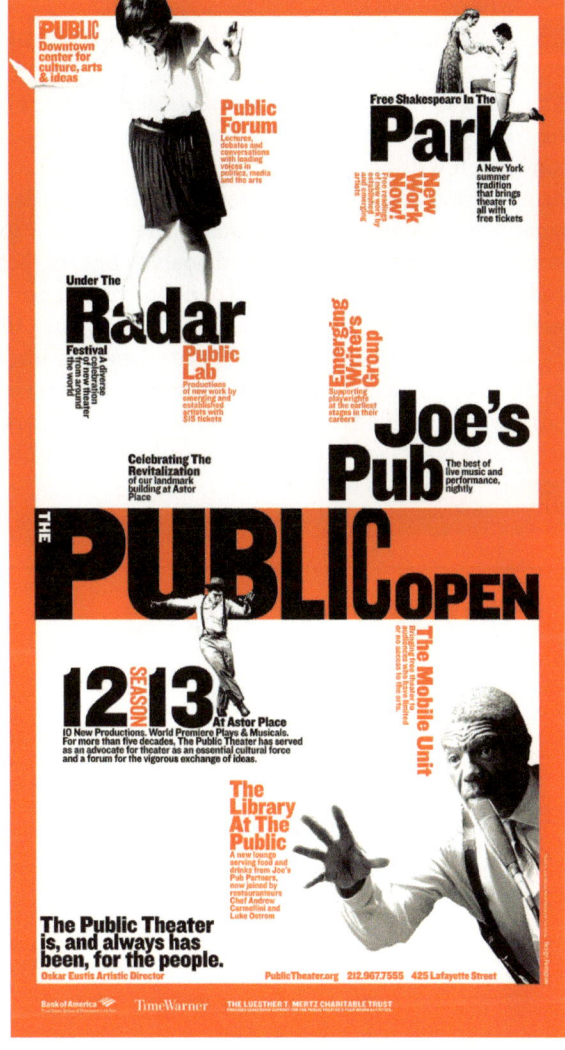

folks take a *central route*. The other side of the model is the *peripheral route*, where people decide quickly based on cues, which are messages and data that do not have much meaning on the real decision, like celebrity endorsement or emotional messages. Audiences make decisions both ways on the continuum depending on education levels, knowledge levels, and emotional states. Messages in the persuasion domains try to position the viewer into taking one route over another. Think about a 30-second ad vs. the white paper.

These ways to persuade are quite valuable to understand and remember when writing for marketing, advertising, and public relations, and should literally guide you. Aristotle teaches us that by using rational reasoning, emotional appeal, or human connection, we can persuade people to buy, act, and believe in something, which are the main objectives of marketing communications. To be persuasive, we need facts, and the way to get them is through research.

2.3 Getting raw material for writing projects

Writing in all forms requires raw materials to use as the ingredients in making words come to life in the roles of explanation, education, and suggestion. Raw materials for producing effective, factual non-fiction writing relies upon research to generate data. In marketing communications, various forms of research yield data used in writing and design of all pieces. Formal research needs to be systematic, using reliable, repeatable methods to capture and analyze data consistently and transparently. Research needs targeted goals to ensure that what is under study is what should indeed be studied, which yields validity. Mix and match quantitative and qualitative methods to decide the best method(s) suited to yielding valuable data for use in marketing communications pieces. Combining qualitative and quantitative approaches to research is a mixed methods approach. Using mixed methods often yields the richest information by revealing different data sets to build numerical and narrative data (Creswell 2003). We use data in marketing communications to help create rational persuasive messages and in the presentation of content in the form of text, which can be technical, persuasive, or news writing.

building data

Client View
briefs
historical research
observations
interviews

User View
heuristic evaluation
copy testing
usability testing

Statistics
databases
reports
websites

Theories
article reviews
book reviews

Quotes & Headlines
content analysis
observations
interviews

Experiences
observations
interviews
focus groups
diaries
case studies

Callout 2B Ways to build data sets for writing and design.

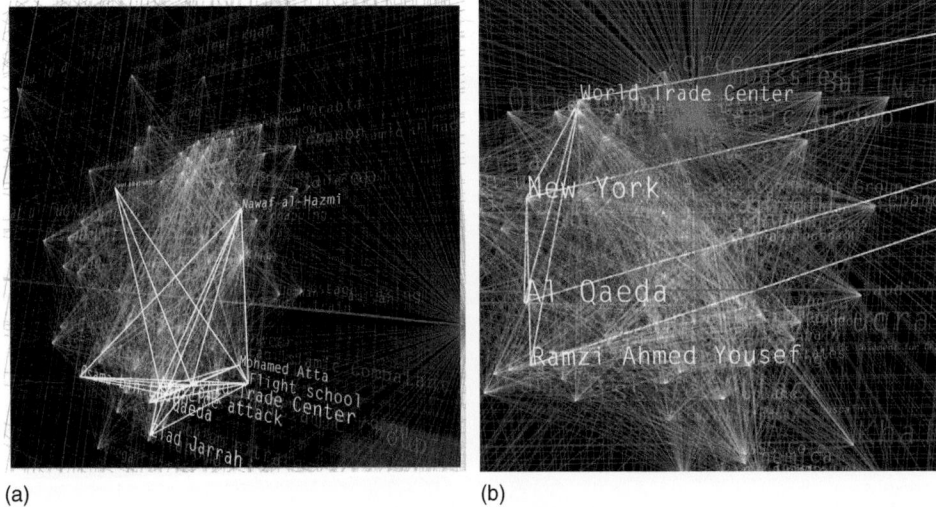

Figure 2.3 **a and b.** Visualizations marry data, writing, and design to make sense and connection of complex information through visual space. Design by Lisa Strausfield. Reproduced with kind permission of Pentagram.

2.4 Marketing communications writing: technical, persuasive, and news

We need three different styles as writers of marketing communications pieces. The variety of projects and subject matter that we work on across touchpoints demands a keen understanding of technical writing, persuasive copywriting, and newswriting. Understanding how to write in these styles is essential in completing marketing communications projects across industries, media, and client types. Let us break them down to see what is unique about each writing approach, when you use them, and what you should focus on in order to execute each soundly and productively.

2.5 Technical writing

Around 1899 engineering schools began establishing separate English departments to serve the unique needs of engineering students, spawning the first book on technical writing in 1908, titled *A Guide to Technical Writing*. (Eilola 2004). Soon after, other books followed and technical writing expanded into technical communication, which focuses not only writing science and technical materials, but also combines research, planning, design, and production into the skills and expertise of the practitioner. Clients in science, technology, healthcare, environmental, and manufacturing need skilled technical writing to generate content across print and web media.

Technical communication

Communication vehicles such as brochures, websites, white papers, manuals, packaging, and reports require writers who can accurately, usefully, and concisely translate technical terms and jargon into meaningful communication. Blake and Bly (1993, 3) define technical writing used for "the

Figure 2.4 Corporations, agencies, and organizations engaged in science and technology products, services, and causes use technical writing in their communications vehicles. IBM and the IBM logo are trademarks of International Business Machines Corp., registered in many jurisdictions worldwide.

literature of science, technology, and systems development" and they classify it as different from persuasive copywriting and news writing. Technical writing becomes *technical* when subject matter is in some specialized area of science or technology, and that subject matter and the text that is written in many cases becomes part of the marketing communications materials like trade advertisements, direct mail, training, and product manuals. Technical writing, news writing, and persuasive writing intertwine in many of the same communication vehicles and require the writer to consider fundamentals of both approaches to bear effective communication that meets the goals of the project and the organization. Can you think of companies that sell technical products and use technical writing in their marketing communications collateral? If you answered with the brands you probably know like Google, IBM, Apple, and Sony, you were right.

Key rules in technical writing and technical communication

There are certain key rules that are unique to technical writing and technical communication. Here are several key rules on technical writing derived from the works of Blake and Bly (1993), Brusaw, Alred, Brusaw, and Oliu (1976), and Lay (2000) that isolate important execution elements.

Figure 2.5 Technical writing is the core writing style in technical communication, practiced by corporations, agencies, and organizations engaged in science and technology products, services, and causes. Here, this dog-eared Lego manual offers the framing, preparation, and steps needed to complete the task and create the intended design – without needing words.

Writing must be accurate and useful

The person who is using the information offered in your technical writing is doing so for a number of important reasons including research, contemplating a purchase, or operating equipment. As well, in training situations safety and compliance is at stake; if inaccurate information poisons the writing, it could be deadly. In all cases, providing accurate, correct information relevant to learning and information-gathering success is mission critical, which means that if it fails, the project could fail. *remember*: Always have multiple editing checkpoints to insure accuracy (Blake and Bly 1993).

When there are steps to follow, there is process, which requires explanation and guidance; this requires technical writing. Explaining a process requires you to first frame the reasons for performing the process in the opening paragraph. Then, explain any necessary preparations. Finally, thoughtfully

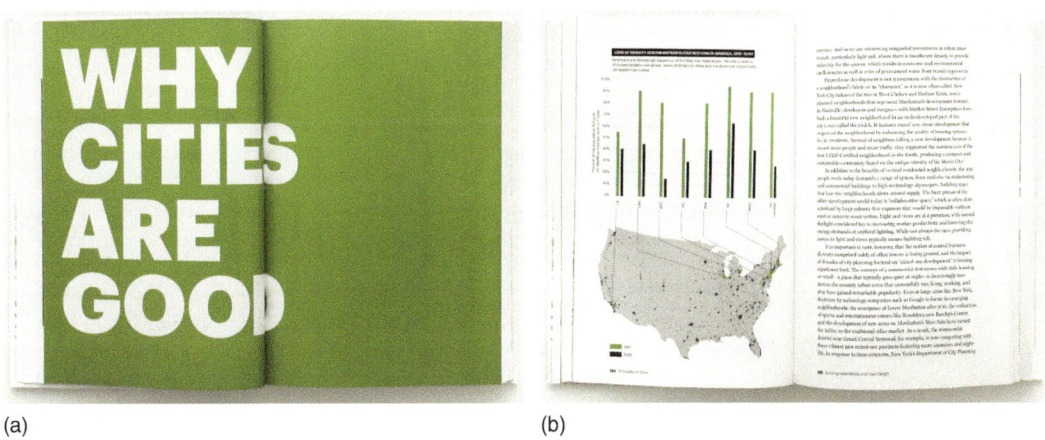

(a) (b)

Figure 2.6 **a and b** Statistics reveal new meaning about the relevance of the data to the reader in the form of well-designed graphics. A collaboration of design, writing, data, and publishing, Pentagram's Michael Bierut and Britt Cobb worked on the design of the book with SHoP Architects' Omar Toro-Vaca and Ryan Lovett, and Metropolis Books publisher Diana Murphy.

Table 2.1 The use of order is critical in technical communication and non-fiction writing. This list is adapted from Blake and Bly (1993, 18–19), who identified common formats for organizing technical material.

Location order	Use location order when proximity is of prime importance. For example, write about science based on relevant knowledge, such as starting a written piece on planets beginning with Mercury and ending with Pluto so that you begin closest to the sun and end with the last planet (p. 18).
Difficulty order	Use difficulty order when learning activities are involved. For example, explain a process beginning with the simplest task and move toward more advanced techniques. This is evident in explaining drawing, which most books begin by first explaining contouring and rough sketching, then moving on to the more difficult aspects of drawing, which are shading and detail (p. 18).
Sequential order	Use sequential order when activities require instruction that relies on following a specific order, such as in equipment installation or setting up a technical product. For example, when explaining the sequence to reboot up a network router and cable modem, which items need to be unplugged or reset becomes paramount to success (p. 18).
Alphabetical order	Use alphabetical order to logically arrange and index a data set with no order that needs a catalog reference. For example, a vendor directory or media list could use this order or a catalog, plan, or brochure might use it in its layout and table of contents (p. 18).
Chronological order	Use chronological order to present events, history, meeting reports, and other time-centric works. For example, history books use chronology and so do case studies and white papers (p. 18).
Problem/solution order	Use problem/solution order with proposals, research, and case studies. Begin with identifying the problem and end with recommending the solution. For example, a product description, marketing text, or advertising copy may need to explain a unique selling proposition position, which makes a product better than another product. One hypothetical case would be showing how brand X cleaned tough stains on clothes 20% faster than brand Y because of special chemical additives. This shows how the product provided a solution to the problem (p. 19).
Inverted pyramid order	Use the inverted pyramid to present the essential facts first … who, what, where, when, why and (sometimes) how in the first paragraph and then weave in the lesser facts in the next paragraphs from most important down to least. For example, reporting on a topic for news materials, articles, memos, and company reports benefit from this order. Use this order in news writing for public relations and journalism (p. 19).
Deductive order	Use the deductive order when you have a generalization that you want to support with facts, evidence and research findings in works including research papers, white papers, and political communications. For example, a writer composing an environmental piece could offer a general statistic, such as xx% of scientists surveyed agree that climate change is real and then cite journal research that identifies temperature changes and flood zones due to melting Arctic ice (p. 19).
Inductive order	Use the inductive order when you are drawing conclusions based on multiple stories or examples based on those personal accounts. For example, a company may have a journalist, publicist, or industry expert write a feature article for a trade-journal that espouses the virtues of certain technologies that have provided parallel success or results to a host of businesses or individuals (p. 19).
List order	Use the list order when you are providing a series of distinct, separate order. Break up points by using subheads, bullets, letters, or numbers. Remember that bullets do not imply a rank, but numbers and letters do. For example, use the bulleted list format for writing fact sheets, resumes, item lists, and slide content (p. 19).

provide useful steps written in small chunks and offer sequence leading to a result. The steps can be numbered or unnumbered and have written descriptions or simply just images representing the steps visually. Use order systems to break down difficult materials so that the reader sees the path to understanding through structure (Alred, Brusaw, and Oliu 1976).

Remember: Frame the reasons, prepare, and explain in chunks.

Use visuals that show data and clarify meaning
Visuals, in all types of communication, show something. In technical communication, visuals drive understanding of complex information. We call these *visualizations.* They help yield answers to unspoken reader questions by allowing data to be more easily absorbed (Lay 2000).

Remember: If there is an image that can valuably represent the data, use it to communicate the main point better.

Use the imperative mood, to tell people what to do
Write instructions and other information documents in the imperative mood, which is the most direct language possible. The imperative becomes active by using verbs at the beginning of the sentence, rather than burying them passively in the middle. You want your technical writing to command action with concrete verbs activating nouns (Blake and Bly 1993; Lay 2000).

Remember: Activate verbs and be imperative.

Here is an example of how to transform sentences to the active voice.

Passive
Instructions and other information documents *are written* in the imperative, which is the most direct language possible.

See the problem: ARE WRITTEN makes this passive and does not activate the verb. When you put the verb and the noun close together, at the front of the sentence, the sentence activates.
Fix the problem: Action activation…move the verb (write) to the beginning of the sentence.

Write instructions and other information documents in the imperative mood, which is the most direct language possible.

Use order to organize material of all types (Blake and Bly 1993, 18–19)
Order comes in different forms, depending on the type of technical information. Understanding different ways to write about order is essential to providing information in a useful, consistent manner. Order is about organization and structure; master it for truly effective technical, persuasive, and news writing. *Remember*: Outline early to get order into your work.

2.6 Persuasive copywriting

Persuasive copywriting is about developing a core message that finds its way into the mind of the consumer and prompts them to act. One of the first masters of persuasive copywriting was Richard Sears (2015), who used printed mailers to advertise his watches and jewelry way back in 1888 (searsarchives.com). Other pioneers in persuasive copywriting were people like W.A. Dwiggin who

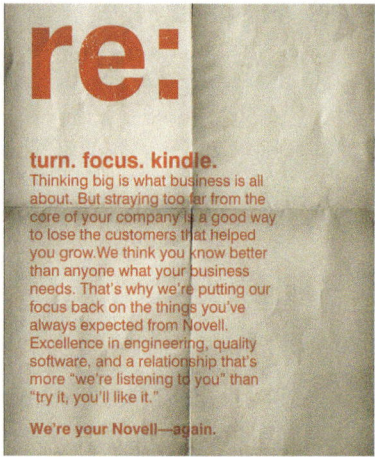

Figure 2.7 Good persuasive copywriting grabs the reader and makes them look closer. Notice the "you" viewpoint " being used to "reconnect" with a vibrant customer base. Design by Turnstyle. Reproduced with kind permission of Turnstyle.

coined the term advertising design as early as 1922 as commercial art became a standalone profession (White 2007). The modern age of persuasion brought in are the infamous mad men who made advertising creatives the rock stars of the business and social world. Copy gurus like Leo Burnett, Bill Bernbach, and David Ogilvy moved copywriting and creative prose to new heights during the 1950s, 1960s, 1970s, and 1980s and were influential icons that helped further the idea that language is a key element in design and that words matter in making things happen. Using a delicate combination of emotion, facts, and suggestion, good copywriting educates and solidifies communication between the consumer and brand, without eschewing the writer's personal opinions. In simple terms, persuasive writing should be interesting, convincing, and believable, a tenet put forth by E. St. Elmo Lewis):

> "The mission of an advertisement is to attract a reader, so that he will look at the advertisement and start to read it; then interest him, so that he will continue to read it; then to convince him, so that when he has read it he will believe it." (1903, 124)

Persuasive copywriting embeds itself in many touchpoints using brand language, which is a conglomerate of words, structures, values, and purpose that come together to create a campaign. Copywriters work closely with designers and account managers to build creative strategy for the client that establishes the touchpoints. A tool for advertising, corporate identity, product design, promotion, and marketing, persuasive copywriting sells a product or service, but can also sell an idea or a candidate; such is the case in political or institutional advertising.

Writing to sell using FAB and USP

Making a connection with the reader to establish communication that drives commerce requires emotional and rational messages. To bring the reader closer to the subject, we educate, stimulate, and translate FAB and USP so that we can create copy that makes things happen.

FAB (features, advantages, and benefits). The features describe the factual components of a product or service, while the advantages offer reasons to use the product or service over another method or product, and benefits are what the product or service does to help the user because of the features. According to master copywriter Robert (Bob) Bly, writing copy that sells is to write first about benefits, rather than pushing features (2006).

Table 2.2 Persuasive copywriting FAB and USP table.
You should try this exercise with a familiar product to begin to think in FAB terms when taking about a product. Here is a FAB and USP list for the website PortfolioVillage.com, which provides a do-it-yourself (DIY) website builder.

Features	Benefits	Advantages (USP)
PortfolioVillage provides Free hosting and a web SiteMaker	Eliminates financial obstacles to creating a website	More accessible than fee based systems
PortfolioVillage provides a graphic design environment in a DIY shell for creating websites	Allows robust design features with do-it-yourself simplicity	Better design tools and content resources than academic systems for creating web portfolios and websites

USP (the unique selling proposition). It is the "advantage" in FAB and is also known as "position." The USP offers product or service advantages over another method or product (Malickson and Nason 1982). It is, in essence a proposition to have someone buy because it is better. Uniqueness becomes the USP. It is the brand advantage and is what makes the product and service different from the competition and says "what the competition cannot say or is not saying at the present time" (Malickson and Nason 1982, 62). USPs are generated by first understanding the client through the briefing process, then understanding audience and competition through research, and finally by understanding how the product or service solves a problem better than another solution through analysis.

Here is a technique for building a FAB and USP platform for your writing. Create a three-column list that presents features first, benefits next, and then advantages in the last column. After doing some research on a product, complete the FAB list by describing the most compelling features, then the benefit and finally the advantage it may have over other methods or competitors.

Key rules in persuasive copywriting

Here are some key rules on persuasive copywriting derived from the works of the Rule of Three Copywriting Studio (2015), Mark Shaw (2012), DiMarco (2010), Drewniany and Jewler (2011), Malickson and Nason (1982), and Bendinger (2009).

Always draft a brief before creating (DiMarco 2010; Shaw 2012)
You should always work from a creative brief, which is a summary of information from the client and research, before you start to design or write. The brief can take on different forms for different purposes. The most common types for persuasion writing are the copy brief and the design brief. The core elements of the copy brief should include an audience profile, core message, and why the target audience should be interested. For design briefs, the main components are goals, audience, concept, message, image, style, and theme, easily remembered by the acronym developed by DiMarco, GACMIST. You can, and will edit the brief as things change in the project and scope of work. Chapter 4 covers briefs.

Create headlines with strong creative hooks (Drewniany and Jewler 2011)
The headline has one purpose, which is to grab attention and turn a glance into an immersive experience for the viewer. Headlines enhance visuals and lure the casual viewer into a commitment to read persuasive body copy. Types of headlines include direct benefit, factual, curiosity, news, command,

question, repetition, word play, and figures of speech. Ask if the headline is selling what it is intended to sell and how it plays across multiple media, including social. Is the headline oo long to Tweet? Use these types as a guide when you are trying to come up with headline ideas. Keep refining and editing your headlines until they are mercilessly clear, informative, and engaging.

Find words that work using concentric circle technique (DiMarco 2010; Curtis, 2002)

The concentric circle technique helps isolate words that connect to the emotional center of the viewer. The words become keywords in the establishment of concepts and campaigns and lend themselves to inclusion into a brand word bank, which is a collection of valuable words for usage in touchpoints and brand expression across media. Create a list of words that represent the experiences, problems, and needs of the audience. Then, using a four-ring circle, place the words that are most emotional and connected close to the center. This will help isolate terms that will pierce the attention of the viewer and engage their feelings and thoughts.

Think three for slogans (Rule of Three copywriting studio, UK)

Slogans are short snippets used in taglines, campaigns, and add voice to a brand. Using three words to create them can be magical in persuasive copywriting. The virtues of the mysterious power in the number three is seen in persuasive copywriting as well as subjects such as religion, physics, music, and art. Using three-word slogans requires a calculated, keen approach to wordsmithing. It has become hallowed ground in an advertising copy.

Three-word slogans with punch:

- Snap, crackle, pop (Kellogg's Rice Crispies)
- Just do it (Nike)
- I'm lovin' it (McDonalds)
- The Real Thing (Coca-Cola)
- Discount double check (State Farm)
- I Love NY (NY State Tourism)
- Coke is life (Coca-Cola)
- Finger Lickin Good (KFC)
- Pure Chewing satisfaction (Wrigley Spearmint Gum)
- Quicker Picker Upper (Bounty)
- That was Easy (Staples)
- I'm feeling Subway (Subway)

Become a reductionist (Bendinger 2009)

Keep ads to one idea only; be a reductionist. Reductionist thinking is about simplification of focus on one, highly visible benefit. The idea is that single-minded ideas are easier to understand and are highly repeatable. Think about Geico's "fifteen minutes could save you 15 percent" spots and the hammering of one lone idea mercilessly into the audience in a variety of ad deliveries, including a talking gecko, cave dwellers, and a money-covered motorcyclist.

Use the active voice, present tense (Malickson and Nason 1982)

As with technical writing, and all writing, stay active in the voice and revert to the past tense deliberately, only for special effect. Staying active means keeping subjects and verbs close together and being on the constant lookout for passive language that drags down the reader. You will see this rule repeated throughout this book; without an apology, it is that important.

Figure 2.8 This brochure for Seattle University shows off technical, persuasive, and newswriting with a crisp concept that initiates action with meaningful headlines and one unifying word…"here." Design by Turnstyle Studio. Reproduced with kind permission of Turnstyle.

2.7 News writing

News writing is a staple in writing for all types of mass communications including newspapers, magazines, books, websites, radio, television, and mobile. Its most notable roots, however, are in newspapers. At the start of the Revolutionary War in the late 1700s, only a few dozen newspapers had circulations throughout the colonies. The writers were propagandists, who today carry the titles of public relations professionals. Their writings helped crystallize public opinion and became a major force that denounced reconciliation with Great Britain and persuaded colonists to fight for independence and create a new republic. This was the start of a common trait between PR and journalism — the ability to write news. Practitioners in journalism and public relations use news writing to tell non-fiction stories with consideration of truth, ethics, and credibility. News writing consists of long form, which is 1000+ words and short form, which is usually around 250–1000 words (Heller 2012). Essays, articles, scholarly papers, book chapters, and complete books all make up long form writing while captions, blurbs, press releases, web copy, social media, brochures, and short columns make up short form. News writing involves reporting, which is "the accumulation and presentation of facts through eyewitness accounts" (p. 59) and criticism, which is critical or analytical and may include interpretation. In pure journalism, reporting is the method. In public relations, reporting, criticism, and interpretation may be part of a written piece also. In either application, the tenets of good news writing are to inform the reader on vital facts that allow processing of an informed opinion or stimulus to act.

Identifying and defining news

We all read the news to get information, which is the essence of what news is, a "full and current information that is made available to an audience" (Metz 1991, 8). Journalism is a process that incorporates first hand reporting of evidence, fact checking, editorial oversight, copyediting, and distribution of a work. It requires a group of people and technically only a single person cannot carry it out, as with as peer-reviewed scholarly articles, which receive examination, commenting, and editing for substance, clarity, and format by a group of peers. In the bulk of public relations writing assignments (press releases, fact sheets, pitch letters), we often work alone or only with a client. In these cases, we are not practicing journalism; we are performing newswriting for public relations. Public relations specialists are now beginning to marry both instances, like in brand journalism, where company innovation, history, and challenges become a pathway for substantive written works that utilize a journalistic process, rather than just newswriting. A published book on the history of a company

Figure 2.9 The news magazine is written and designed to gain maximum interest while still providing newsworthy information relevant to readers' lives. This spread from the "Brave Thinkers" list in *The Atlantic* shows the marriage between design and news writing. Design by Luke Hayman, Pentagram. Reproduced with kind permission of Pentagram.

Table 2.3 Qualities that make news.

News quality	Description and identification
Timeliness	Reporting on what is happening right now. Is the story getting coverage elsewhere? Is it part of a social event or problem currently discussed in the mainstream news and social media?
Proximity	Reporting on where something is happening. Is the story local, national, or international? Will it affect certain groups based on their locations?
Consequence	Reporting on the short- and long-term ramifications of an event or action. Is the story going to cause potential harm or benefit? What is affected — environment, groups of people, societal norms, legislature?
Prominence	Reporting on the personal and professional activities of eminent people in society. Is the person famous or infamous? What is the severity and consequences of the event or action?
Human interest (oddity)	Reporting on the emotionally connected and intellectually intriguing stories that do not influence the world. Is the story going to illicit a heartfelt or enigmatic response from readers? Will they feel sorry, outraged, or glorified? Will they seek out new information to add to their knowledge on the subject? Remember the ice bucket challenge?

Source: Adpated from Metz (1991).

would be an example of brand journalism. In all instances, news must meet criteria, which is what makes it reportable and gives value to the reader.

Gatekeepers are people in prominent positions who can open or close the gate on news because they work for major media outlets who reach billions of people collectively (Metz 1991). They have the ability to decide what gets published and what does not. They are the reporters, editors, producers, publishers, bloggers, and social media thought leaders who have an audience. It is their job to inform the public accurately, objectively, factually, and completely. They have one problem; they need content to fill their platforms, so places where hard news was dominant are now sharing generous space with soft news and publicity pieces. That is where the public relations specialist comes in. They provide the news that ultimately helps the gatekeepers by giving them content to fill their articles, broadcasts, tweets, and talk shows. However, to get through the gate, the content must be newsworthy. Because news is an account of an event, or a fact, an opinion, it is open to interpretation. Eliminating all bias is impossible, which makes the *angle (focus)* of so many stories slanted beyond pure objectivity. A news act or occurrence must have news qualities in order to be worthy of reporting as news, which in simple terms is "a current event that is important to a group of people" (Palser 2012, 7).

Key rules in news writing

Here are some key rules on news writing derived from the works of Gutkind (2012), Clark (2006), Zappala and Carden (2010), Bly (2005), Metz (1991), and Zinsser (2006) and accented with my experience teaching students how to write better.

Fact checking and accuracy (Gutkind)
When you write news copy you are creating non-fiction work that needs to be factual, otherwise you will lose your credibility as a reporter and writer. Certify the accuracy of facts in all cases of

news releases, feature stories, white papers, and media alerts, especially those pieces of data that cannot be blurred by someone else's perception. Things like locations, dates, times, names, publicly reported information is verifiable, and checked for truthfulness. You do not have to be objective in your narrative, but your information must be trustworthy. Fox News and NBC News have both had their news organizations exposed and discredited for poor editorial and managerial oversight in the blatant inaccuracies of Bill O'Reilly and Brian Williams in their public statements and works.

Report and write for scenes (Clark)
Realism is built on a scene-by-scene account in news reporting. When you write for news and storytelling of any kind, think in scenes, single snapshots of one instance in time. It follows how we watch movies and it makes for a strong approach to writing stories for news or persuasion.

Leads (Metz, Zappala and Carden)
Aside from headlines that grab attention instantly, the lead is the most important part of the story in public relations news writing because it gets the attention of the editor or reporter who will open the gate for distribution to major audiences. It is vital to the journalist because it gets the attention of the reader, and invites them to absorb the story's words further. The classic rule for leads is to use the inverted pyramid, which offers the five Ws and the H. This is the most common approach to lead writing and works well for both PR and is a standard for journalism. In public relations, leads are sometimes shy on the five W's (who, what, where, when, why) and focus instead on the items with the greatest public relations value. This may be okay for internal publications, but try to avoid this type of news writing when submitting to wires and news organizations. Whenever possible, use the five Ws and the H in PR news writing; editors and reporters will reward you with more placements. Keep leads brief, but with punch, trying to write them under 60–70 words is a good strategy; brevity should become clarity. Remember, localize and emphasize the most important part of the news in the lead aside the other critical (ws) information.

Inverted pyramid (Metz)
Born during the Civil War as a way to get "hot news" through the communication channels of the notoriously unreliable telegraph lines, the inverted pyramid provided a specific way to funnel information in news writing by importance, rather than chronology; today, it is the standard format for writing news. It is a simple idea that creates an information hierarchy for readers and writers. Writing using the inverted pyramid dictates that a news story starts with the bulk of the critical details in the beginning and then tapers down to the least important information at the bottom. It has several advantages including quick organization of stories, fast scanning for editors, and allows readers to get the gist of the story without making it through the entire article. Always use it for public relations and news writing.

Quotes and attribution (Zinsser)
Take clear notes when interviewing someone, as it is "your ethical duty to the person being interviewed is to present his or her position accurately" and when quoting, be sure to "single out the sentences that are most important or colorful" (p. 108). You should be as accurate as possible, but make sure that your quotes make sense in the piece by adding clarifying words if needed. When using a quote in a paragraph, start a sentence with a quote, rather than leading up to it with an elementary phrase beginning with who said instead of what said.

Start quotes with what said, rather who said.

> Weak: Mr. Borowski said that he liked to "go to the Ranger games and cheer with wild fans until my voice cracked."

> Stronger: "I like to go to the Ranger games," Mr. Borowski said, "and cheer with wild fans until my voice cracks."

2.8 Writing tool belt — essential skills

As you move along creating ideas with words, there are certain tools you will want to add to your repertoire to build better process and polish. Here are some essential skills to attach to your writing tool belt.

Activation of verbs — voice and tense

Activation of verbs entails careful examination of sentences to remove the passive voice. Touted, as a guaranteed way to make your writing stronger and measurably better by countless writing books, using the active voice by activating your verbs is one of the best writing habits you can pick up. The first thing to understand is that tense and voice are not related. Tense explains time and voice shows relationship. What makes a verb active or passive? It is all about the subject and if it is giving or receiving the action of the verb. Once you identify givers and receivers, activating verbs becomes part of your arsenal of writing and editing tools. Always use the grammar check in Microsoft Word so that your passive sentences are underlined for you when you go back to edit your work, or as you are writing.

Voice — who or what gets the action?
Subject gives action of the verb — active verb

> Kim delighted John. (active)
> The ball hit Jack. (active)
> Consumers enjoyed the product. (active)

Subject receives the action of the verb — passive verb

> John was delighted by Kim. (passive)
> Jack was hit by the ball. (passive)
> The product was enjoyed by consumers. (passive)

Subject does not give or receive the action — linking verb

> Kim *seemed to be delighting* John. (linking)
> Kim is *to be delighting* John. (linking)
> Kim *was delighting* John. (linking)

If you can substitute a form of *be* (*was, is, or am, are, be, being, been, has been, may be, might be, should have been*) as the verb, it is a linking verb and it is not active or passive. It is also grammatically correct.

Verb tense — When is the action happening?
We write in relationship to time and when we do not represent time properly in the form of verb tenses, the readers suffer. Verb tenses include the three main categories of present, past, and future and the four subcategories of simple tense, progressive tense, perfect tense, and perfect progressive tense. Knowing the basics of verb tense fosters making the right tense automatic in your writing. I referred to Thurman's treatment (2003, 57–59) to create a useful tense table that offers quick reference and clarification on verb tense.

Simple tense — the standard
- I ride my bike. (present tense)
- Happening now and happening again
- I rode my bike. (past tense)
- Happened
- I will ride my bike. (future tense)
- Happening again

Progressive tense — the now and the future
- I am riding my bike today. (present progressive) AM, IS, ARE with an -ing verb
  Happens at the time it is written
- I was riding my bike yesterday. (past progressive) WAS, WERE with an -ing verb
  Happens in the past
- I will be riding my bike tomorrow. (future progressive) WILL BE with an -ing verb
  Happens continuously and in the future

Perfect tense — the past and the now
- I have ridden my bike today. (present perfect) HAVE, HAS
  Happened in the past and but is continued in the present
- I had ridden my bike for two years before I entered the race. (past perfect) HAD
  Happened in the past before another action happened
- I will have ridden my bike for more than four days before crossing the finish line. (future perfect) WILL HAVE
  Shows future action happening before another action happens

Perfect progressive tense — the past, the now, and maybe the possible future
- For the past two years, I have been riding my bike. (present perfect progressive) HAS BEEN or HAVE BEEN + "-ing" verb
  Happened over a period in the past, then kept going in the present, and maybe will continue in the future.
- Before I rode my bike, I had been running on the treadmill for the past decade. (past perfect progressive) HAD BEEN + "-ing" verb
  Happened continuously and was done before another past happening

- Next year, I will have been riding my bike for more than a decade. (past perfect progressive) WILL HAVE + "-ing" verb
  Happened continuously and will be finished sometime in the future

Outlining and flowcharting

Organizing your ideas is an important step in writing all types of documents, especially in non-fiction writing, where order is paramount. Make it a habit to use hierarchy tools such as outlines and flowcharts for establishing and generating tentative blueprints for writing and interactive projects.

The outline is the perfect organization tool for linear writing. It is simple to use, built in to many word-processing software programs, and is familiar (think table of contents or Facebook Status strings). The key to a good outline is using a structure with one to three levels, without over sub-heading unwarranted ideas that are not at the top of a thought. Use the outline flexibly, move things around, and cut, cut, cut to get to the point.

Flowcharting is great for creating a visual structure for your data and content. It presents a graphical outline that is non-linear, with boxes and lines to represent the flow of information throughout the document, app, or site. The flowchart, like the outline, creates easily in MS Word or MS PowerPoint, and is a familiar item in our information lives (think web site, gaming, sales kiosks, and app navigation menus).The key to good flowcharts is establishing the proper structure, without over stuffing the top level. Use the flowchart dynamically. Place top-level content according to how high it sits in the hierarchy, and how much metadata it holds, which is sub data or data about data.

Chunking and progressive disclosure

The reader more easily digests small paragraphs that present chunks of information than large volumes of words that fail to offer a clear point or obstruct the point simply with too much meaningless information. Try to keep paragraphs tight, use chunking, a way of writing popular to educational content that espouses delivering one point or idea per chunk. In printed work, the next chunk comes from the next paragraph or set of steps. In web pieces and interactive writing (games, presentations, e-learning), the next chunk usually comes from a link to "more >," or "continue >," which allows the reader to move to the next piece of information if he or she wants to, creating time for absorption and a level of discoverability that encourages further exploration. Publishing uses chunking with designs using small multiples, which are multiple, small chunks of information used in a layout. This type of composition is effective for creating a macro/micro reading that shows "micro" pieces of data that are part of a larger "macro" topic or idea.

"You" viewpoint

The "you" viewpoint is a way to write in a manner that is audience centered and focused on the reader and not the writer. We see the "you" viewpoint in promotional copy and technical communication the most. Business writing also utilizes the "you" viewpoint in correspondence and other written items like notices, policies, and reports. This is because using the "you" viewpoint in your writing communicates intimately and directly with the reader to get them to act. It is less formal and more conversational. Whether it is an advertisement for lip balm, or instructions on how to assemble a baby crib, using the "you" is in many cases needed to create a path for reader action. Newswriting typically does not employ this technique because it is neutral in angle and looks to inform, rather

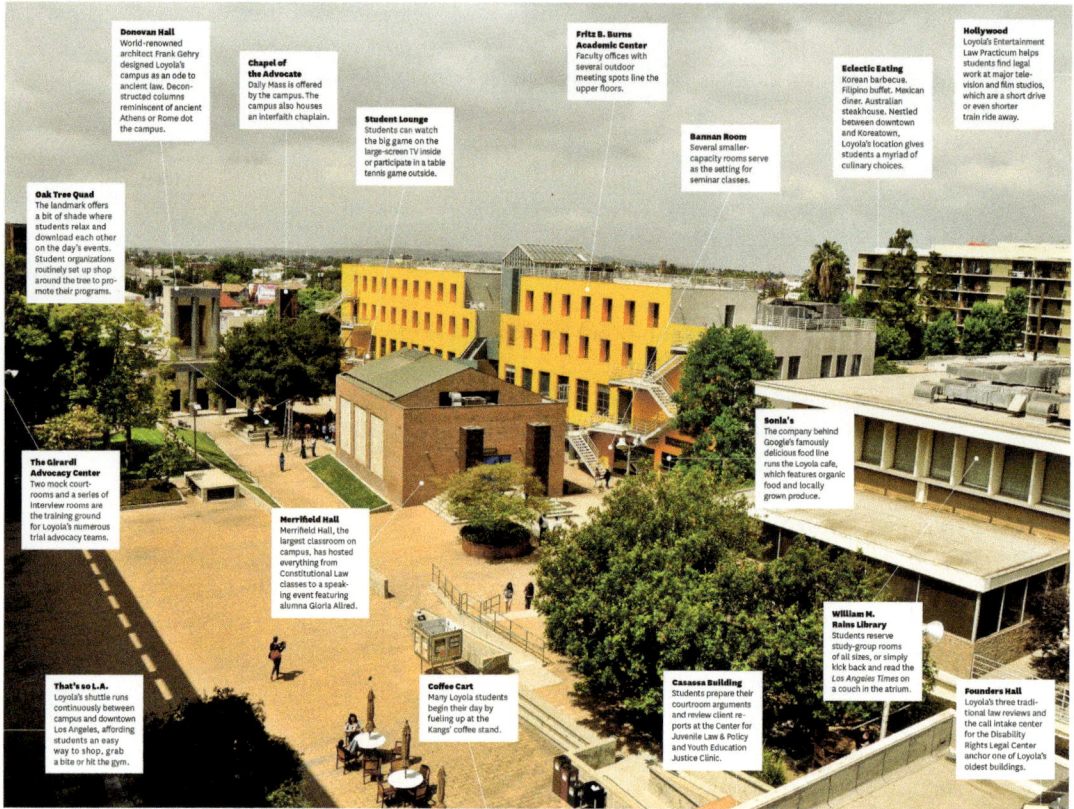

Figure 2.10a Small multiples with birds-eye view
This spread provides small multiples of chunked information in a macro-micro driven layout that gives a birdseye view (macro) coupled with data from the ground (micro). Design by DJ Stout, Pentagram. Reproduced with kind permission of Pentagram.

than persuade. The use of "you" must be consistent throughout the text and is typically offset with an existence of the writer and their organization in the form of *we*, *us*, or, *I*. This more personalized approach creates trust and connection through pronouns that make meaningful messages. Here is a small sample of using the "you" in action.

> In this book, I hope to bring new information and skills to *you* with the outcome being *your* success in marketing communications.

Expressing data

Data drives decision-making because it offers evidence that purports to be accurate and representative of the problem at hand. We move toward data as a foundation of information when we are deliberating a decision or forming an opinion. If represented data contains obfuscation or is less than genuine, decisions drawn from it can have serious consequences. Be accurate. Always check data for source credibility, and determine who has disseminated the data and why. Be wary of information

Figure 2.10b Micro/Macro design. This table of contents spread uses micro headlines in a small multiple layout that guides the reader across the macro message that Drexel University produces outstanding research. Design DJ Stout, Pentagram. Reproduced with kind permission of Pentagram.

from a non-governmental or non-academic source. Corporations send out data reports and research findings frequently. These may be for public relations or marketing purposes, rather than simply to add to the knowledge base and research literature on the subject. When showing the data make sure that you focus in on the most important statistics that have meaning to the audience and can be understood by a general population, rather than using jargon exclusively and losing the reader.

Crafting headlines and subheads

Headlines and subheads are very important to any written piece for several reasons. First, think of headlines as little billboards or in some cases, enigmas for the viewer that satiates their appetite for information. Second, a good headline and subhead makes the reader think and react, with either emotion or further engagement in the form of reading the entire article and then maybe even looking further for new information. If this is an editor looking to pick up a story for their outlet, the headline can be the element that grabs their attention. Third, subheads offer extended teases to the inquisitively ready reader by revealing a little more. Finally, headlines and subheads are vital to search engine rankings and indexing on the web. Headlines contain keywords. Google rakes up the keywords and ranks the sites they connect to in their search engine. Headlines and subheads on press releases and other marketing communications are especially reliant on headlines and subheads as these come over the wire services and journalists, editors, and producers across media pick them up. Be simple and direct. Do not exaggerate or use words that are too big and will confuse readers. Your headlines should have rhythm to their words and avoid awkwardness at all costs. The best way to learn

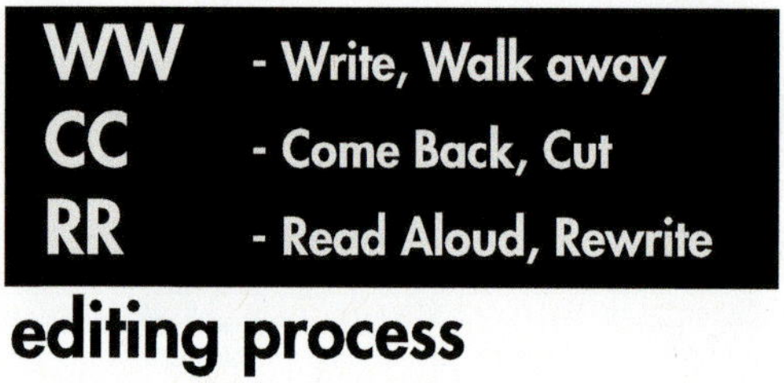

WW - Write, Walk away
CC - Come Back, Cut
RR - Read Aloud, Rewrite

editing process

Callout 2C Editing process simplified. *Source*: Adpated from Metz (1991).

how to write great headlines is to read them, from all media, especially newspapers, magazines, and advertisements, which all thrive on the power packed in headlines.

Editing and rewriting

Rewriting, the product of editing, is part of writing, no way around it. Editing requires cutting words and reshaping sentences to tighten and connect them, presenting ideas in a simpler, more meaningful way. Copyediting is designing words into stronger messages. The editing process is essential in all art forms and is usually a separate job. Think about the film editor who turns a series of "shots" into a movie and the photo editor who decides on which images make it into the pages of a magazine. In all cases, we act as our own editor, especially in writing, where the goal of editing is to rewrite or recreate for eliminating clutter, which frees language of "unnecessary words, circular constructions,

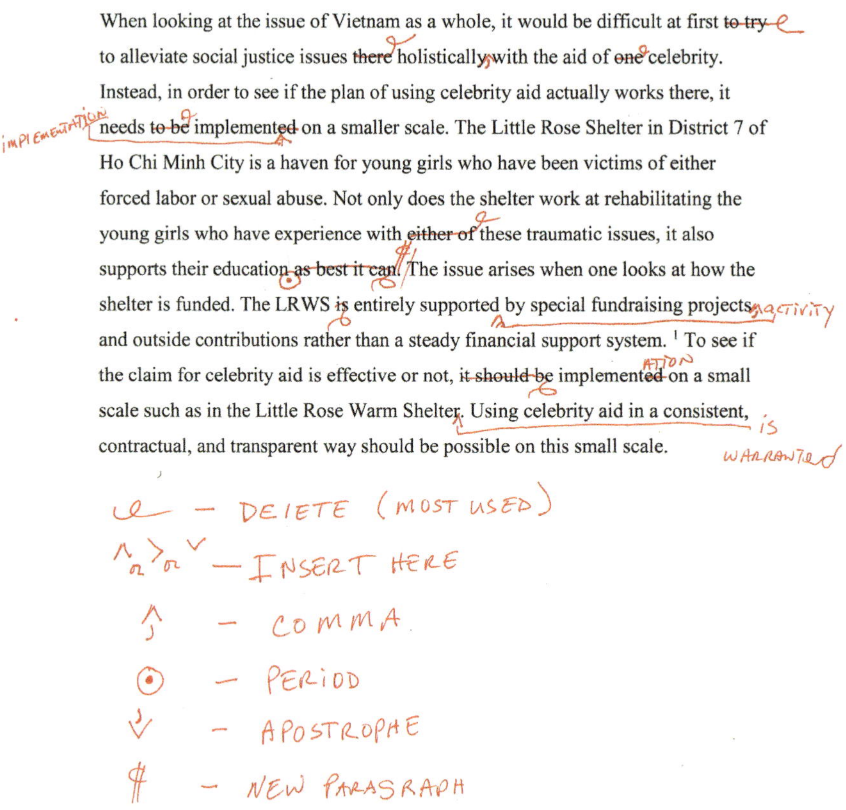

When looking at the issue of Vietnam as a whole, it would be difficult at first to try to alleviate social justice issues there holistically, with the aid of one celebrity. Instead, in order to see if the plan of using celebrity aid actually works there, it needs to be implemented on a smaller scale. The Little Rose Shelter in District 7 of Ho Chi Minh City is a haven for young girls who have been victims of either forced labor or sexual abuse. Not only does the shelter work at rehabilitating the young girls who have experience with either of these traumatic issues, it also supports their education as best it can. The issue arises when one looks at how the shelter is funded. The LRWS is entirely supported by special fundraising projects activity and outside contributions rather than a steady financial support system. ¹ To see if the claim for celebrity aid is effective or not, it should be implemented on a small scale such as in the Little Rose Warm Shelter. Using celebrity aid in a consistent, contractual, and transparent way should be possible on this small scale. is warranted

Figure 2.11 Editing on paper Use these common symbols when editing using a paper copy or proof.

- ℓ — DELETE (MOST USED)
- ∧ > or ∨ — INSERT HERE
- ∧ — COMMA
- ⊙ — PERIOD
- ∨ — APOSTROPHE
- ¶ — NEW PARAGRAPH

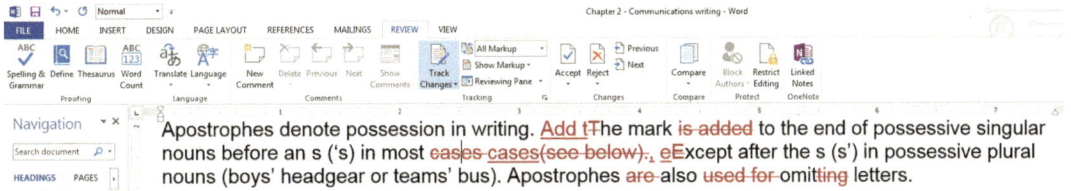

Figure 2.12 Editing in Microsoft Word using track changes. Use track changes in Microsoft Word to keep a running record of edits throughout the life of a document. You look at markup, original, or both. See your edits and draft simultaneously.

pompous frills, and meaningless jargon" (Zinsser 2006,6). Never take writing for granted. It is hard work that demands that you craft sentences a second, third, or even a fourth time to ensure all the fat is trimmed and only the delicious meaning exists. If possible, get a fresh eye to look at it, which is another person who can read the piece to illuminate any bumpy passages.

Give your words the careful attention they deserve. When I ask students to become their own editors, I give them this simple process to use. Whether editing on paper or electronically, editing is the most important part of good writing.

2.9 Essential grammar rules

We learn grammar initially in elementary school, however with time, we forget. The assembly of solid sentences is difficult because we need to make choices based on these grammatical conventions. We struggle with instances of pronouns like *them* or *they*, and are unclear about presenting verb tenses for example, *was going* or *went*? The wrong choice can make your work unclear, choppy, and unsuccessful. Here is an adapted list of utmost essentials on grammar, usage, and style derived from Zinsser (2006), Thurman (2003), and from the seminal work on grammatical execution, *The Elements of Style* by Strunk and White (2009), to clarify critical grammar situations so you make better choices and you will actually have a "grammatically correct" reason why.

Usage and style for common punctuation marks

In writing marketing, advertising, and public relations pieces, a practitioner comes upon many instances where understanding usage (when to use) and style (how to use) need clarification. Here are some frequently seen items in marketing communications writing that we need to master for fluid grammatically sensible, writing.

Parenthetical punctuation

Strunk and White evangelize that these particular rules below "cover the most important principles that govern punctuation" and recommend, "they should be so thoroughly mastered that their application becomes second nature" (p. 7). The rules below explain different scenarios of parenthetical expressions, which are words, phrases, or sentences that explain or modify a thought. Separating parenthetical statements is about placing commas and other punctuation, but knowing where and when to use them is the key. You must make a decision if a text string is parenthetical or restrictive. Parenthetical gets a comma, but restrictive does not. The difference is simple.

The Comma

Table 2.4 The comma (derived and adapted from Strunk and White's *Elementary Rules of Usage*)

Rule	Correct examples	Incorrect examples
Enclose parenthetic expressions between commas. This essential rule is sometimes difficult to apply. Remember that to use a comma, an English snippet must explain or modify a thought, which makes it parenthetical, otherwise, it is restrictive. Restrictive words and phrases do not offer new explanation or modification to the subject. When simply continuing the thought or with restrictive terms, eliminate the comma.	*Explaining or modifying a thought is parenthetical* The best person for the job, unless you disagree, is Jack. [The best person for the job], [unless you disagree], is Jack. [parenthetical] *Dates are parenthetical* January to April, 2015 April 10, 2015 Thursday, April 10, 2015 *Abbreviations, academic degrees, and titles are parenthetical* John DiMarco, Ph.D. David Fitzsimmons, CPA., Accountant David Smith, President	The best person for the job unless you disagree is Jack. (incorrect) January to April 2015 (incorrect) April 10 2015 (incorrect) Thursday April 10, 2015 (incorrect) John DiMarco Ph.D. (incorrect) David Fitzsimmons CPA. Accountant (incorrect) David Smith President (incorrect)
Never delete one comma and leave another (one comma only) as Strunk and White proclaim, "there is no defense for such punctuation" (p. 2).	Identification terms are restrictive with one meaning and word order *No commas* Attila the Hun The Fresh Prince of Bellaire The artist formerly known as Prince *Restrictive, no comma* John DiMarco Jr. (Jr. is restrictive) A person with diabetes shouldn't eat candy in excess. (*shouldn't* is restrictive) The car that is running is in the street. (*that* is restrictive and tells which one)	 Attila, the Hun (incorrect) The Fresh Prince, of Bellaire (incorrect) The artist, formerly known as Prince (incorrect) John DiMarco, Jr. (incorrect) A person with diabetes, shouldn't eat candy in excess. (incorrect) The car, that is running is in the street. (incorrect)

Table 2.4 (*Continued*)

Rule	Correct examples	Incorrect examples
	Conjunctions (which, when, where) with time and place are parenthetical and need a comma	
	The student group, which had first been concerned, became more comfortable as the day continued.	The student group which had first been concerned became more comfortable as the day continued. (incorrect)
	In 1934, when Frank was born, New York City was growing rapidly.	In 1934 when Frank was born, New York City was growing rapidly. (incorrect)
	In the church, where David was baptized, masses were held nightly.	In the church where David was baptized Masses were held nightly. (incorrect)
Place a comma before a conjunction in a two-part sentence When you have a two-part sentence (independent clauses) that are connected by conjunctions add a comma before them: as but yet so for nor or unless as long as as soon as because before if when which, where, wherever, while once since providing that though although so that so long as than and You should add a comma if the statements are parenthetical (new explanation or modification). If the two sentences are closely related (restrictive) and use *and* do not use a comma.	*Two-part sentences with conjunctions, add comma* I want you stay, but you said it is important to get home. Please leave the room, while I get dressed. I left the lights on, so you can find your way around. The concert was packed, yet the donations were not very substantial. I want you to stay, as I cannot be without you. Make sure the lights are off, because the electricity bill is expensive. Our company will grow, as long as we keep revenues rising. *Close relationship sentences with and No comma* He has extensive communication skills and is a strong writer. Jack bought five pairs of jeans and two belts. She has five dogs and two cats.	I want you stay but you said it is important to get home. (incorrect) Please leave the room while I get dressed. (incorrect) I left the lights on so you can find you way around. (incorrect) The concert was packed yet the donations were not very substantial. (incorrect) I want you to stay as I cannot be without you. (incorrect) He has extensive communication skills, and is a strong writer. (incorrect) Jack bought five pairs of jeans, and two belts. (incorrect) She has five dogs, and two cats. (incorrect)

(*continued*)

Table 2.4 (Continued)

Rule	Correct samples	Incorrect samples
Do not break sentences in two with periods, unless it offers emphasis. To make sentences more meaningful and vivid, refrain from using periods for commas, unless it is for emphasis.	*Turn two sentences into one with a comma and conjunction* Joe was an interesting political candidate, *because* he had a flair for debate. (better) The teacher provided well-researched lessons in math, *since* she took her job very seriously.	Joe was an interesting political candidate. He had a flair for debate. (weak) The teacher provided well-researched lessons in math. She took her job very seriously. (weak — lacks connection)
	Only break thoughts into two sentences when you need emphasis, or are reporting short passages. The man fell off his bike and hit his head. He was killed instantly. (better)	The man fell off his bike, hit his head, and was killed instantly. (weak — lacks emphasis on outcome)
Comma clarity derived from Strunk and White's Elementary Rules of Usage		
Use commas in a series of three or more for each item except after the last. Separate all items with commas, unless they are related. Even if they are, using a comma before the last item does not make it incorrect, only less eloquent and specific.	*A common mistake, only omit the last comma when the last two item are related.* Dr. Smith carried his stethoscope, tongue depressor, and charts. The corporation was engaged in banking, securities, and insurance. (all different use commas) The corporation was engaged in banking, stocks and bonds. (related, last two items don't need a comma) I ate a sandwich with pickles, peanut butter and jelly. (related, last two items don't need a comma)	Dr. Smith carried his stethoscope, tongue depressor and charts. (incorrect) The corporation was engaged in banking, and securities and insurance. (incorrect) I ate a sandwich with pickles, peanut butter, and jelly. (incorrect)

The Semicolon

2 Writing Technical, Persuasive, and News Communication | 35

Table 2.5 The semicolon

Rule	Correct sample	Incorrect sample
Use a semicolon or period to connect compound sentences without a conjunction. When you have two grammatically complete sentences not connected by a conjunction, but are connected in thought, you should NOT add a comma, but use a *semicolon*.	*Two-part sentences without conjunction* Add a semicolon or a period for less connection and more emphasis: The company is healthy; profits are on the rise.	*Two-part sentences with commas are called comma splices* The company is healthy, profits are on the rise. (incorrect)
It is also correct to write those sentences separately with periods replacing the semicolons.	Our staff has a light workload; several projects closed recently. Our staff has a light workload. Several projects closed recently.	Our staff has a light workload, several projects have been closed recently. (incorrect)
	The concert was unsuccessful; therefore, the donations were not very substantial. The concert was unsuccessful. The donations were not very substantial.	The concert was unsuccessful, therefore; the donations were not very substantial. (incorrect)

The em dash

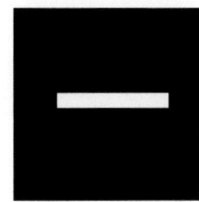

Two kinds of dashes

Em dash — sets off an interruption or summary.
He cried out — I can't breathe — the crowd stopped and stared.
En dash — aka hyphen, hyphenates words in passage and on end lines. Step-by-step.

Table 2.6 The em dash.

Rule	Correct sample	Incorrect sample
Use an em dash to separate, interrupt, or announce a summary within a sentence. When other punctuation does not seem strong enough to show a break inside a sentence, use an *em dash.* —	*Add dashes to set off phrases that need "separation stronger than commas, less formal than colons, and more relaxed than parentheses" (p. 9). Think of pop-up ideas that need to be blurted out in a sentence.* We are working diligently — and getting things done — I might add! The store was crowded — oops! I just stepped on someone's leg. I know you closed the deal yesterday — that matters most.	

Making en and em dashes.

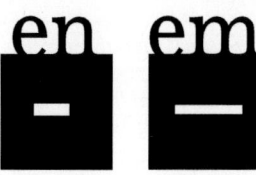

– em

Windows

Make an em dash in Microsoft Word for Windows.

– Ctrl + alt + - (keypad) = —
– Alt + 0151 (keypad)
– Type two dashes in Word next to each other

Make an en dash in Microsoft Word for Windows.

– Type a dash – (keypad)
– Alt + 0150 (keypad)

Mac

Make an em dash in Microsoft Word for Mac.

– Option + shift + - = —
–

Quotation marks

Quotation marks act as a container for something unique. There are two types, double quotation marks "quote" and single quotation marks 'quote'. Double quotation marks enclose a direct quotation from a person. Use single quotation marks when quoting inside quotation marks.

Punctuating a sentence with a quotation
What to remember

      Commas and periods — place quotation marks outside.
      Semicolon and colon — place quotation marks inside.

"Students can show real evidence within portfolios," says Professor John DiMarco in *Career Power Skills*.

"Students can show real evidence within portfolios"; Professor John DiMarco offers examples in the book *Career Power Skills*.

Indirectly, mid-sentence
What to remember — do not capitalize a quote mid-sentence.

All the professor would say is that, "they find great ways to create a personal brand."

Multiple paragraphs
What to remember — place double quotation marks at the beginning of each paragraph, but only one at the end of the paragraphs.
"It is the invention I spent two years finalizing in Brooklyn.

"I am sitting in my workshop, cultivating ideas, and walking in the sun forgetting that my angel investor needs a prototype by this week.

"In Ohio, no one would understand the pressure I have put on myself and my family."

Use of irony
What to remember — set off ironic words and short phrases using quotation marks.
Everyone in the house "cleans" my car after long road trips.

Enclose titles of articles, speeches, poems, short stories, and books:
What to remember — set off names of printed works in double quotation marks. Use double quotations after the words *titled, the word, referred to as, or designated*.

The professor had a new book coming out titled "Career Power Skills," which outlines how to research careers and create professional communication.

Apostrophes

Apostrophes denote possession in writing. Add the mark to the end of possessive singular nouns before an s ('s) in most cases, except after the s (s') in possessive plural nouns (boys' headgear or teams' bus). Apostrophes also show the omission of letters.

Plurals that do not end in s
What to remember — add an apostrophe with an s when you have possessive nouns.

We went to see all the wrestler's matches.

Expressions
What to remember — add an apostrophe with possessive third-party references.

>He stayed on the team, despite everyone else's complaints.

>She built the company with somebody else's money.

Joint possession present
What to remember — add an apostrophe when two or more possess something jointly.

>The company examined Woodward and Bernstein's articles.

Joint possession not present
What to remember — add an apostrophe to the last noun when two or more are not in joint possession.

>The company examined Wood's and Bern's expense accounts.

Proper nouns with s at the end
What to remember — add an apostrophe between the s's with proper names ending in s. Or, add the apostrophe after the s. Both are grammatically correct.
>The publisher lauded Brooks's novels. (This looks weird, but is okay.)
>or
>The publisher lauded Brooks' novels. (Also correct and has less tension.)

Letters, figures, symbols
What to remember — add an apostrophe before the s with alpha or numeric entries. Publishers also suggest that dropping the apostrophe is acceptable also if the snippet is clear and understandable.

>She taught him the ABC's of being a salesperson. / She taught him the ABCs of being a salesperson.

>He was born in the 1800's. He was born in the 1800s.

Inanimate objects
What to remember — add an apostrophe before the s with things that are not alive and have possession.

>He was knocking on heaven's door.

Contractions
Apostrophes have another role to play in grammar. It is within contractions. When we contract two words, we join them and eliminate letters. The apostrophe takes the place of those erased letters and acts as a sign to the reader that the language in the text is more relaxed. Keep in mind that contractions turn formal writing into informal writing. Watch your usage of them in technical and news writing, but embrace them in persuasive writing, which frequently connects with eyeballs and hearts using personal language.

>You won't believe your eyes!
>Opposed to: You will not believe your eyes!

2.10 Five common writing mistakes to avoid

I review many student-writing assignments and frequently see the same communication debilitating errors. These mistakes are common, but may be committed out of a lack of editing and careless desire to simply, "get the work done." Poor writing dampens your star in the professional world, so keep these mistakes out of your text at all costs because they proclaim a lack of caring.

1. *Do not capitalize words that do not require it.* Unless it is a required style, acronym, proper naming, or grammar point, do not capitalize words for emphasis, or any other unknown reason. Use the styles manuals *AP Style Guide* and *Strunk and White's Elements of Style* to verify capital letter usage if you are unsure.
2. *Do not use complicated words to attempt to dazzle the reader.* The most intelligent writing communicates clearly and efficiently. On the other hand, we can say... The most intelligent writing communicates perspicaciously and swimmingly. Use words that you and the reader will know, without question.
3. *Do not write all your ideas in one long paragraph.* Break up ideas into smaller paragraphs or chunks. One big paragraph scares off the reader and suffocates their ability to ingest your main ideas cohesively.
4. *Do not use clichés unless they have contextual relevance.* Commonly overused expressions, or clichés, cheapen writing because they expose a lack of thought by the writer. With contextual relevance, clichés add depth to a story, as with a quote that contains a cliché or a connection to experiences or events that warrants use. Look up clichés in Google to get infinite lists of these poor phrase choices when you are not sure. Do not be guilty of using one. Instead, write an original thought. If you avoid clichés, you are good to go and will be all you can be — the proof is in the pudding!
5. *Do not confuse verb tense.* Keep tenses consistent throughout each paragraph and within each document. Tense is critical to writing coherently so give the reader a consistent timeline of action to follow. Check tenses for consistency and clarity during every editing stint.

2.11 Five steps to find writing success

The GROWN process

> Getting started is always the most difficult," students lament as they explain their trepidations with writing. Successful writing means that you completed the process, and ultimately generated the intended writing product. Good writing takes a good amount of time, but the results can be magnificent. Here are the five steps to getting something written successfully. I use the mnemonic GROWN to help you remember that if you do not follow these steps, your words and ideas will sink below the surface of the reader's interest and attention due to lack of process. Follow GROWN to build a successful writing process.
>
> Get to know — get to know the assignments or project on paper by identifying your communication goals (educate, persuade, inform, entertain), the intended audience, the tentative or required length, and required style.
>
> Research — research to gain source data, quotes, background information, existing works, and dissemination routes. Write notes with source references to consolidate ideas for

written pieces. Research is so important in MARCOM because in most cases, we are explaining something to an audience, and we need to be correct in what we state. Decide which methods are best to collect the data needed to communicate your points. Determine if you need generalized quantitative population data, or narrower, qualitative information about a group or person, then build data sets. Use programs like REFME.com, which allows you to cite works for research and add notes for later reference.

Outline — outline your idea hierarchically so that you have a structure for your work. Make each new section in the outline a paragraph heading and then flow ideas into each paragraph, chunking new ideas and expanding on questions and secondary information later in the work.

Write — write a draft first and assume that it not a finished piece of text. Free write or labor over each sentence, whichever way you feel comfortable. Either way the text is still not finished until you come back to it for editing and revisions.

Now edit — after you write, always say to yourself ... now edit! You need to push yourself to complete this very critical step. Edit and rewrite twice in two separate sessions for maximum quality. Walk away from the work. Now come back and edit. Walk away, and come back and edit again. Three times is great, but two times are a bare minimum. When you skip editing, your writing suffers.

2.12 Chapter exercises

The exercises offer writing practice in different types of treatments for industry sample projects that you will learn more about in later chapters in the book. Broken down into the three types of writing most used in marketing communications, exercises are short and precisely target mechanics and foundation skills.

Technical writing

1. Professor interview and article

    Role: Act as a technical writer for the college or university magazine.
    Assignment: Write a bylined (by you) short 250–300-word article on an interview with a professor on the topic of writing process.
    Include
    - Lead paragraph
    - Two quotes
    - Three to four takeaway tips
    - Anything else to add to the story
    - Brief biographical statement (about you the writer) after the piece.

    Process
    (a) Interview a published professor in your college outside of your major to discover their writing process. Ask about business documents such as emails and memos and ask about academic works like articles and books. Take meticulous notes and record if allowed (ask before recording).

(b) Prepare a list of 5–6 questions that extract information covering these topics:
- How do they research and outline writing projects?
- What styles do they use?
- How many edit and revision sessions do they perform on shorter business documents vs. longer academic works?
- Write using the GROWN process

2. Love letter / Break-up letter for a technology product

Role: Act as a technical copywriter developing copy treatments for a product brochure.

Assignment: Write two short letters (150 words each) that resemble a love letter for one product and a break-up letter for a competing product. Choose two technology competitors (GoDaddy vs. Network Solutions, Ford vs. Chevrolet, IPhone vs. Android, Mac vs. Windows computers, Bulova vs. Rolex, Samsung vs. LG, etc.) to be used, one for each respective letter.

Include
- In the love letter talk about the virtues of the product in relationship to your needs and happiness, as if you were serenading the one you love with words.
- In the break-up letter, explain why you are so unhappy and why you need to break up.
- Use the technical features or specific product information in each letter.

Process
Research product specifications features and advantages (go to the product websites to get perspective and data). Try the products yourself or have others try them and give their opinions in some informal research trials. Take notes or record loves and hates. Use your social media channels to get some opinions from friends and family on what they love or hate most about the chosen products. Write thoughtfully, based on a combination of fact and emotion.

Persuasive copywriting

3. Create the name and tag line of a new chain restaurant.

Role: Act as a brand strategist and copywriter for a new restaurant.

Assignment: Write a GACMIST brief that outlines a new concept and formal business name, which includes Goals, Audience, Concept, Message, Image, Style, and Theme. You will generate a brand new name and a short tag line that replaces an existing brand or creates a new one. For example, Domino's Pizza changed their name to Dominos in order to reflect their addition of menu items beyond pizza. You will choose an existing fast food restaurant chain and make up a new name with tag line to rebrand it. Alternatively, make up a new restaurant chain name and tagline to compete against existing chains.

Include
- GACMIST
- In G (goals), you will list what the goal of the name change is and why it should be done. Or, why there needs to be a new chain (requires analysis)
- In A (audience), you will list who the audience is that will absorb this communication. (requires research)
- In C (concept), you will list the new name and defend the concept. (requires creativity)

- In M (message), you will list the new tag line. Make it short and memorable — try for three words or less. (requires logic)
- In I (images), you will write the types of images and artwork needed to support this new concept and message. Obviously, you will have a new logo, but what other graphic elements? Restaurant signage…what else? The Dominos' commercial for the new name showed the old signage torn down from Dominos' stores with ferocity and the spot cutting to the new signage with the new name and logo mark — the announcer chimes in…Domino's Pizza is now Dominos! (requires research and art direction)
- In S (style), describe the mood, what colors should be used, what sort of typeface might work. Short of actually designing the logo and other elements, try to describe what you see in your head. (requires research and art direction)
- In T (theme), describe the story behind the idea and supporting it in a short paragraph. (requires storytelling)

Process
- Free write new names and ideas out on scrap paper as you brainstorm the new brand name.
- Build a list of potentials and then cross off the ones that are weak until you find the winner.
- Ask others for feedback on the names.
- Put the names up against existing names in the industry for comparisons.
- Remember, you are renaming an existing brand or making an entirely new one so use your knowledge of people and culture, coupled with research, to help find a creative solution.

Some possible restaurant chains to rebrand or compete against:

McDonalds, Burger King, Panera Bread, Jersey Mikes Subs, Subway, Chipotle, Fridays, Applebee's, Hooters, Taco Bell, KFC, Pizzeria Uno, CICI's Pizza, Panda Express, Quiznos, Dairy Queen, Arby's, Auntie Ann's Pretzels, Hardee's, Carl's Junior, Checkers, Sabarro Pizza, Pizza Hut, Cracker Barrel, Ground Round, Denny's, and Chuckie Cheese.

4. Create a FAB and USP chart of your favorite chain restaurant.

   Role: Act as a copywriter for your favorite restaurant.
   Assignment: Create a FAB and USP chart that provides a simple table with features, advantages, and benefits for your favorite restaurant chain. See Table 2.2 for an example.
   Process
   Research the chain and create a chart showing specific features, advantages, and benefits.

News writing

5. Writing leads for your favorite celebrity or athlete

   Role: Act as a public relations writer developing lead paragraphs for a music magazine section titled "Artist Watch."
   Assignment: Write a series of lead paragraphs (3) that reports on your favorite celebrity, athlete, or artist over the last 12 months. What have they been doing for the past year? Chronicle the artist's activity with a tightly written summary that offers the most newsworthy items and other valuable information (the vice ws and the h) in one well-composed lead paragraph (less than 150 words). Use sources, but make the piece in your own words.

Include
- Gigs, appearances, charities, awards, and other newsworthy items in the leads. Create separate leads for each special news item.
- Write two different versions that highlight different newsworthy activities or issues in the person's life.
- Make sure to include a headline and subhead.

Process
- Research the person in focus and make a short list of the most notable occurrences (good or bad) in their life.
- Outline the main points of the lead matching up who what, where, when, and why.
- Write. Walk away. Now edit. Make the paragraphs tight and fact filled.

Chapter references

Alred, Gerald J., Charles T. Brusaw, and Walter E. Oliu. 1976. *Handbook of Technical Writing*. Boston, MA: Bedford/St. Martins.

Bendinger, Bruce. 2009. *The Copy Workshop Workbook 2002*. Chicago, IL: The Copy Workshop.

Bivins, Thomas H. 2011. *Public Relations Writing: The Essentials of Style and Format*, 7th ed. New York: McGraw-Hill.

Blake, Gary, and Robert Bly. 1993. *Elements of Technical Writing*. New York: Maxwell Macmillan International.

Bly, Robert W. 2006. *The Copywriter's Handbook: A Step-By-Step Guide To Writing Copy That Sells*, 3rd ed. New York: Henry Holt.

Clark, Roy Peter. 2006. *Writing Tools: 50 Essential Strategies for Every Writer*. New York: Little, Brown and Company.

Creswell, John W. 2003. *Research Design: Qualitative, Quantitative, and Mixed Methods Approaches*, 2nd ed. London: Sage.

Curtis, Hillman. 2002. *MTIV: Process, Inspiration and Practice for the New Media Designers*. Indianapolis, IN: Peachpit Press Publications.

DiMarco, John. 2010. *Digital Design for Print and Web: An Introduction to Theory, Principles, and Techniques*. Hoboken, NJ: John Wiley & Sons, Inc.

Drewniany, Bonnie L, and Jerome A, Jewler. 2011. *Creative Strategy in Advertising*, 10th ed. Belmont, CA: Wadsworth.

Eilola, Johndan. 2004. *Central Works in Technical Communication*. New York: Oxford University Press.

Gutkind, Lee. 2012. *You Can't Make This Stuff Up: The Complete Guide to Writing Creative Nonfiction — From Memoir to Literary Journalism and Everything in Between*. Boston, MA: Da Capo Press/Lifelong Books.

Heller, Steven. 2012. *Writing and Research for Graphic Designers a Designer's Manual to Strategic Communication and Presentation*. Beverly, MA: Rockport.

Lay, Mary M. 2000. *Technical Communication*. Boston, MA: Irwin/McGraw Hill.

Lewis, E. St. Elmo. 1903. "Advertising Department: Catch-Line and Argument." *The Book-Keeper* 15.

Lupton, Ellen, and Jennifer Cole Phillips. 2011. *Graphic Design Thinking: Beyond Brainstorming*. Baltimore, MD: Maryland Institute College of Art.

Malickson, David L, and John W. Nason. 1982. *Advertising–How to Write the Kind That Works*. New York: Scribner.

Metz, William M. 1991. *Newswriting: From Lead to "30": From Lead to "30"*. Upper Saddle River, NJ: Prentice Hall.

Palser, Barb. 2012. *Choosing News: What Gets Reported and Why*. Mankato, MN: Compass Point Books.

Petty, Richard E., and John T. Cacioppo. 1986. *Communication and Persuasion: Central and Peripheral Routes to Attitude Change*. New York: Springer.

Sears Archives, History. 2015. *History of the Sears Catalog*. Accessed June 23. http://www.searsarchives.com/catalogs/history.htm (accessed June 23, 2016).

Shaw, Mark. 2012. *Copywriting : Successful Writing for Design, Advertising, and Marketing*, 2nd ed. London: Laurence King.

Strunk, William I., and White E B. 2009. *The Elements of Style with Revisions, an Introduction, and a Chapter on Writing*. 50th ed. Boston: Pearson.

Three, Rule of. 2011. "What Is the Mysterious 'Rule of Three'? | Copywriters of Distinction." *Copywriters of Distinction I Rule of Three — The Copywriting Studio (Copywriters of Distinction)*. http://rule-of-three.co.uk/what-is-the-rule-of-three-copywriting/ (accessed June 23, 2016).

Thurman, Susan. 2003. *The Only Grammar Book You'll Ever Need: A One-Stop Source for Every Writing Assignment*. Edited by Larry Shea. 2nd ed. Fort Collins, CO: Adams Media.

Wheeler, Alina. 2009. *Designing Brand Identity: An Essential Guide for the Whole Branding Team*. 3rd ed. Chichester: John Wiley & Sons, Ltd.

White, Alex W. 2007. *Advertising Design and Typography*. New York: Allworth Press,U.S.

Zappala, Joseph M. 2010. *Public Relations Writing Worktext: A Practical Guide for the Profession*. Edited by Ann Carden. 3rd ed. New York: Routledge.

Zinsser, William Knowlton. 2006. *On Writing Well: The Classic Guide to Writing Nonfiction*. New York: HarperCollins Publishers.

3
Communication Design

Visual communications of any kind, whether persuasive or informative, from billboards to birth announcements, should be seen as the embodiment of form and function: the integration of the beautiful and the useful.

Rand 2014

Chapter objectives

After completing this chapter, you should be able to:

- apply communication design concepts into creative projects.
- identify and define the visual anatomy of communication design pieces.
- understand how design and writing connect in mass communication.
- analyze aesthetic enhancing design rules.
- create simple design pieces exhibiting visual and rhetorical focus.

3.1 Communication design solves problems

Design solves problems, and for communication designers these problems relate to core client needs in persuasion. The segments of graphic design and advertising design listed below are the pillars of practice in solving client marketing communication (adapted from White (2007, 1).

Marketing communications problems

Focused on solving client needs:

    Advertising
    Corporate identity
    Public relations
    Product promotion
    Product design

Communications Writing and Design: The Integrated Manual for Marketing, Advertising, and Public Relations,
First Edition. John DiMarco.
© 2017 John DiMarco. Published 2017 by John Wiley & Sons, Ltd.

Communication design

Professional practices requiring a creative director or design manager:

> Advertising and marketing
> Editorial and publishing
> Product packaging
> Digital, interactive and web
> Training and development

Graphic and advertising design

Six design disciplines requiring an art director:

> Typography
> Photography
> Illustration
> Copywriting
> Product design
> Architecture/Interior design

3.2 Design direction

Art and creative directors

Being an art director is not so much about being an artist, but it is about knowing great design. Heller and Vienne (2009, 23) espouse the idea that "not every designer can (or will) be an art director — great or otherwise. Many great designers are simply ill suited to manage others; they prefer to do the design things themselves rather than oversee other people's work." This puts the idea of the creative team into the art director role in context to help you decide if you want to design, or manage.

Creative directors and design managers have a wider challenge that goes beyond art direction into management of the entire creative strategy across client needs, vendors, and multiple media. Creatives manage art direction staff, account staff, production staff, and budgeting for campaigns. They are the leaders in connecting business and design.

Understanding the traits of a good art director and creative director will help you if you are one, or when you work with one.

Art directors must:

- Be able to listen to many ideas and see great ones
- Be able to steer a project to success with visual control and confidence
- Be able to delegate design decisions to talented team, members, thoughtfully
- Be able to let others design
- Be able to instigate and evaluate contributions of ideas
- Be able to make proper managerial decisions on time
- Be able to explain design decisions to clients, managers, and staff who are inexperienced in visual communication

Creative directors must:

- Be able to listen to many ideas and see great ones
- Be able to steer sets of project teams to success with overall creative control and financial prudence

- Be able to delegate design decisions to multiple teams and vendors
- Be able to communicate confidently with clients, upper-level management and executives
- Be able to take responsibility for the entire campaign, its projects, people, progress, and outcomes.

3.3 Communication design components

When I worked behind a desk in the persuasion industry, I held several titles throughout my corporate career. Communications Coordinator, Assistant Marketing Manager, Marketing Communications Manager, Director of Advertising, and finally Creative Director, when I ran my own shop. Regardless of the title, the location, or the organization, whether it was writing *and designing* a press release, or developing a full color brochure, I engaged in communication design. When you perform communication design, you may be doing it for a number of different graphic communication reasons, under a plethora of titles, and many clients' foci. The goals of your communication pieces could support education, persuasion, entertainment, or information — or a combination of them. Regardless of the goal, communication design has specific components that are universally important to understand. Become familiar with *layout, typography, images, color, and motion/animation* as these elements occupy the communication design project you will work on during your career.

3.4 Layout

Think about all the layouts you encounter each day on paper and screens. Each time you interact with a new element of media, there is a layout that offers visual composition, which attempts to adhere Gestalt principles. Based on the studies of early twentieth-century German psychologists, Gestalt laws suggest the way the human brain sees objects, orders them and arranges them in their thought process (Golombisky and Hagen 2010). The goal of a strong layout is to utilize the parts in the composition to create a whole image that has continuity in the mind's eye. To do this, layouts need to be composed using structural elements such as grids and adhere to a variety of design rules, like BANGPP.

Layouts are seen everywhere and are created for all mediums including print, web, mobile, desktop, tablet, kiosk, video player, audio player, forms, games, and any other device you can think of that is digital. Layouts are different for multiple media, with the most common substrates being good old paper and our constant companion at home and on the road, the screen. Data-in these two realms imprints via ink or pixels.

Figure 3.1a Advertising layout. Using a typographical play with the word "any," this outdoor advertising campaign and graphic program focuses on persuading tourists and city dwellers to visit the observation deck at the top of 30 Rockefeller Center, the landmark 70-story skyscraper in New York. Design by Michael Gericke, Pentagram. Reproduced by kind permission of Pentagram.

Figure 3.1b Editorial layout. Creating interest for information through enigmatic imagery and clean typography, this editorial page, designed by Pentagram, highlights the commitment of the *New York Times* to the marriage of thoughtful and impactful writing with superior design. Design by Michael Bierut, Pentagram. Reproduced by kind Permission of Pentagram.

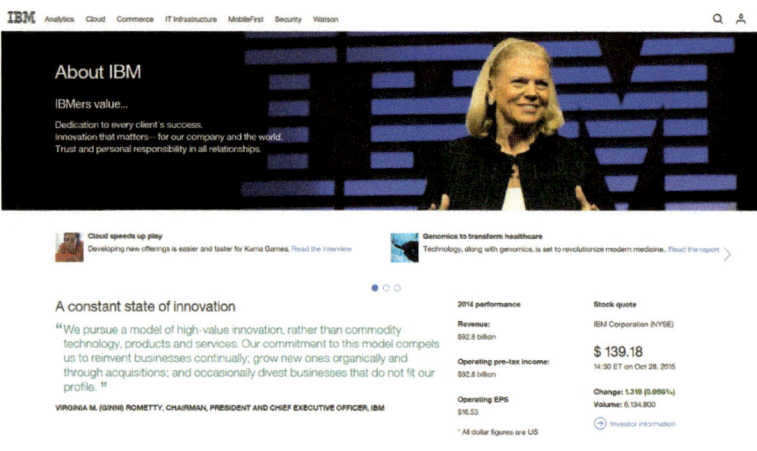

Figure 3.1c Public relations layout. Driven by facts and company pride, this pressroom, public relations layout presents the virtues of IBM, its people, mission, and products through facts, writing, and design, http://www.ibm.com/ibm/us/en/. IBM and the IBM logo are trademarks of International Business Machines Corp., registered in many jurisdictions worldwide.

Figure 3.1d Marketing layout. Driven by san serif typography, this identity for DRY Soda Co offers a marketing platform form signage, retail packaging, and visual merchandising. Design by Turnstyle. Reproduced with kind permission of Turnstyle.

Grids — rule of thirds and the law of thirds

Using grids is critical to web, mobile, and print design. White (2005, 203) defines the grid as "a skeletal guide used to ensure design consistency," which means that grids are critical to design because they provide frameworks to apply Gestalt principles in designs with the goal of achieving consistency and visual closure, making multiple parts one whole image.

There are many different types of grids that can be used in a composition, but the one grid that "provides a wide range of variation for exploration within a controlled system of organization" according to grid systems guru Kimberly Elam (2004, 7), is the 3 × 3 grid. The 3 × 3 column grid allows you to understand the rule of thirds and apply the law of thirds (DiMarco, 2010), which is a great way to figure out where to place elements on a page or screen to help create good design.

The rule of thirds is a go-to layout concept you will need to achieve better visual layouts throughout your career. The technique goes like this: divide the medium into a 3 × 3 grid of nine rectangles and four intersections. The primary design elements should sit within the grid and have dominance in the intersections. Use a secondary design element for balance. The law of thirds dictates that elements do not have to sit directly at the intersections. Elements can be in close proximity, where attention occurs naturally (Elam 2004).

BANGPP — a visual layout rubric

The vitality of a design is dependent on the use of type, image, and space. It is no wonder, as a design educator, the most frequent question new and inexperienced communication designers ask me is "where do I put things on a page?" Well, the grid and the rule of thirds is a great start. You also need a method for evaluating the page or screen design after creation. Using BANGPP, a design rubric developed by DiMarco (2010) you can look at the composition or the collective elements and make decisions on where to put items on the page or screen in the final layout. The criteria, based on sound design principles, help you create or analyze a well-structured page layout. These tenants, coupled with the 3 × 3 grid, provide an easy way to understand layout, and make your compositions better.

B (balance) is the distribution of weight in a composition. Create visual balance by positioning elements on opposite sides of the page. Alternatively, use centering and white space to isolate elements to create less or more visual weight.

A (alignment) is the lining up objects with proportionate distribution. Object and text alignments sit either left, right, center, or justified. Left alignment is most often-used and rarely fails visually, so

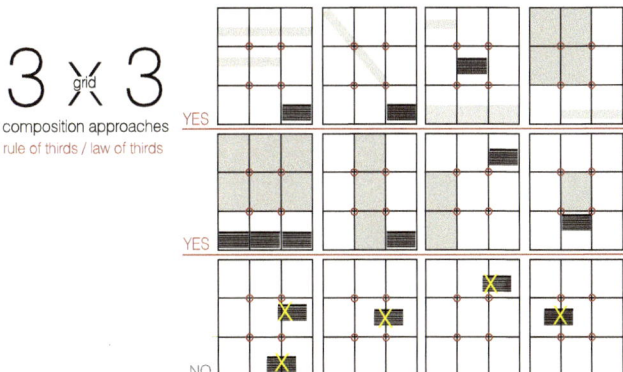

Figure 3.2a Grid usage rules. Understand the 3 × 3 grid rules first, and then break them to explore new approaches. Any element placed on the page must occupy one, two, or three full (with margin) vertical, horizontal, or diagonal sections of the grid. Design elements including type, image, or interactive objects should not land in the middle of a grid square or extend across a portion of it. The red circles represent where naturally the eye is drawn.

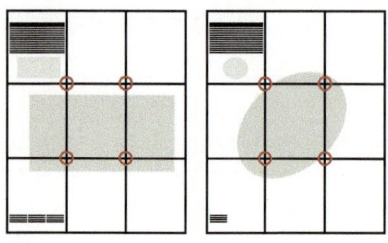
(b)

(c)

Figures 3.2b and c Grids in action. The grid in 3.2b clearly organizes the text in this publication, which uses a three-column grid on the left side and a two-column grid on the right. In 3.2c, a book spread exemplifies the rule of thirds and the law of thirds. Notice how the dominant elements intersect the red circles, where attention is highest. Design by Turnstyle. Reproduced with kind permission of Turnstyle.

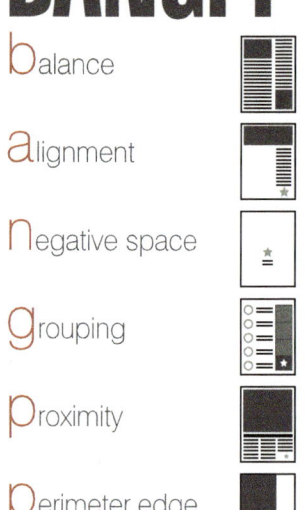

Figure 3.3 BANGPP checklist. BANGPP offers a simple checklist of criteria when looking at a layout. Use BANGPP with a 3 × 3 grid to have a reliable visual approach to designing anything on paper or a screen. Design by John DiMarco.

Figure 3.4 Balance example. Design by Paula Sher, Pentagram. Reproduced with kind permission of Pentagram.

Figure 3.5 Alignment example. Design by Michael Bierut, Pentagram. Reproduced with kind permission of Pentagram.

Figure 3.6 Negative space example. Design by DJ Stout, Pentagram. Reproduced with kind permission of Pentagram.

Figure 3.7 Grouping example. Design by Njenworks.

Figure 3.8 Proximity example. Design by D.J. Stout, Pentagram. Reproduced with kind permission of Pentagram.

Figure 3.9 Perimeter edge example. Design by DJ Stout, Pentagram. Reproduced with kind permission of Pentagram.

use it as your default alignment. Use centering with caution and have a solid reason to do it. Use right when you need a clean visual line on the on the side of the page or for balance. Alignments are also known as "justification," with left alignment having a ragged right edge and justified alignment having a sharp right edge.

N (negative space) is the space that does not contain image or text within a composition. It is the empty part of a composition, also known as the ground, while the text and images make up what is known in art language as the "figure." Figure and ground make up the pieces of a composition. Negative space is vital to good design and contributes to balance. Use negative space to isolate page elements or to emphasize or minimize them.

G (grouping) is the colocation of elements in a composition. The grouping of objects, or closeness, becomes an important way to connect elements in a layout, such as a logo and a website address for example. Another way grouping aids a composition is when combining or connecting graphic elements in a way to create a new and different image from the structured parts.

P (proximity) is the location of elements to each other and the composition. Proximity dictates where things go on a page relative to other elements. Headlines, for example have a certain proximity to a graphic or the body of text in a page. Buttons and links may occupy other proximities to be effective. Where headlines and images are placed in a composition affects the visual quality of the layout. This means that proximity of pieces in a page or screen needs scrutiny and visual planning. Proximity and scale become intertwined in good design.

P (perimeter edge) is the live space for the design and refers to where text or an image bleeds (goes off the page) or uses margin within a composition. Bleed off the page or screen creates a dynamic look, with motion and rhythm, while wide margins create negative space and isolate visuals within the boundary of a layout.

3.5 Typography

Type is more than just placing the cursor on the page and typing using default values, in fact, Meggs (1989, 17–19) said type is "an exact art of measurement and proportion, message and form." Type creates the written word in communication design and fonts are the letterforms we use in typography. Type exists on a page or a screen through fonts, which are single typefaces with a style. Fonts contain the letters, numbers, punctuation marks, and special characters needed for written communication and have varied styles, which collectively create a font family. So for example, Helvetica Bold is a font, and its alternate styles Helvetica Italic, and Helvetica Black are all part of the Helvetica font family. Styles of fonts within families include roman, regular, bold, semibold, italic, book, oblique, heavy, black, condensed, thin, and bold italic. Not every font family contains all of these styles so if you need bold and the font you picked does not have a bold style, choose a different font.

The way we place type on a page means something. Communication designers know this and because typography is so critical to good design, they are literally obsessive over it. This means following rules and using grids to ensure layouts with text are consistent, hierarchal, and communicate clearly, without question.

Remember, fonts are files installed on a PC (Mac or Windows) and are specific to computers and not programs, so do not expect the same fonts to be on all computers. Digital page layout programs such as Adobe InDesign have a feature to collect fonts for print output, which ensures what you designed is what prints. Programs like Adobe Photoshop and Adobe Illustrator allow exporting and flattening images, embedding fonts or converting them from being in an editable text document into a single, flat image for final output.

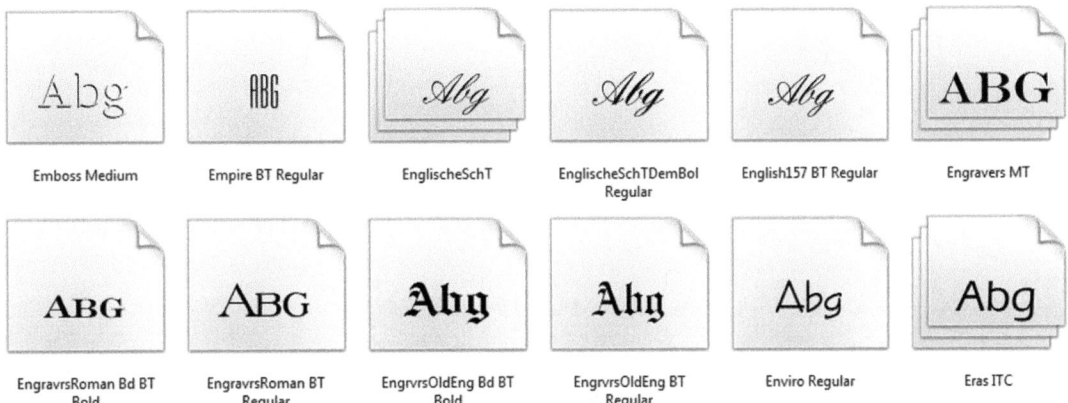

Callout 3A Fonts are files too.

Choosing fonts

There are two main types of text in a communication design; display text (also known as headline text) and running text (also known as body copy). Seven common type categories exist and give us a wide range of faces to use in our designs. Knowing which face to use is always a challenge, but identifying different face types and following some simple rules will help you make better typography decisions. When choosing a typeface, first consider what the tone of the message is and decide if your font needs to whisper or yell, and should they be naturalistic (serif) or industrial (san serif)? Understanding the audience will help you determine tone and form. Finally, what fonts do you have on your computer to use? Download fonts with varying usage rights from font farms like DAFONT, or purchase fonts through classic foundries like MonoType. Fonts also come bundled with various software packages.

Setting type

We use computer software to set type digitally. Writing a press release in Word, laying out a publication spread in InDesign, creating an infographic in Photoshop, and designing a logo in Illustrator all require digital typography. In Word or PowerPoint, use the formatting palette to set type. For Adobe applications, the standardized type palettes look and act the same. Regardless of the program, setting type relies on understanding the attributes for characters and paragraphs. Character attributes in digital design programs dictate the way text looks on a page. Paragraph attributes manage how lines of text are set in relationship to each other and the page itself.

Type attributes
The attributes of type change the way it looks on the page. We can manipulate both character and paragraph attributes. Character attributes that can be manipulated using digital tools include:

Character attributes
A. *Font*: the name of specific typeface and style. Helvetica Bold Italic, for example.
B. *Size*: the height of the font in either pixels or points. Remember there are 72 points in one inch, which equates to a 72 point letter totaling one inch in height. Fonts sizes range from 7 point to

set in Garamond Book Italic Condensed 60 pt.

Garamond 10 pt. regular
Garamond 10 pt. italic
Garamond 10 pt. bold
Garamond 10 pt. bold italic

Times New Roman 10 pt. regular
Times New Roman 10 pt. italic
Times New Roman 10 pt. bold
Times New Roman 10 pt. bold italic

Bodini BT 10 pt. roman
Bodini BT 10 pt. bold condensed
Bodini BT 10 pt. book
Bodini BT 10 pt. book italic
Bodini BT 10 pt. italic
Bodini BT 10 pt. bold
Bodini BT 10 pt. bold italic

Figure 3.10 Stay in the font family for consistency. Font families contain various styles of a typeface (Futura, for example) such as bold, book, black, heavy, oblique, plus more. Use fonts in one family for an easy way to achieve consistency when you are unsure of how to mix fonts.

Garamond 36 pt. bold italic

Times New Roman 36 pt. bold

Bodini BT 36 pt. bold condensed

set in News Gothic BT Bold 46.67 pt.

Avant Garde BT 10 pt. book
Avant Garde BT 10 pt. book oblique
Avant Garde BT 10 pt. medium
Avant Garde BT 10 pt. medium oblique

Gill Sans MT 10 pt. regular
Gill Sans MT 10 pt. italic
Gill Sans MT 10 pt. bold
Gill Sans MT 10 pt. bold italic

Futura BT 10 pt. medium
Futura BT 10 pt. medium bold italic
Futura BT 10 pt. extra black
Futura BT 10 pt. extra black condensed
Futura BT 10 pt. Extra Black Condensed Italic
Futura BT 10 pt. Extra Black Italic
Futura BT 10 pt. medium condensed italic
Futura BT 10 pt. heavy
Futura BT 10 pt. heavy italic

Gills Sans MT 36 pt. bold italic

Avant Garde BT 36 pt book

Futura BT 36 pt. extra black

12 point for running text, with type larger than 18 point used for display text such as headlines, subheads, type as image, and logos.

C. *Kerning*: adding or removing space between pairs of characters. Kerning is used primarily on display text because at large sizes letters tend to have inconsistent spacing. When this occurs, tightening or loosening of kerning helps the letterforms sit properly. One typical pair that needs leading is the **TT** letter combo or the **To** combo, so look out for these when setting display text over 18 point.

D. *Horizontal scale*: stretching letters horizontally by percentage. This attribute should rarely be touched, and only for display type. Never use this on running text (body copy).

E. *Baseline shift*: shifting type above or below the standard baseline. The baseline is where the type sits on a line. Lower-case letters with descenders go below the baseline, as with the lower-case letter "y."

F. *Font style*: font families can have various styles including bold, italic, semi bold, black, and oblique, among others. These are the actual font styles, rather than the faux styles you can add.

G. *Leading*: the space between lines. Leading typically needs to be 2 points larger to avoid spacing issues, however, this depends on the typeface and use of capitals or lower-case.

H. *Tracking*: adding or removing space between all characters within a block of text to create incremental space between letters or words. Tracking allows you to fit text into a space and is measured in ems, which are a proportion of type size.

I. *Vertical scale*: stretching letters vertically by percentage. This attribute should rarely be touched, and only for display type. Never use this on running text (body copy).

Figure 3.11 Fonts that go beyond serif and sans serif: Slab serif, Script or cursive, Black letter, Decorative, Symbol.

J. *Color*: change font color here by accessing the color picker in Photoshop to attach a CMYK, Pantone/spot, or RGB color the type.

K. *Faux type effects*: applying a "fake" bold, italic, strikethrough, and small caps allow you to enhance text when the font style you want is unavailable. Use these at a minimum.

Paragraph attributes

Figure 3.12 Characters and type. Character palette from Adobe Photoshop. Once you understand the basic attributes of type, you can apply your knowledge across applications.

Paragraph: space created by pressing the enter key. Paragraphs, based on page attributes, may or may not have text on them. Their empty size can be manipulated using font size. Show hidden characters and highlight the mark, then make font size changes have invisible spacing options.

M. *Alignment*: the left, right, center, or justified edge of text. Setting alignment is critical in creating clean visual edges for the eye to follow.
N. *Left indentation*: the space in or out of a block of text. Indentation can be left or right, or both.
O. *Hanging indent*: the first line indent of a paragraph.
P. *Space before paragraph*: static space added before a paragraph.
Q. *Hyphenate*: keeps or removes hyphens in a text block.
R. *Right indentation*: the space in or out of a block of text. Indentation can be left or right, or both.
S. *Space after paragraph*: static space added after a paragraph.

Drop cap: drops one or more capital letters down within a set number of lines and characters in a paragraph.

Columns: separate rows of text paragraphs that allows paragraphs to be broken up for easier visual digestion. Columns are used in grids, with the 3 × 3 being an industry standard.

Baseline grid: the grid that creates a standard baseline within a publication.

Two kinds of type: display type and body text

When we set type on a page or screen we need to consider the two kinds of type pieces. They are display type and body text. Display type is text set larger than 18 point and is considered a focal point of interest in a design. Body text is set lower than 18 point and typically set between 7.5 and 12 point for long passages beyond a few words. The *New York Times*, for example may set text for an article in the newspaper to 9 point, while brochure copy might be set to 10 or 11 point. The default size on most word processors is 12 point — do not keep it though, use 9–11 point body copy for a clean,

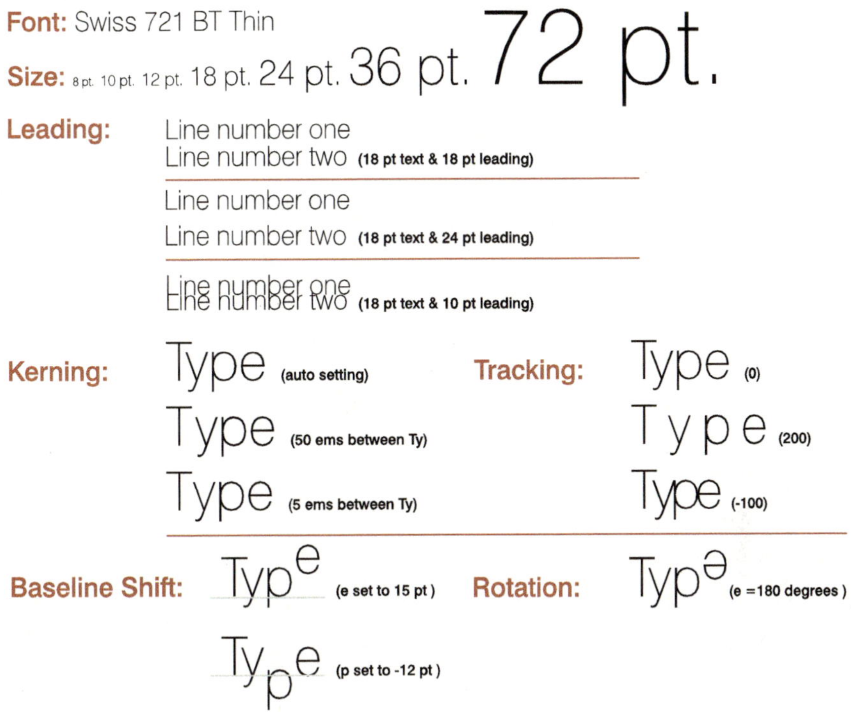

Figure 3.13 Type attributes. Typography is the art of setting type. It requires understanding and keen appreciation of characters and the attributes that give them beauty and uniqueness.

Font: Swiss 721 BT Thin

Size: 8 pt. 10 pt. 12 pt. 18 pt. 24 pt. 36 pt. 72 pt.

Leading:
Line number one
Line number two (18 pt text & 18 pt leading)

Line number one
Line number two (18 pt text & 24 pt leading)

Line number one
Line number two (18 pt text & 10 pt leading)

Kerning:
Type (auto setting)
Type (50 ems between Ty)
Type (5 ems between Ty)

Tracking:
Type (0)
T y p e (200)
Type (-100)

Baseline Shift: Type (e set to 15 pt)
Type (p set to -12 pt)

Rotation: Type (e = 180 degrees)

legible look in print. For screens, experiment with slightly larger sizes for typography in video games, presentations, videos, kiosks, websites, and mobiles. This is critical, as you need to test various fonts for use on different screen sizes. With paper, we print a proof to see how type looks. For the screen typography, we perform prototyping and usability testing to see how communications appear and perform on various size screens, operating systems, and delivery platforms.

Display type is highly readable, attention-getting, brash, and attractive. Headlines are display type; subheads can also be set as display type or may be better as body text, depending on the need for clarity. Graphical type such as logos and type illustrations are display type. Display type can be

Figure 3.14 Paragraph positioning. Paragraph attributes palette in Adobe Photoshop. Once you understand the basic attributes of paragraphs, you can apply your knowledge across applications.

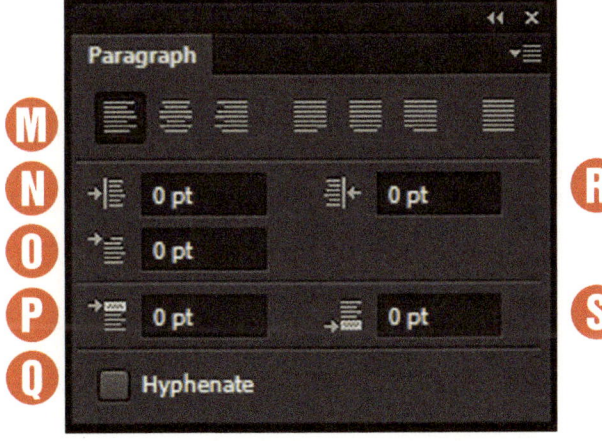

60 Communications Writing and Design

Figure 3.15 Display type and body text. The display grabs the reader visually (readability) and the body explains the details clearly (legibility). The prop for the anniversary poster for AIGA/NY is a mix tape the designer created for the organization's launch party in 1983. Design by Michael Bierut, Pentagram. Reproduced with kind permission of Pentagram.

enigmatic, elegant, old-fashioned, modern or any other graphical style that will communicate with your audience and deliver the message.

Intermediate type is between sizes, typically a subhead and can be styled after either display or body text attributes, with manipulations.

Body text is highly legible, information delivering, vividly clear, and easy to read. Body copy also known as running text should be highly legible so that it is easy to read, without hesitation or confusion.

Readability and legibility

In addition to the various physical attributes seen in typography such as font, size, leading, and kerning, which have numerical values, there are also two capacities that become critical in looking at type as an information delivery system (White 2005). They are readability and legibility.

Your goal for any piece is to improve the readability and boost the legibility of the type to maximize a visual, emotional, and rational connection with the viewer or reader. Make every headline highly readable and do not settle for the default font — care about type and the reader will respond.

Readability refers to the level of "attention-getting" delivered from type on a page or a screen. Legibility refers to how easy type is to read. We combine readability and legibility to create visual attraction, visual contrast, and clear information delivery in a communication vehicle. Headlines are typically very readable, which makes eyes gravitate to a page, while body text is very legible, which makes reading longer passages easy on the eyes and brain.

Readable type ... what to remember

It grabs readers visually and creates an "overall reading experience" (White 2005, 131), which is "macro-typography." High readability makes a piece interesting, but in many cases produces low legibility, which is the ease type can be read under normal reading conditions (White 2005).

- Use it in display type.

    Make the readability of headlines, type illustrations, logos, and other display type shine by considering size first and then other text attributes. If text is larger than 18 point, make it display type and give it the attention both as a designer and as a visual element it deserves. Take care to set display type diligently and remember type of 18 point and above should be kerned for maximum letter spacing

- Use it to connect to the audience's self-interest.

    Headlines for a medical magazine article for doctors would include some visual medical reference, like veins running through the text, while headlines for a skateboarding magazine designed with young adults in mind might utilize tagging as a headline theme. Think about the audience, what they know, or would attract them.

- Use it for short and memorable copy only

    Keep uses of display type for short pieces of text, as we mentioned. Headlines, some subheads, logo type, graphical type, and type illustrations are all worthy of display type.

- Use a design program to create display text.

    Making headlines graphical is an excellent way to explore fully creating display type. Use Photoshop to make a graphical headline and drop it into a page layout program like MS Word or Adobe InDesign.

Legible type...what to remember

It guides readers and creates a high fidelity information delivery experience, focusing on letters, words, and lines, which is "micro-typography" (White 2005, 131). High legibility makes a communication piece easy to discern, and allows the reader to absorb it seamlessly and dynamically with their eyes so they can move to the next logical input. If something is illegible, the mind stops the thought as it has to help the eyes decipher the message and meaning before understanding can occur.

- Use it in body text.

    Make the legibility of body text vividly clear by considering font, size, leading, and color each time you set body text. Body text can bea range of sizes with mice copy at 6.5-7 point and main copy text from 8-12 point. Start at 10 point body text and work up or down to find the right fit and feel. Never settle for using only the default size of 12 pt.

- Use BANGPP as a guide

    When you look at body text on a screen or page, you want it to be visually comfortable. When setting margins and columns think about balance, alignment, negative space, grouping, proximity, and perimeter edge (DiMarco 2010).

- Use it for long copy only.

    Be mindful and use clear body text for text-heavy works (anything over a paragraph) in marketing, advertising, public relations, and journalism. Long form like books and magazines and shorter marketing communications pieces like brochures and catalogs require strong attention to body text.

- Use style sheets to keep body text consistent and hierarchical.

    Keep uses of body text consistent by using style sheets in your layout programs. Any time you have more than one paragraph, it is a good idea to make a basic style sheet that you use as a guide when setting section heads (not headlines), subheads, and body text.

    Call out 3B Keeping it consistent with styles. Style sheets in page layout programs provide consistency and hierarchy for long form typography.

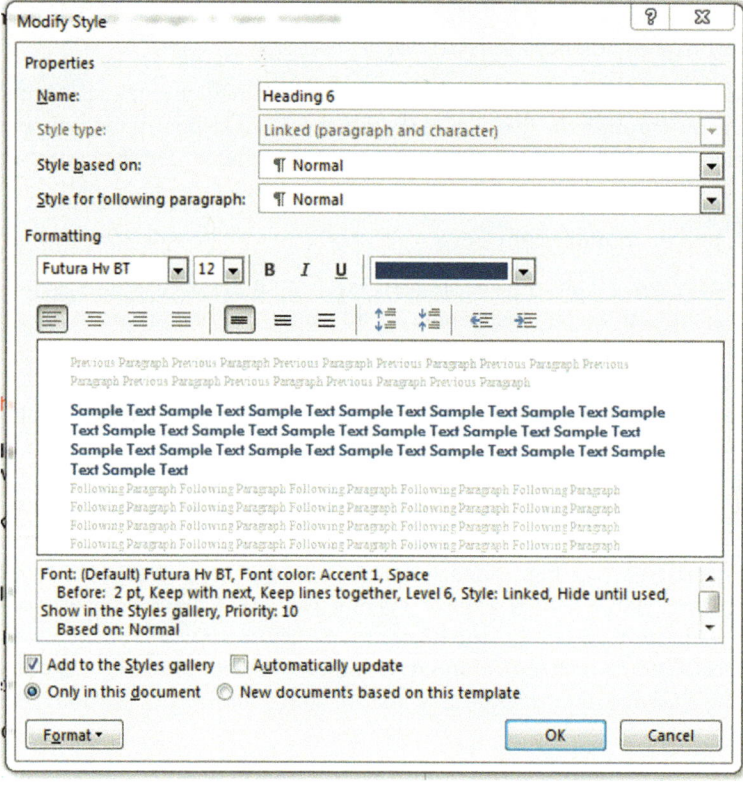

Remember, if you are using a page layout program such as Microsoft Word or InDesign, utilize style sheets for long documents or short ones with lots of text. Style sheets provide standardized text and paragraph settings. Character and paragraph styles, named and applied, allow you to manipulate

Figure 3.16 Readability and legibility in harmony. This book design presents New York City's design guidelines for promoting physical activity in the urban environment, to help address the twenty-first-century health concerns of obesity and related chronic diseases. Design by Luke Hayman, Pentagram. Reproduced with kind permission of Pentagram.

individual attributes each time you want them applied to a text selection. Setting style sheets is easy. Highlight the text, apply the attributes, and then name and save the style in the style sheet palette of whatever page layout program you use. The styles can be set up and edited to allow you to control the typography globally within the document, which greatly contributes to consistency and fewer typographical errors from incorrect attributes and position.

Hierarchy and consistency

Hierarchy
Placing display text and body text on a page or screen can be a free flowing and random process when we are using type as a design element. However, when we are setting long form documents (anything over a paragraph), hierarchy and consistency play a key role in facilitating visual harmony. Hierarchy dictates top-down structure, with power at the top and descending importance. In the case of typography, the top-down structure usually takes the form of headline, subhead, and body copy in publications for marketing, advertising, or position to imply hierarchy. For documents that are text laden, text size should vary with styles to imply an outline of sorts so that established levels of information are stacked in story form. The head (not headline) may be 16 point, the subhead may be 13 point and the body copy 10 point. This size variance establishes a visual hierarchy for the reader and sets the "top-down" structure for the document.

Consistency
Putting things that are alike in the same place, as the same style, and in the same way each time is how you achieve consistency. Style sheets help you do this, but most important is the commitment and diligence from the designer. You must not take consistency for granted; otherwise, your work will suffer. Visual anomalies (or mistakes) cripple the impact of designs tremendously and are the difference between professional-level and sub-pro work. Things like too many varying font faces or sizes,

Figure 3.17 Hierarchy and consistency help readers digest. This spread for the Fact Book for USC's College of Letters, Arts, and Sciences creates visual hierarchy and structure using typography choices of font, size, color, and placement. Design by DJ Stout, Pentagram. Reproduced with kind permission of Pentagram.

coupling images that are different styles, and requiring viewers or users to rely on recall rather than simple recognition detract from consistency. Think about visual contrast, how you can create consistent looking documents, while highlighting critical information points. The typefaces you choose and their usage foster a consistent look and easy digestion, or a jagged look, which is cumbersome to decipher, much like a ransom note.

To obtain consistency, stick to a few simple rules:

- Use a maximum of two typefaces per project. You can vary the styles of the fonts (bold, italic), but confine yourself to one family. Type should be the same, or completely different.
- If you use two fonts, they need to be completely different and cannot be similar where they could be mistaken for each other. For example, you would not use Times and Garamond together because they are very similar in their serif style. Using Helvetica and Arial would be a mistake also as they are almost identical in stature. However, if you combine Helvetica and Garamond, we can see now see a nice interplay between serif and san serif faces that creates visual contrast.
- If you are not sure about type, use one font family with varying size and one family style (bold preferably) to keep it simple.

Responsible typography in action

Typography is a skill and a craft, executed by professionals who study communication design, graphic arts, publishing, and letterforms with meticulous veracity. This should not scare you, but inspire you to care about text and typography throughout your career. Make a commitment to every project you execute that you will take care and consider the typefaces you use, how you use them, and how the audience will breathe in the text on their way to understanding the message and story.

Typography considerations

The combination of display type and text type make up most communication pieces. The display type and the text type need to work together as visual elements to first draw in the reader, and then communicate the message. In his book, his book *Thinking in Type: The Practical Philosophy of Typography*,

3 Communication Design | 65

Figure 3.18 Typography elements in beautiful harmony. This spread by Luke Hayman for *Time* magazine illustrates all the critical elements of readability and legibility. The exploded view shows responsible typography in action and breaks down what components need serious consideration when setting long form type. Can you find examples of each element?

typography guru, art director, and author Alex V. White suggests concentrating on the following elements to achieving both readability and legibility in typographyi: I have added some suggestions to this adapted list with the goal of providing some simple guidelines for the beginning designer.

1. Type size
   The size of the type is critical to the visual cohesion of the composition and the clarity of the message. When creating display type (headlines), the type should be set larger than 18 point to provide hierarchy and dominance. When creating text type, use 9–11 point type for maximum legibility. If the text type is too large, it hurts the Gestalt and looks incorrect.
2. Type weight
   The weight of the type refers to heavy, medium, light, or thin. Medium-weight text provides the maximum legibility and heavy weight provides high visual contrast and works well for display type. Lightweight works well for a less heavy page layout.
3. Type posture
   The posture of the type is the style of the type, for example italic or slanted, which is harder to read than roman (standard), so it should be avoided.
4. Line length and columns
   The length of a line should be around two alphabets' worth of letters (52 characters) to create an optimal reading experience. Longer lines create more difficult legibility because the desire to keep reading after a few lines is diminished. Smaller line lengths create an easier, quicker read for the viewer to recognize the message. Use multiple column grids to ease the reader's eyes and keep the text flowing.

5. Letter spacing and word spacing

    Good letter spacing is transparent from the design and eases visual digestion of words. Using tracking to manipulate word and letter spacing in a word and kerning to manipulate space between two letters are ways to experiment with letter spacing and word spacing in display type. Use kerning and tracking tools carefully so you do not ruin the uniformity and clarity of text type. Never put two spaces after a period. There is no such thing as a double space in digital design. Never use the space bar (adding multiple spaces) in place of using tabs or indents.

6. Line spacing

    Leading is space between lines, also known as lines spacing. For leading to be set properly it must create neutral spaces between lines that enhance legibility. Leading can also be varied to create an effect (compressed or extended) with display type.

7. Justification

    Justification refers to the text lines being ragged (left aligned ragged right) or going to the same edge at the end of the paragraph (justified). Ragged lines are easier to read, but justification creates an engaging aesthetic to the form of the text by creating implied lines. Use left aligned-right ragged in most cases and be sure to include at least six words per line when using justified type to avoid uneven word spacing.

8. All caps vs. lower case

    All caps are more difficult to read than lower case, so avoid using all caps in text type. You can experiment with using all caps in brief display and intermediate type, but be sure to use the approach sparingly.

9. Type and background

    Keep text and image high contrast for maximum readability and legibility. Avoid using reverse text for small sizes. This means white text on dark backgrounds. Small reversed out serifs are hard to read. Use san serif typeface (without tails-straight edged) when using reverses.

10. Serif vs. sans serif

    Serif typefaces have horizontal stokes (tails) at the bottom and the top of the letters and are commonly used in text type because they are easy to read. The newspaper is set to Times New Roman, a serif face that has eloquent legibility and is very easy for the eyes to digest. Serif fonts are more organic because of the flowing forms that exist in serif typefaces. Sans serif typefaces have sharp edges and a modern look. They work well in headlines (display type) and in reverse type (text type or intermediate type). Mixing serif and san serif typefaces, (the right mix) creates visual contrast and helps the eye recognize primary, secondary, and intermediate type elements in the composition.

3.6 Images

Visual content, sometimes called "art" or "image" in the creative industries, are the visual components used in communication pieces. All "art" needs to be conceptualized, chosen, developed, commissioned, and edited. Regardless of the kind of asset needed, creative directors, designers, marketing managers, publicity directors, advertising account executives, photographers, editors, publishers, art directors, and illustrators work together to produce images for use in marketing, advertising, public relations, and news projects. Images can be photographs, type graphics, illustrations, animations, motion graphics, or full video. Different types of images require the use of different software for design and output. Professionals work at all levels of production, management, editorial, sales, and distribution to create billions of communications that become touchpoints for an infinite number of big and small brands.

Photographs

Born around 1855, the practice of photojournalism and the development of the halftone in the 1880s (Heller and Vienne 2009) captured the world differently forever and gave rise to a humankind culture that is fascinated and persuaded by images. Since the formal creation of the fields of photojournalism, direct advertising, and public relations in the in the late 1800s to early 1900s, the persuasion and news industries have relied on photos to tell stories, sell products, and change public opinion.

In electronic media production terms "bitmap image " or "raster file " are their digital species. In traditional terms, they are photographs, or halftones. They create interest in communications pieces and are a vital part of messaging. Using photography effectively in communication projects relies on shooting and sourcing photographs that will make a connection with the message and persuade the reader or viewer to think, act, or buy in a way that is predetermined. Images need to convey meaning beyond the words on the page. For advertising, images need to be thought provoking (How will this help me?) or disturbing (How will this hurt me?). In public relations, photographs should portray visual evidence and create a perception, sometimes beyond reason. In marketing, photography visually presents a target consumer, a product, its features, and potential benefits to the consumer.

Crossing the line of consumer and professional, photography is required to create content for most creative projects in marketing communications. However, do you need a professional photographer to take good photos? Yes and no. Professionals add a higher level of sophistication to a body of images. They also have expertise in lighting, framing, and shooting in unique situations, like sports or public venues, so they usually do not miss important shots because of lack of knowledge or technical messes. Many professional photographers now perform image retouching and file conversions so images are ready for placement into publications right away, without additional steps. If you have a budget, hire a pro to shoot your photos for commercial applications. The next best thing to having a pro shoot live is to use stock photography from an agency that offers royalty-free images. Companies like Getty Images, Dreamstime, and Photostock offer high quality images for virtually any genre or application. Their libraries are deep and continue to grow as photographers worldwide constantly contribute their images to these repositories.

This does not mean that others who have not studied photography formally cannot take great images for professional use in the creative field. With the cost of DSLR cameras at feasible levels and the rise of smart phones with sophisticated cameras, understanding how to shoot photos at events, for product pieces, and for news is a valuable skill for all communications professionals to possess. You can visit the companion website of this book in the appendix section to read a short primer on photography by Rex Thomas. It will help you get started and explain the most common terms. Another suggestion is to take a photography or photojournalism class at a local college or camera store to get a hands-on learning experience to shoot photos under the supervision of an expert.

Illustrations

Known traditionally as drawings, technically as vector artwork, or in generic form called clipart, illustrations have a special place in marketing communications. They can stand alone and provide attention-grabbing intrigue as with photographs, and they can tone down images that would otherwise be too graphic or disturbing in photographic form. Illustrations can also offer exploded

Figure 3.19 The need for photography. Photography is a critical element across marketing, advertising, and public relations pieces as it is a main source of content. Design by Turnstyle. Reproduced by kind permission of Turnstyle.

technical views of complex processes and products and coupled with animation and video create compelling communication experiences. Heller and Vienne (2009, 40–43) describe illustrators as having one of two approaches to design, either contemporary or retro. Contemporary illustrators are working within their time, with focus on the moment and the now. Digital imagery, geometry, pop culture, and social commentary frequent contemporary work, while retro illustrators focus on styles embedded in the past. Satire, imitation, and the recreation of past styles are the trademark of retro illustration.

Using illustrations effectively relies upon the quality of the illustration, its intent, and the audience. Illustrations take various forms including logos, packaging graphics, TV bugs, line drawings, infographics, digital paintings, complex technical diagrams, collages, and hand-drawn art. Illustrative forms need digital files for placement into a print, web, or motion design application. Editing and final output are critical steps, which require clean files. This means that they need to be technically sound regarding resolution and scale. In addition, illustrations need to communicate the message in an intriguing, understandable way that goes beyond a photograph or text description. If you need to explain the illustration, it does not work. Remember, an illustration should explain and represent on its own.

You can create illustrations on your own using applications such as Adobe Illustrator and Photoshop. Another way to gather illustrations for your layouts is to commission an illustrator to create them. Finally, you can buy the rights to use royalty-free digital illustrations from stock agencies, many of which also sell stock photographs.

Figure 3.20a, b, and c The value of illustration. Illustration is used in marketing, advertising, and public relations to visualize information, create visual identity, and alter realism. Logotypes, brandmarks, charts, and drawings are all illustrations. Packaging uses illustrations extensively. Design by Turnstyle. Reproduced with kind permission of Turnstyle.

Motion graphics and animation

Motion graphics incorporates multimedia components including text, still (two-dimensional) graphics, three-dimensional modelled graphics, audio, video, and animation into a four-dimensional, time based composition. Communication designers who develop motion graphics use time based design to integrate video, audio, and sometimes animation to create the illusion of change over time and graphics "in motion." The most prevalent use of motion graphics and animation is in video gaming, television and film, and now on the web in sites and corporate content. Titling sequences, television show intros and bumpers, television graphics, web banners, opening film credits, gaming sequences, and your cell phone start-up screen all-incorporate time based motions graphics.

Using motion graphics effectively relies on visual quality, message, and most importantly, time. Time is a critical element in motion graphics and requires a designer to be mindful of rhythm and space to insure the work properly communicates in the specified media. To accomplish this, motion graphics work incorporates a variety of multimedia tools and integrates animation into motion pieces.

Visual quality is important in all screen and print media. But most importantly, narrative value, character and story, is paramount in animation. Production value is paramount in motion graphics. Just think of the quality of artwork (or lack of) put forth in popular animated television series such as *Beavis and ButtHead* and *South Park*. The popularity of those shows did not come from dazzling visuals, but from solid narrative connection based on highly creative writing. Those animated shows are presented technically through sequencing of created frames, not a montage of media resulting in motion graphics. Three-dimensional animations require both narrative value and production value, as seen in high budget 3D animation blockbusters that integrate animation and live action such as *The Lego Movie* and *Jurassic World*.

Another facet to animation and motion graphics is interactivity, which is an interaction between a user and a product or experience. Interfaces provide the user navigation dashboards that deliver options and pathways to access more information or allow execution of actions (like rolling a bowling ball on a Wii or racing a car the Fast Five mobile game). Once designers and artists create characters or wire frame screens, which are prototype layouts of interactive products like websites and apps, motion designers and programmers add functionality in the form of actions, which are coded instructions that allow users to interact with the digital product and offer data exchange (things like log-ins, user accounts, and high score lists). The quality of the user experience based on the interface design is known as usability. Think about apps and websites you visit. Are the highly usable? When you engage with these digital environments, do they make you think too much about how to do things or are they offering a seamless experience that operates on recognition, rather than recall? These are the questions asked by usability experts when testing digital products including websites, games, apps, kiosks, operating systems, programs, and any ither digital interface.

Motion graphics and animation are occasionally lumped together, or interchanged with each other in definition. Granted, there are similarities between the two. Some professionals may converge the terms. On the surface, they seem to be the same; however, there are distinct differences between the two techniques. Differences, which are critical to executing or managing content development and production for screen based, moving media.

Similarities
(a) Motion graphics and animation both use multiple media to deliver the message.
(b) Motion graphics and animation both use time, space, and rythym in compositions.
(c) Motion graphics and animation both use compositing and keyframing of media in a timeline and layers.

Differences
1. Animation typically involves characters or objects coming to life as the main content. Motion graphics uses design elements, images, and typography to deliver a message. Animation should tell a story.
2. Character animation projects rarely use type, except for titling sequences, and even then, many times frames are illustrated. Animating type is an animation technique that is used heavily in motion graphics. When we speak of animating type, we are bringing type to life. Motion graphics projects rely heavily on type and type animations.
3. Animations can be simple frame-by-frame compilations, which create change over time through sequence, and create message through the artwork, opposed to message through motion. Motion graphics incorporate moving elements for message.
4. Motion graphics for the web may include interactive components, such as links or dynamic user controls. Animation is cinematic in nature. Motion graphics in many instances is interactive in nature.
5. Motion graphics uses identity elements including logos and product artwork. Animation uses characters mostly or animates type or objects.

Figure 3.21 Motion graphics are used in interactive and web projects and require attention to rhythm, timing, and space.

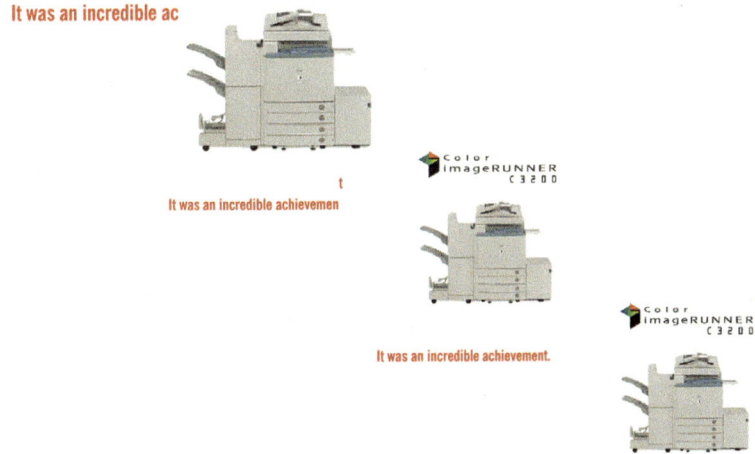

3.7 Color

Color is an important part of communication design. Using color, vividly delivered within marketing communications through screen has become an important skill for professional communicators.

Color sensation and attention

When we think of color, we think of grabbing the attention of the viewer. Color does create attention, but first it creates sensation, which is an actual physical event that causes the body to respond to a stimulus. Sensation is just the beginning, as the brain next must engage in perception, which identifies and defines the object relevant to other elements in the environment. Color is secondary to recognition, meaning that we first recognize of the object against its background then we get the sensation (Holtzschue 2006, 30–34). This contributes to the fact that people are selective in their attention and will visually gravitate to images and colors, depending on how involved they are in the task (Weinschenk 2011, 39–40). Color can aid in that process by creating sensation as images lure viewers in.

Color matters in design because it connects people and brands. Brands have used color as a device to stimulate memory in consumers forever. Color makes brands distinct and carries tradition such as the Coca Cola logo, with its red background with reverse (white) text, which has stood proud for over a century. Another great example is Target, with its red bull's eye that dominates its branding across media. Think about Big Blue, IBM, which has made blue (PMS300) a part of every corporate their corporate identity. On the other hand, the absence of color is also an approach to sensation. Using black and white adds a timeless feeling to a piece and can create an elegant or somber mood. Black and white, combined with color, can highlight content and drive visual attraction to a communication. Initially, developed logos need to "work" in black and white, and then development of color versions begins.

Color usage reinforces an idea, and in many cases turns that idea into an idiom. An idiom is an idea understood through common speech, with a simple route to comprehension (White 1990). Think, "the sky is blue," or "hell is red," "the Fourth of July is red, white, and blue," and "Halloween is black and orange." These common perceptions make color decisions easier and offer a starting point for thinking of how people react to color in design.

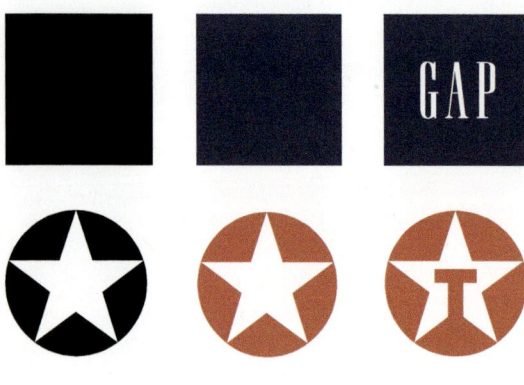

Figure 3.22 Shape, color, and form in sequence. We see shapes first, and then color, and then we make sense of form (Wheeler 2006). This illustrates how important the design of a mark is to the identity and cognition to consumers.

Understanding color terminology

Color, based on light, comes from a host of illuminated sources including the sun, light bulbs, neon signs, projectors, and monitors. Light energy is transmitted in waves of various amplitudes (lengths), Comknown as wavelengths. These wavelengths corresponding to various colors, are received by the eye, and then a signal is transmitted to the brain that signals recognition of a particular color (Holtzschue 2006). Computer applications for digital imaging and painting are a canvas that allows mixing in the color domains using the artist colors of red, yellow, and blue with the additive colors of RGB. Then, software allows translation for printed output to CMYK colors, the subtractive color model, based on ink pigments, which are cyan, yellow, magenta, and black.

The basic terminology of describing color in action in design includes the terms hue, value, shade, tint, saturation, and contrast.

Hue is the name of the color, also known as pure color. Brown, red, purple, orange, green are hues. Consider all slight variations as hues also.
Value is the lightness or darkness of a hue.
Shade is a hue when it is made darker (adding black).
Tint is a hue when it is made lighter (adding white). We can use hues in different values to create tints or shades of that hue. A tint is a percentage of a color with added white. One hundred percent black gives you black. Fifty percent black gives you gray.
Saturation (also called chroma) is the vividness or dullness of a color, which enhances or minimizes the intensity of the color.
Contrast is the result of comparing values. Black and brown have low contrast. Black and yellow have high contrast. We choose and manipulate hue, value, shade, tint, saturation, and contrast when we create digital design compositions for print and screen.

The artists' color wheel (ROYGBP)

The artists' color wheel is a spectrum (range) of visible hues (colors) in order. The color wheel consists of six (**R**ed, **O**range, **Y**ellow, **G**reen, **B**lue, **P**urple) or 12 colors (ROYGBV plus the in-between colors).

The six-color wheel contains

Primary colors   red (r) in RGB = 255, 0, 0
                                     yellow (y) in RGB = 255, 255, 0
                                       blue (b) in RGB = 0, 0, 255

Using these three primary colors, secondary colors (in-between colors) are made by an equal mix of two of the three primary colors.

Secondary colors green (b + y) in RGB = 0, 255, 0
orange (r + y) in RGB = 255, 155, 0
purple (r + b) in RGB = 155, 0, 255

The twelve-color wheel adds another layer of colors with tertiary colors, which lay intermediate to primary and secondary colors on the wheel. Mixing the three primaries in different percentages creates tertiary colors.

Tertiary colors

orange — red
yellow — orange
yellow — green
blue — green
blue — violet
red — violet

Choosing color using wheel schemes

You need to decide on colors before and during development of a print or screen project. The color wheel reveals a multitude of visual color choices to create a simple palette. We can describe different color groupings on the color wheel as color schemes, which offer a standardized way to start a

Figure 3.23 The artists' color wheel (ROYGBV). Color wheel with primary, secondary, intermediate, warm and cool colors. Design by Kristen Crawford. Reproduced with kind permission of Kristen Crawford.

color palette or stick to a simple approach to matching colors, without having to think too extensively about your subsequent choices. Color wheel schemes include warm and cool, monochromatic, complimentary, analogous, contrasting, achromatic, and black plus.

Warm and cool color

In some cases, color schemes offer a way to describe the sensory attribute of a color residing on the color wheel. This becomes important when we are trying to evoke feeling through a piece by using color as a guiding element in a design. If the headline of a piece was a cliché like "It's getting hot in here," what colors would you use to communicate that idea? When talking about color, one common metaphor identifying colors or palettes as **warm or cool color**. The "visual temperature" of color makes its warm or cool.

Monochromatic color schemes

Simplicity is virtuous in design and quite useful in making color choices. One way to eliminate extensive color decision-making is to use one basic hue that may or may not contain variations in lightness

Primary colors:
    warm: red and yellow.

Primary colors:
    cool: blue.

Secondary colors:
    warm: orange

Secondary colors:
    cool: purple and green.

Figure 3.24 Warm and cool colors.

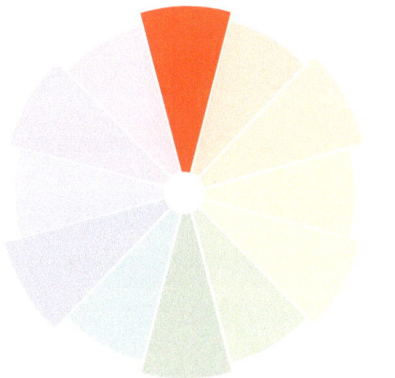 

Figure 3.25 Monochromatic color example. Design by Turnstyle. Reproduced by kind permission of Turnstyle.

(tint) or darkness (shade) — this is monochromatic color, *Mono* meaning one, and *chromo* meaning color.

Complimentary color schemes use hues that sit directly opposite each other on the color wheel. This creates contrast. Think about these examples from sports. For example, the Los Angeles Lakers use purple and yellow to create contrast. The blue and the purple are the quieter color, therefore dominant.

Analogous color schemes use hues that are located close together on the color wheel. The closeness of the hues creates harmony, but uses only one dominant color and the other color acts as a supporting color to avoid visual confusion.

Contrasting color schemes use hues that have three colors between them. These colors should contrast, not clash visually. Use more bright colors as accents and less bright colors for backgrounds and solid areas of color.

Achromatic color schemes (also called grayscale color schemes) use black, white, and grays and are absent of colored hues. This is the type of scheme used when creating images in grayscale. Contrast becomes paramount, as the values of the grays, black, and white must create a discernable figure and ground relationship.

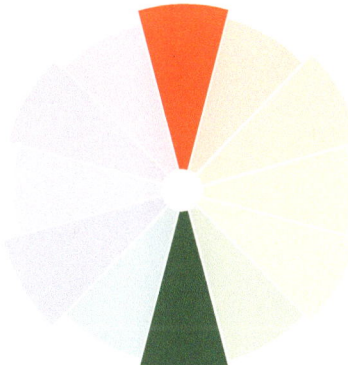 

Figure 3.26 Complimentary color example. Design by Turnstyle. Reproduced by kind permission of Turnstyle.

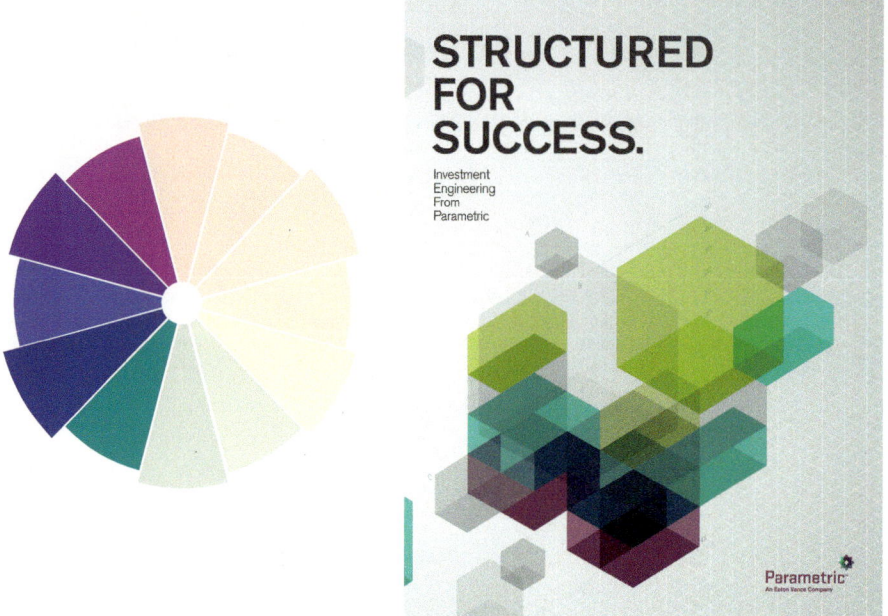

Figure 3.27 Analogous color example. Design by Turnstyle. Reproduced with kind permission of Turnstyle.

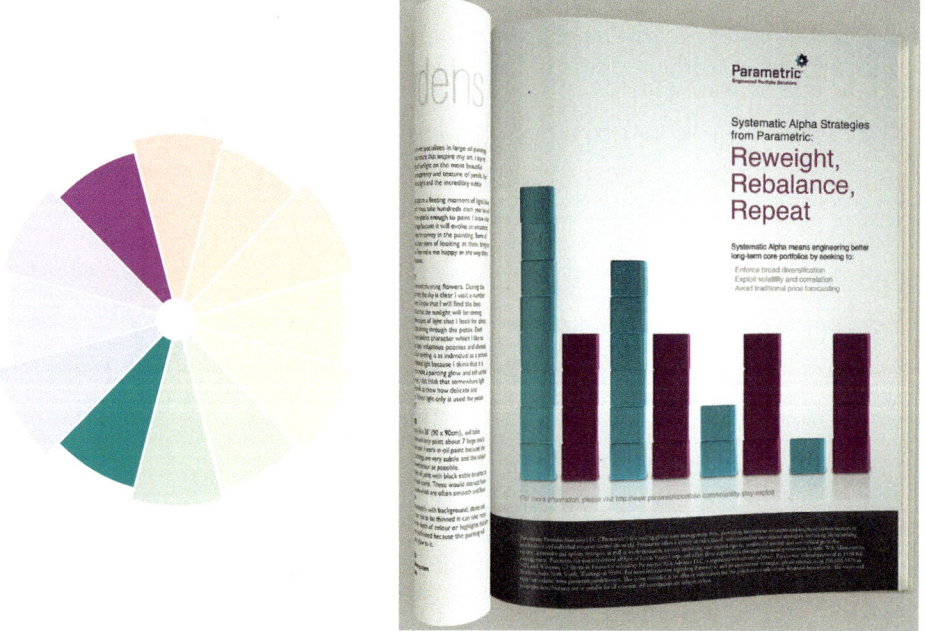

Figure 3.28 Contrasting color example. Design by Turnstyle. Reproduced with kind permission of Turnstyle.

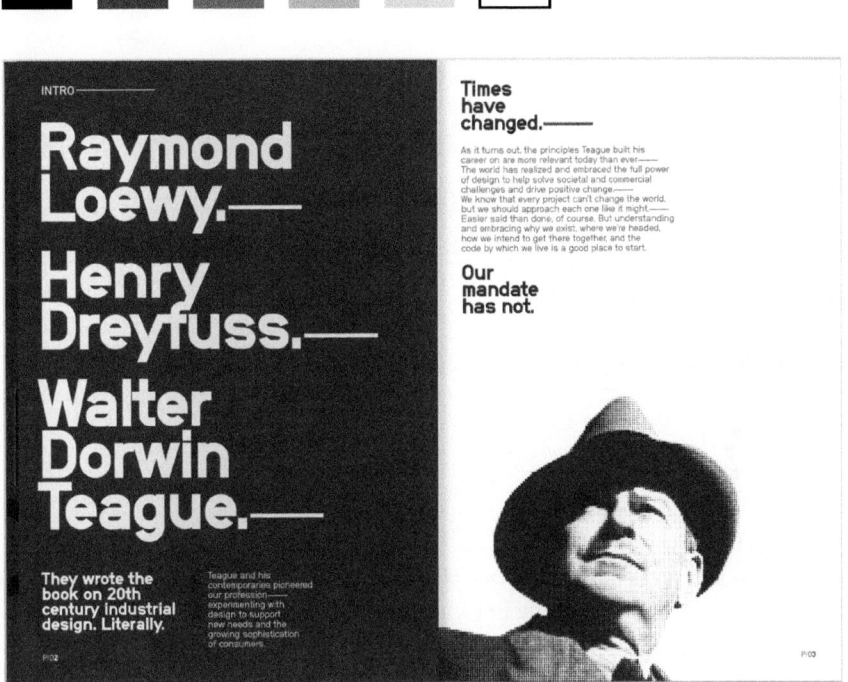

Figure 3.29 Grayscale color example. Design by Turnstyle. Reproduced with kind permission of Turnstyle.

Black plus color schemes use black, white, a palette of grays plus one hue. In digital design using two colors, the hue is typically a Pantone color. Using tints and shades of black and the Pantone color, designers can create richer color documents that have similar impact to other color pieces but cost considerably less than four-color process printing jobs because they only use two colors. The classic example of black plus one color are the traditional Yellow Pages telephone directories (now the Yellow Book has color ads too), which used only black, yellow, and grays for artwork.

Choosing color based on content

Content drives color choices. This means that if a communication piece is historical, you may need to use the same colors that were evident during that period like a sepia tone or grayscale (pre-1950), or maybe pink and teal (1950s), or a tie-dye color mash (1960s). To find historical colors to fit a project, you need to do some research. Look at photos and films that depict time-periods and pull colors and patterns out to emulate in your swatches. Alternatively, if a piece has an environmental angle, you may decide to use colors derived from nature or a specific physical setting. The brown color of bark coupled with the dark green color of a maple leaf might be effective for piece on say, Canada, or the environment, for example. Think about the "genre" of what you are creating. Ask the following question. Would this communication piece, from a style point of view be considered dramatic, instructional, children's, comedic, or news/information? Once you have somewhat pinpointed that classification, look at other works (TV shows, films, catalogs, book covers, artworks, photos, and magazines, in that genre to get inspiration on color choices for developing color palettes for your project.

Color is an element of design that requires careful handling. Color guru Jan V. White wrote in his classic text *Color for the Electronic Age* (1990, 9): "Color should not be used just because it is available.

Figure 3.30 Black plus one. Black plus one color scheme using a knockout (reverse logotype) over black. Design by Turnstyle. Reproduced with kind permission of Turnstyle.

Potentially, it can do more than merely make reports, letters, and charts eye-catching. We must be discriminating and avoid acting like children with a new box of crayons. Color should not be used to dazzle but to enlighten and thus add value." The availability of color and colorization tools available to the designer is enormous. The most important thing is to use color with intent, and in many cases restraint, so as not confuse communication.

White (1990) suggests some guidelines for using color prudently and effectively:

Use color for a certain purpose other than "liking a color"
Use color to guide the reader
Use color to intensify a visual message
Use color to speed up interpretation
Use color to accentuate positives
Use color to establish mood
Use color to make sense and clarify ideas
Use color as a distinguishing characteristic
Use color as a locator signal
Use color to explain and persuade
Use dominant colors supported by accent colors
Use predetermined color schemes instead of guessing about color

Color palettes and color harmony

When we think of color palettes, we should think about harmony. Beyond just "matching" colors, think about mood, emotion, urgency, and tranquility. These factors should play a role in choosing colors and developing a color palette for each piece or brand. Color palettes hold colors used consistently throughout a piece for text (heads, subheads, drop caps), editorial elements like call outs, and to tint or colorize photographs, images, or page backgrounds. To create a color palette, pick two to

Figure 3.31 The personality of color. These snowboards show a range of color palettes with different visual appeals. Design by Turnstyle. Reproduced with kind permission of Turnstyle.

four colors (hues) that will act as top-level colors for primary information. Then you can experiment with different shades of those hues to establish second-level colors for less critical page or screen elements. When establishing palettes, be sure to write down the color values and color space to insure consistent usage.

3.8 Common design mistakes to avoid

As I review many student designs, I see many of the same issues contributing to weak work. Weak, meaning that the design does not adhere to design rules, is sloppy in its execution and production, or is lacking is thoughtful creativity. Here are some common mistakes to avoid:

Incorrect image proportions and resolution

Make sure to scale proportionately images in page layout and digital imaging programs. Nothing screams inexperience more than a person's head being egg shaped in an image within an advertisement or other communication piece. Every object in nature has an aspect ratio, which is the height-to-width relationship. To keep this natural ratio, be sure that when you scale any image that you hold down the shift key and grab the corner while dragging to size. This keeps the height and the width at 100% each. Resolution is part of the equation so make sure you follow the simple rules: 72 ppi (pixels per inch) for screen and 300–350 ppi for high-resolution print output.

Uncaring typography

All computer programs that let the user place text on a page have default settings for type size and attributes. Typically, MS Word sizes to 12-point Arial by default. Now this is fine if you are sending a memo or typing notes. Nevertheless, if you are designing something, which you feel anytime you touch a creative tool, you should take care to perform typography with care and consideration. The first way to execute that is to avoid using the default font and size for every document you create. Use typefaces that fit the communication need. Sans serif fonts elicit a look that is masculine, industrial, and for clarity purposes, are very legible for heads and subheads, and sharp at small sizes. Serif fonts elicit a look that is feminine, naturalistic, and looks best in body copy sizes where extensive reading is the function. Mixed, a serif and sans serif (Helvetica and Times for instance) can create a beautiful and functional page. Finally, do not fall in love with one font and use it on project after project. Explore and buy new typefaces that extend your creative options. Type foundry websites are all over the web. You can find free fonts and full font families for purchase at these sites: Google "type foundries" and "free fonts." Monotype is the largest foundry in the graphic world. Free fonts are available with various usage condition at sites including Dafont.com and 1001fonts.com.

Using color for the sake of color

Make color count. Get in the habit of creating a color palette that is well thought out and based on some reasoning, rather than just, "I like green." Remember that color affects perception and mood, and with that persuasion. Research the subject matter to reveal how color is part of the environment, people, and culture of whatever you are presenting visually. Experiment with different combinations to create a targeted palette for each project. Use the color wheel schemes: monochromatic, analogous, complimentary, black plus one, contrasting, and achromatic schemes, to make creating color easier.

3.9 Chapter exercises

Execute these exercises using markers and paper, or electronically using any digital page layout tool including MS Word, PowerPoint, Adobe InDesign, Photoshop, or Illustrator. You may want to work with marker and paper first to develop ideas and then transfer them to the computer.

1. *Analyzing grids in publications*

    Role: Act as a communication designer performing page layout research.
    Assignment: Using high-end magazines such as *Vogue, ESPN, SI, SELF, GQ*, and *Time*, find advertisements and editorial pages that utilize the 3 × 3 grid. Using a marker, draw lines on the pages where the designers worked inside the 3 × 3 grid. Notice where page elements lie in the designs and how many ads are similar in their compositions.

    Process

    Go through the publication and find three examples of where the 3 × 3 grid was used and three where a different grid was used. Clip out the pages and make notes as you compare them to see how the designs differ.

2. *Creating a product poster focusing on type and image*

    Role: Act as a communication designer developing layouts for a product poster.
    Assignment: Using one letter and one image, create a product poster (8.5 × 11 or 8.5 × 14) for a familiar tool in your life. A pencil, for example would use the letter P in the composition, with an image or images of a pencil of some type. Imagine the work is on display at a trade show for the pencil industry. Soap, would use the letter S, and so on. Keep the brand out of it and focus on using the letter and the image as the design components. You can add three words to the piece. You pick the words that connect with the tool (maybe history, uniqueness, importance). It is about the generic object, rather than the brand of the object.

Process

1. Experiment with designs using a sketchpad initially and then use any digital tool of your choosing to complete the design.
2. Make a few palettes of variations of color and consider scale, font, layout, repetition, rhythm, and composition when making the designs.
3. Use the 3 × 3 grid and focus on BANGPP in your layout. Think critically about how to best place elements on the page.
4. Think about image form, and how people recognize shapes, text, and symbols.
   Pick a favorite common product and then research different images to use. Use only one image in the composition and one letter. Repetition is allowed, and so are backgrounds if they add value to the design. The goal here is to inform and persuade the audience of the power and value of the tool in people's lives.

3. *Creating a color palette for a seasonal event poster*

   Role: Act as a communication designer developing color palettes for a seasonal event poster.
   Assignment: You need to create a four square palette that acts as the color standard and background element for a seasonal event poster. The colors should be useful in the poster also. The event will be represented by text only (or text as graphic), with the background seasonal colors. The colors should communicate the season with the event name typeset in the center.

   Process

   Experiment with palettes using a Pantone swatch book or digitally in Photoshop, Illustrator, or InDesign.
   Arrange the four colors in squares symmetrically, either with or without dividing lines, to make a color set. Create more than one and then narrow it down to a single swatch set of four together.
   Layout the colors in a background design in any digital design program. Layout event poster.
   Critique, revise, review again.
   Output the final poster to a .TIF file for printing. Save layers to have an editable file for the future.

Chapter references

DiMarco, John. 2010. *Digital Design for Print and Web: An Introduction to Theory, Principles, and Techniques.* 1st ed. Chichester: John Wiley & Sons, Ltd.
Elam, Kimberly. 2004. *Grid Systems: Principles of Organizing Type (Design Briefs).* 1st ed. New York: Princeton Architectural Press.
Golombisky, Kim, and Rebecca Hagen. 2010. *White Space Is Not Your Enemy: A Beginner's Guide to Communicating Visually Through Graphic, Web and Multimedia Design.* Amsterdam: Focal Press/Elsevier.
Heller, Steven, and Veronique Vienne. 2009. *Art Direction Explained, At Last!* London: Laurence King.
Holtzschue, Linda. 2006. *Understanding Color: An Introduction for Designers.* 3rd ed. Hoboken, NJ: John Wiley & Sons, Inc.
Meggs, Philip B. 1989. *Type and Image: The Language of Graphic Design.* New York: Van Nost. Reinhold.
Rand, Paul. 2014. *Thoughts on Design.* San Francisco, CA: Chronicle Books.

Weinschenk, Susan. 2011. *100 Things Every Designer Needs to Know About People: What Makes Them Tick?* Berkeley, CA: New Riders Publishing.

Wheeler, Alina. 2009. *Designing Brand Identity: An Essential Guide for the Whole Branding Team*. 3rd ed. Chichester: John Wiley & Sons.

White, Alex W. 2005. *Thinking in Type: The Practical Philosophy of Typography*. New York: Allworth.

White, Jan V. 1990. *Color for the Electronic Age*. New York: Watson-Guptill Publications.

4

Creative Research Methods

Creation of a mandala, much like creation of a research design requires looking at the "big picture" as well as tremendous attention to detail.

John W. Creswell 2003

Chapter objectives
After completing this chapter, you should be able to: • define the seven steps in the design process. • identify and define a set of universal design research methods. • understand when, why, and how design research methods work. • apply design research methods to solve creative problems. • build a toolset for design thinking that complements writing skills.

4.1 Understand, research, then execute

We focus on concept and execution in communication design and writing. Before we can engage in execution, the concept must be powerful. The relationships between the creative team and the stakeholders (clients) are a shared vision, predicated on a vision of success for the project, and driven by the concepts they generate and agree upon together. Getting to strong concepts requires research and design thinking to develop solutions to problems that the client simply cannot resolve on their own, but need and want to be part of the solution-making process. Research yields data to serve as a foundation for new concepts. Research is the engaged search for knowledge by asking questions in a deliberate systematic way to gain data. In marketing communications, research helps creatives to understand audiences and markets, so crafted messages carry maximum efficiency. In writing and design for marketing, advertising, and public relations, research yields nuggets of information that can ignite a concept for design or establish a direction for copy and messaging. Once developed, work needs editing, revision, filtering, and refinement to be ready for delivery. The quick start menu of design research and conceptualization techniques crystallizes ideas, which is essential for conceptualization, the most important piece in a communication campaign.

Communications Writing and Design: The Integrated Manual for Marketing, Advertising, and Public Relations,
First Edition. John DiMarco.
© 2017 John DiMarco. Published 2017 by John Wiley & Sons, Ltd.

4.2 Design process—seven steps

The design process starts with a stakeholder (client) and a problem. The process to solve the client communication problem includes:

1. *Identify* audience, problem, and communication goals. Create a client creative brief during this stage.
2. *Research* the audience and media to gather data that can be used in messaging. Execute design research methods during this stage.
3. *Target* the emotional center of the audience by establishing words, themes, and style to elicit a response. This is the thrust of concept development. Execute design research methods during this stage. Create a GACMIST design brief during this stage and use this step to establish concepts and keywords that will drive the execution.
4. *Conceptualize* brainstorm on paper developing sketches, storyboards, outlines, flowcharts, and rough layouts to establish layout, composition, and functionality.
5. *Create* mockups, proofs, prototypes, and treatments that exhibit the design solution.
6. *Revise* work to filter content and force the design team to justify design decisions critically to enhance the final product.
7. *Evaluate* against the goals of the project outlined in the creative brief and measure the success of the piece to inform future projects.

4.3 Briefs: creative, design, and scope

Client creative brief

The creative brief is a jointly authored document between client and design team that acts as an upfront agreement that defines the essence of a project and key messages (Phillips 2011). The creative brief, done first, initially establishes a path to synergy between the client's vision and designer's interest and capabilities. After an initial meeting, the design team works on three steps to write the creative brief, which will then be subject to interpretation and changes based on the client needs and desires.

Steps
Different agencies and shops use varieties of creative briefing processes and document templates, but the critical aspects of developing the creative brief include:

1. Posing client questions
   - What are the outcomes the client wants?
   - What problems have created the client's needs?
   - Who is the audience?
   - Who is the competition?
   - What has been done before?
   - Who will implement and maintain the project after launch?
   - What makes the client and their product, services, and problem unique?
2. Conducting client research
   - Seek to understand the client, audience, and industry.
   - Research people and information inside and outside the client circle.

- Use ethnography (field trips with note taking) to gain a point of view of the client environment.
- Partner with your client to learn as much about them as you can throughout the project.
- Pull critical data nuggets that may have resonance in message making.
3. Writing a statement of client goals
   - Combine what you learn from your research and client interpretations to write a one or two-sentence statement of goals description of the project's imperative criteria. The mission statement is concrete and understood by both the design team and the client.

GACMIST design brief

Once the creative brief has identified and defined the client problem and vision, a solution needs to be developed and chronicled using a design brief, which acts as a list of content and message components that will occupy the design solution. Distill the most important aspects using the GACMIST design brief, which narrows the elements needed to solve the problem into an easy-to-remember acronym (DiMarco 2010). Before the creation of the design brief, design thinking and research leads to development of strong concepts (the "C" in GACMIST). The concept creation process can utilize a host of design-thinking methodologies to come up with ideas that can solve a problem using visual and written elements to deliver a message with the goal of persuading, informing, entertaining, or educating an audience.

Steps

Complete the GACMIST design brief as design research is happening, after the client and design team signs off on the client creative brief. The client creative brief puts specific mutual expectations in writing, while the GACMIST design brief outlines conceptual solutions and acts as a guide to developing the communication piece.

The GACMIST design brief combines the client brief with design research to provide a focused outline of the conceptual project components.

Client name:
Project name:

GOALS What are the project communication goals? Are you trying to: persuade, inform, educate, or entertain, or a combination of some? This is where you pull from the client creative brief to establish the client needs and project purpose.
AUDIENCE Who is the target audience? Who are they descriptively and in what assumed scenarios are they receiving this communication?
CONCEPT What is the big idea that connects the goals and audience? What are the words that hit the target audience in the emotional center?
MESSAGE What is the unique selling proposition that influences the audience? What are the taglines, copy, and headlines that may have resonance?
IMAGE What images present a magnetic attraction to the audience, and communicate the message clearly? What visual puns can captivate the audience with clever, intelligent, clear ideas that lead to action?
STYLE What visual framework fits here? What is the graphic style? Should the work incorporate features of a time, environment, or contemporary visual approach?
THEME What is the story that drives the message? If your communication told a short story, what would it be?

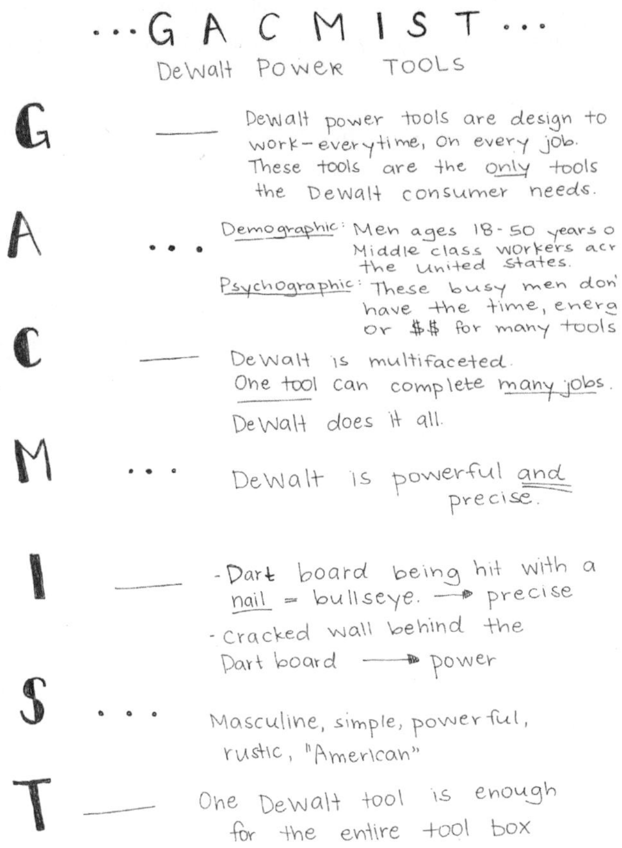

...GACMIST...
DeWalt Power Tools

G — DeWalt power tools are design to work – everytime, on every job. These tools are the <u>only</u> tools the DeWalt consumer needs.

A ...
- Demographic: Men ages 18-50 years o Middle class workers acr the United States.
- Psychographic: These busy men don' have the time, energ or $$ for many tools

C — DeWalt is multifaceted. One tool can complete <u>many jobs</u>. DeWalt does it all.

M ... DeWalt is powerful <u>and</u> precise.

I —
- Dart board being hit with a nail = bullseye. → precise
- Cracked wall behind the Dart board → power

S ... Masculine, simple, powerful, rustic, "American"

T — One DeWalt tool is enough for the entire tool box

Figure 4.1 GACMIST, put forth by DiMarco (2010), provides a vital starting point for establishing the components needed for a visual communication. Design by Elise Cruz. Reproduced with kind permission of Elise Cruz.

Project scope document

Once the creative brief and design brief outline the elements to follow, a scope brief (also known as a scope document) lists the technical tasks and offers a timeline with dated deliverables that act as a project schedule for the production team. When the project changes, the scope changes, and so should the scope brief. When this happens, and it does much of the time, this is scope creep. It is when the project criteria change to include more work it creeps forward. It is important to establish timelines and tasks as they become vital to project considerations such as printing and delivery schedules and client billings, if necessary and to help avoid unneeded scope creep. The project scope verifies the roles and expenses and acts as a contract of work between the client and design team outside of a formal proposal.

Steps

Complete the Scope brief after the client creative brief and the GACMIST design brief. The scope is a technical document that may elaborate design and digital tasks, outline further research, or list duties and responsibilities for the whole project. This document can take any form, and is usually created based on the project type and typical milestones agreed upon by the design team and client.

1. *Write down important tasks and add notes and deadlines* in the project process. The draft date is when the task begins. The final proof date is when the task ends. The approval date is when the client says OK, this is done.
2. *Update the document as the items are approved or if there is scope creep.* Do not forget to add information as needed so that the scope document reflects the exact stage of the project and when the deliverables can be expected. If deadlines for deliverable change, make a note and update the Scope document.

Project name: 11 × 17 Identity Brochure
Client name: Miller Consulting

Client contact information: N/A

Start Date: 10/1/2015

Task (*milestones)	Team member	Draft date	Final proof date	Approved by	Notes
Research keywords using CC method	JD	11/5/2015	11/15/2015 11/16/2015	Mr. J – manager Mr. X—client JD—designer KD—art director	On schedule
Write draft outline / GACMIST	KD				Need 500 words or less
Revision #1 copy	JD				Check technical terms
Create 11 × 17 page spreads (3 versions) layouts using keywords from CC method for 4c brochure	JD				Need to resize logo for better placement on the page
Make first round design revisions	KD				Check PMS colors
Create matchprint, or digital proof	KD				Get AD (art director) and CD (creative director) sign off
Revision #2 full revisions	JD, KD				Check text, images, and layout
FINAL REVISED PROOF	JD				This is the last approval before final output
Quote and order brochure printing from ABC co.	KD				quote 500 100 2500 quantities
Deliver job and invoice client	KD via UPS ground				Set payment terms before starting job

Figure 4.2 Scope document.

4.4 Design and market research methods

In the purest sense, design research methods help define the problem so that design solutions can be determined to yield a successful communication design that solves the problem. Research is critical to design and writing because it can help define a problem and guide a writing or design solution. It guides the creative team to discover hidden meanings, establish process, and build a cache of usable content. Research is simply a process of using our senses to observe, record, and analyze, and report data. We research everyday informally, as we do with clients and vendors during a project. We also may be involved in formal research, which is rigorous in method and execution. Both qualitative and quantitative methods are useful and used in market research and design research alike.

When we perform data collection during the study using field techniques, we are engaged in primary research, which allows a "collection of new information designed to fit specific needs" (Wheeler 2009, 104). When we refer to data collected by others, existing research, we are performing secondary research, which allows "interpretation and application of statistical, demographic, or qualitative data" (Wheeler 2009, 104). In either case, we perform inquiry using a method (see the chart below), then build data in the form of numbers and narrative to guide conceptual and design decisions. For the numbers, we use quantitative methods and for narrative (text) we use qualitative methods. The quantitative approach builds measurable, statistical data derived through, surveys, polling, and experiments. The quantitative approach helps writers and designers gain an initial understanding, by building data from larger populations. It can also provide numbers that are used to establish creative concepts in advertising, marketing, and public relations campaigns. Numbers are critical because they provide fact-based credibility to a message.

For narratives and understanding the true layer of meaning below the surface, qualitative methods build data from smaller groups. The humanistic, qualitative approach uses experiences, observations, content analyses of documents (print and A/V), focus-group results, and interview findings to generate concepts and narratives that offer feelings and emotions in a pure form.

The first responsibility we have as communication designers is to collaborate with the client and other stakeholders to define the problem. Exploratory research, initially executed and highly flexible, helps build awareness to situations and people who are part of the communication problem and solution. The problem leads to other questions that we make assumptions about in the quest for knowledge. These are hypotheses, which are guesses based on assumptions of information that we possess. To qualify and clarify these assumptions, we need methods that will help isolate the essential factors (variables) in the communication process. Three methodologies exist: quantitative, qualitative, and mixed methods, which combine the former. Mixed methods are most effective yielding multiple data sets that create a research spiral that funnels down to grounded conclusions supported by reliable (repeatable) and valid (genuine to task) data collection techniques. Communication problems can include persuading, informing, education, or entertaining with the solution consisting of a calculated message in the form of a design. Quantitative techniques serve to establish a definition of the core concepts surrounding the problem. These include asking audience questions (surveys, questionnaires) brainstorming, and concentric circle exercises. Qualitative techniques dig deeper into the audience experience using ethnography, which relies on observation, interviews, and focus groups in an effort to go below the surface of larger populations to find out what people are thinking and feeling. Ultimately, any method can used at any phase of a project. Sometimes revisiting research methods can help steer a project that needs additional creative boost or identifies new problems not identified during initial stages.

Solving problems using design methods activates divergent and convergent thinking in tandem. With convergent thinking design methods, the path to a solution is broken into a number of steps to solving the problem, with a mechanized formula guiding the process. Visual research, for example, is a technique utilizing a convergent thinking process that calls upon the creative researcher to collect content and gather visual evidence of patterns, repetition of words or concepts, themes, and anomalies. The evidence, further analyzed, becomes available for data visualization, which presents raw data in a universally understood way so that understanding transcends into clear, unambiguous information.

Use divergent thinking when the path is unclear, as we do not know what we are doing, and need to analyze and tinker with approaches that may or may not provide a successful solution. Divergent thinking usually comes first, and then leads to convergent thinking once a direction is established. We may use divergent thinking along the convergent route as well. The divergent approach lends itself to spraying ideas out in any phase of the design process, as it is a free flow of ideas, which transform into calculated design solutions. Utilize the design research techniques below to build data sets that you interpret into usable facts to help establish concepts, messages, images, styles, and themes for communication design projects. The research technique "everything from everywhere" is an example of this approach, which asks the researcher to be aware, observe, and absorb visual, natural, contextual, spatial, cultural, and societal happenings. Then parlay the visions into ideas that bring historical and contemporary thoughts to new projects.

Market research

Data gathering occurs using research methods, located through library resources, or bought from other research sources that offer syndicated market data. Each of these methods allows designers and writers to build data sets to use in their work. Library resources include instruments including the U.S. Census, Lexis-Nexis, and Communication Abstracts. These sources offer access to full text articles from business, academia, and the press. Aggregate data sources offer paid subscription to their data sets, which cover lifestyles, product demographics, populations, buying trends, and many other consumer and business variables, which can be used a starting point for a valuable communication campaign. One data set, the VALs 2 (**v**alues, **a**ttitudes, and **l**ifestyles), gauges and classifies consumers into eight categories as explained by Drewniany and Jewler (2011, 75). It includes:

1. Innovators: successful, sophisticated, and active with high self-esteem
2. Experiencers: self-expressive, young rebellious excitement seekers
3. Strivers: motivated to receive self-definition and approval from others
4. Thinkers: mature, well-educated professionals
5. Achievers: goal oriented, in control, and value respect
6. Believers: conservative, deep moral codes, with modest education and income
7. Makers: suspicious of innovation and physical possessions are not impressive
8. Survivors: narrowly focused, cautious consumers

Market research looks at market trends and customer characteristics to attempt to best plan and project the most effective way to design and promote a successful product. Different methods yield different data types. Wheeler (2009, 104–105) lists market research methods to include the following

Quantitative methods—statistically valid market information
Surveys
Usability testing
Product testing
Eye tracking
Demographic and psychographic segmentation
Standardized data from media research companies
Content analysis

Qualitative methods—customers' feelings, beliefs, motives, and perceptions
Ethnography (recorded observations)
One-on-one interviews
Focus groups
Mystery shopping
Visual research

Twenty questions to target your audience

In her book *Everyone's Guide to Successful Publications*, Elizabeth Adler (1993, 73–79) offers a list of questions that can be used to tailor a piece to an audience. Answering these questions (some or all), which I have adapted below, will help you design for communication by focusing on the information you gain during the research process, rather than simply guessing or tailoring the piece to what you expect instead of what your target audience expects. One question from the list might inspire a concept or direction that becomes paramount to the message.

Questions to ask
1. Who is your target audience? (everyone cannot be an answer here)
2. Are there more men or women? (find statistics)
3. How old are they? (children, teens, adults, seniors)
4. Where do they live? (city or town, state, country)
5. What is their income level? (wealthy, upper, middle, low, poverty)
6. What is their education level? (less than high school, high school, four- or two-year college, masters or doctoral level)
7. What is their knowledge level? (use and sophistication with the product, service, or idea)
8. How are they different from you? (specifically)
9. How are they similar to you? (specifically)
10. What is their attitude toward the product or service? (how they feel so far)
11. What is their background in relationship to the topic. (what they have experienced so far)
12. What are their values? (ethical stance in society)
13. What are their tastes? (refined, middle class, or subsistence)
14. How do they spend their leisure time? (introverted or extroverted)
15. What do they read? (magazines, books, newspapers, websites, blogs)
16. What makes them unique? (special features of the group)
17. When can you get their attention the easiest? (time of day, environment, month)
18. Where will they read or interact with the communication piece? (format and media)
19. What effect do you want to have on them? (what feelings should they have)
20. What do you want them to do? (what actions should they take)

Figure 4.3 Brainstorm to somewhere. Brainstorming sessions need moderators and should conclude with useful flowcharts, mind maps, or lists that illustrate direction in ideas. Photography by Diana Colapietro and Megan Monfiston. Reproduced with kind permission of Diana Colapietro and Megan Monfiston.

Brainstorming

The technique of brainstorming has roots in the advertising industry. Alex F. Osborne is credited with describing the term in 1948 in his book on creativity titled *Your Creative Power* (Phillips 2011) and coining the design thinking term officially in 1953 in his book *Applied imagination* (Martin and Hanington 2012) working at famed ad agency BBDO.

The brainstorming technique involves generating lists of new ideas in rapid fashion to address a single problem in the larger process of design (Curedale 2013), which allows the elimination of creative blocks during the initial phases of a project. Creating lists of ideas is useful, but Ausubel and Novak (1978) suggest using visual frameworks to better utilize brainstorming sessions by generating web diagrams, which show central concepts and questions with supporting facts and ideas and flowcharts, which show actions and interactions between users, messages, and processes within a given design system. When the brainstorming process is visualized with graphic structures that highlight information elements, the design team becomes more aware of problems and has keener insight when suggesting ideas.

How to brainstorm

1. *Establish a group and appoint a facilitator.* The group should be between two and 12 thinkers to gain an effective array of ideas with a manageable size team. One person steps up to moderate the session as facilitator. The job of the facilitator is to write down all ideas offered by the group. Using a white board, flip chart, or a computer, the facilitator writes and categorizes ideas to create a visual palette of ideas. The facilitator must keep the session moving, with quantity of ideas being a critical outcome to the technique. The facilitator should set a time limit and a quantity limit on ideas (our goal is to list ten new ideas, for example).
2. *State the problem.* It is important to narrow the focus of the ideas to meet the needs of the problem. Break the problem down and state it clearly "problems people have at the office," for example is vague. Narrow it by stating "obstacles people encounter during small group co-worker communication at the office." By breaking the problem down, exposure of real issues occurs and serves to eliminate less meaningful ideas right from the start.
3. *Write down all ideas, without issue.* The goal is to generate as many ideas as possible. There are no bad ideas, only ones that are not used. Do not make fun of ideas, not matter how silly, and keep them flowing throughout the session. Combine ideas and concepts to generate useful solutions that capitalize on the groupthink dynamics. Use visualization structures such as flow charts and web maps to illustrate how brainstormed ideas are structured and related.

4. *Rank, record, and recommend.* The session is only as good as the ideas that it generates. It is important to rank ideas in order of value, feasibility, and consensus. Record the findings via visual vehicles plus reporting and distribute them to the stakeholders and design team for thoughts and considerations. Finally, choose the next directions derived from the brainstorming session. Move forward with the next phase of the project by either performing further research or beginning client and design briefs, or the project itself.

Concentric circle exercises (CC method)

The late Hillman Curtis was a prolific designer and skilled writer who taught me some very important design lessons through his writings and the awesome beauty and functionality of his works. One technique that I added to my tool belt from his masterful repertoire was the method of concentric circle exercises to "help in finding the heart of the product and brand, and its emotional epicenter" (Curtis 2002, 42). It is by far the easiest way to identify words that matter when communicating emotional connection. With the value of words being so premium in the design and writing process, this method is highly useful in finding creative gold.

How to use concentric circles
1. *Draw three rings to create a concentric circle* on a plain sheet of white paper or whiteboard.
2. *Using the client, other stakeholders, or creative team members, ask them to provide six to seven words that they associate with their brand or product.* The words are listed on the side of the sheet next to the circles. This can also be done with the design team or as an individual method.
3. *Write in or draw arrows to each word as it fits on the emotional continuum of the client, user, and audience spectrum.* If the word is strong emotionally, place it closer to the center. If it is a less emotionally persuasive word, place it away from the center near the outer rings. The same technique can be used for rational words. Use the technique to narrow down which features or benefits are most important. Cross out words that do not work. Alternatively, use the method to decipher which word in a tagline or headline will elicit a response.
4. *Isolate the word with the most resonance and justification,* which should be the word in the center bull's eye of the circles. Use the chosen word as a platform for new concepts and messaging.

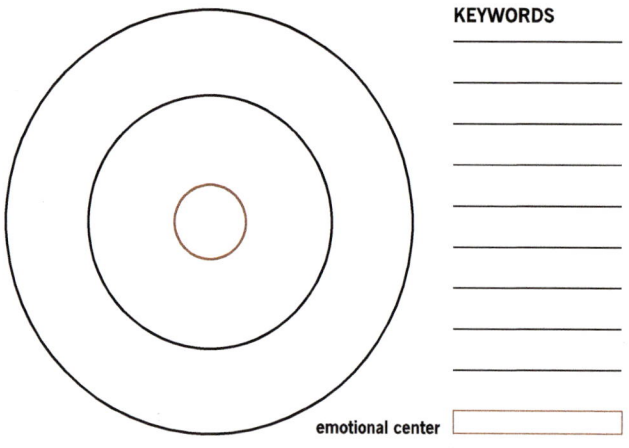

Figure 4.4a Concentric circle method and emotional center. For this method, generate keywords during brainstorming. Then add the keywords and place the most important nearest to the center (emotional center) of the concentric rings. Isolate words that are most important, most moving, and most connected to the potential audience. Then harvest the best words for use in tag lines, ads, and messaging.

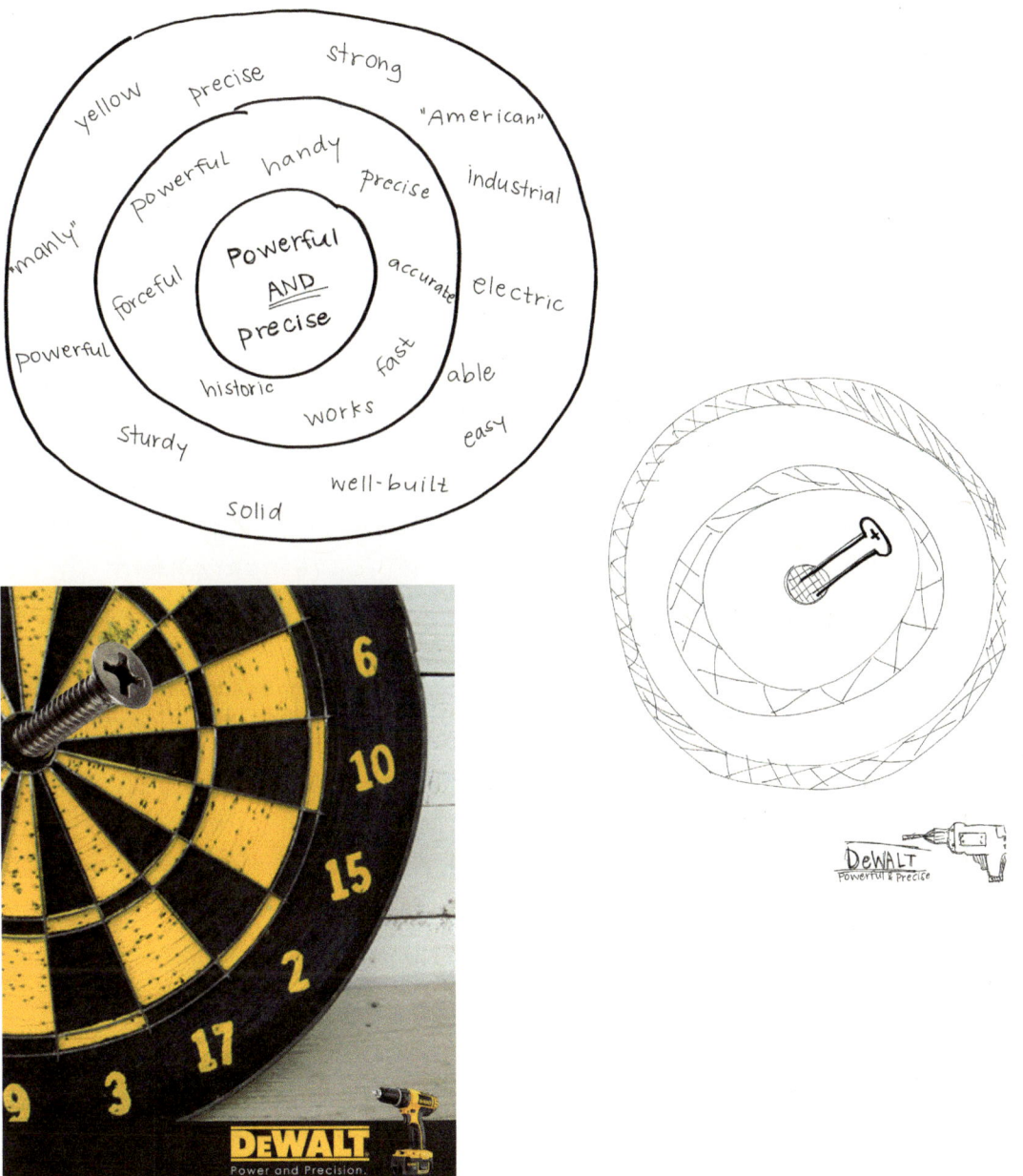

Figure 4.4b Concentric circle exercise in practice. This student spec ad project example shows how the concept process evolves to a digital design comp. Design by Elise Cruz. Reproduced with kind permission of Elise Cruz.

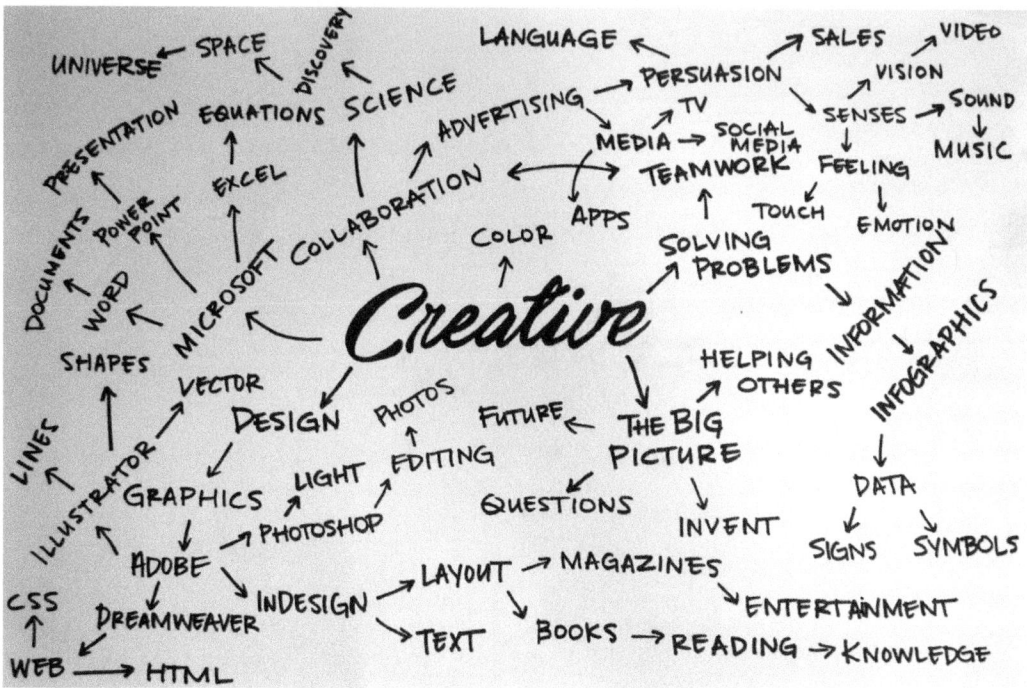

Figure 4.5a Textual mind maps. Mind maps can text to show idea branches. Design by Artiana Winder. Reproduced with kind permission of Artiana Winder.

Mind mapping

Psychologist, Tony Brazen (Phillips 2011, Martin and Hanington 2012), illuminated the technique of mind mapping, which offers designers and writers a method to quickly explore a problem and all its dynamic pieces, while becoming a starting point for design. The techniques uses a non-linear approach, which allows creative teams to freely associate elements in order to make or break connections and visualize relationships between concepts that could be meaningful and useful.

How to mind map
1. *Focus on one element and place it in the center.* Use a landscape sheet of paper or a board or flip chart pad. Use a dry erase marker or pencil so you can erase and move pieces.
2. *Branch out top-level extensions from the center.* Create the first, primary level, which represents the components closest to the center word in both meaning and relevance. Using line connectors add spokes and boxes with words to create clusters. The branches and boxes closet to the center are primary clusters.
3. *Expand, organize, and subdivide new branches out from the primary clusters.* Words that are more distant from the center topic go out further and then generate their own idea clusters.
4. *Examine and strengthen the map.* Look at the mind map critically and then move things around or eliminate items to create a clearer picture. The goal here is to fortify the knowledge and understanding of the creative team so that they are keen to the essence and elements of the problem.

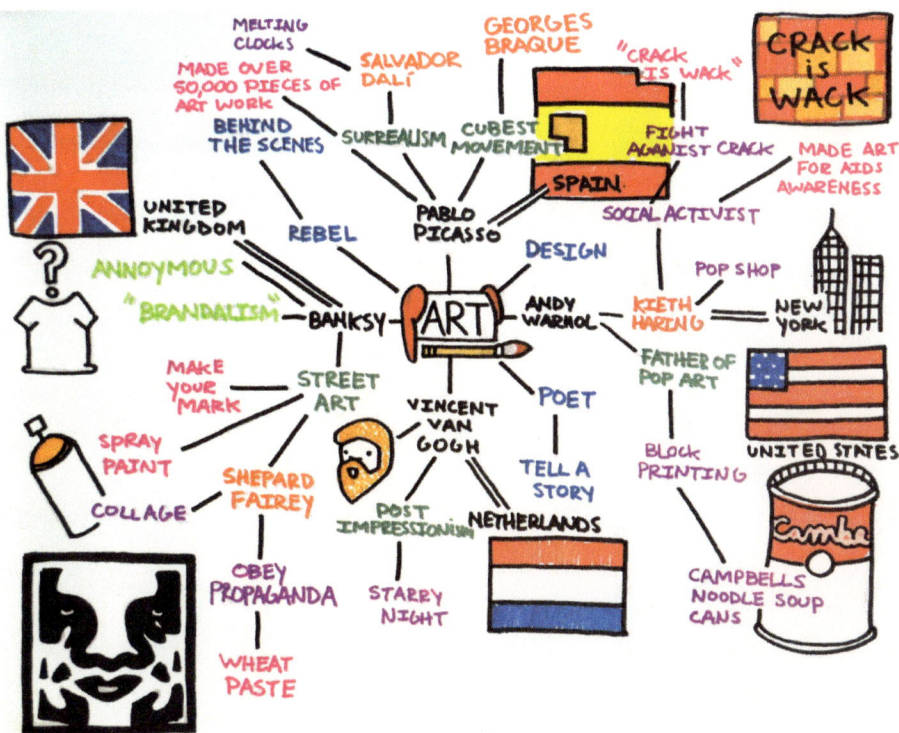

Figure 4.5b Illustrated mind maps. Mind maps can use images to illustrate connections between concepts. Design by Nick Heller. Reproduced with kind permission of Nick Heller.

Design ethnography

Ethnography is a qualitative method in which the researcher studies an intact cultural group, using obtrusive and unobtrusive observation and interviews to collect data (Creswell 2003). The value of ethnographies is that they allow a fly-on-the-wall viewpoint of a person or group within a natural setting and expose lived realities. The products of ethnographies are the creation of personas and scenarios that shine a light on the audience member's needs, desires, and conditions. Ethnography collection methods yield personal data through observing what people do, how their environments and spaces look, and how they act and react. This data collection process also includes interviews with people, one to one, or in groups.

Interviews can be formal (obtrusive), or informal in nature, with field notes and diary entries following interactions when they are "unobtrusive"—not known. To understand workplace technology issues, the researcher (in blue) observes and informally interviews the staff member in her office. Once a relationship is established, a formal interview is conducted with questions built to expand on key research hypotheses from informal observations.

How to perform design ethnography
1. *Get in.* You need to have access to the environment and people that you want to study. Make relationships formally (with clients) or informally (shopping in a client store to see experience, space, and service for example) and stake out where you need to be to collect the most important data.

Figure 4.6a Observation in ethnography. The image above shows an observation of communication confusion using an interface. This provides information on the environment, employee feelings, and customer problems. Use observations as a source of data for interview questions. Interview subjects to gain data on thoughts, feelings, attitudes, and emotions.

Figure 4.6b Interviewing in ethnography. Interviewing people in their environment is a great method for revealing what is under the surface. Photography by Diana Colapietro and Megan Monfiston. Reproduced with kind permission of Diana Colapietro and Megan Monfiston.

2. *Observe and record using the diary method and field notes.* You should first get the environment inventoried by observing and making notes about what you see. After explicit notetaking/photographing/recording in field (who, what, where, when, why, how), then remove yourself and write a diary entry that offers your "gut" feelings, highlighting reactions from you and others, and isolating moments that seem out of the ordinary day-to-day activities. Look beyond the obvious to open new pathways to ideas and hypotheses further investigated through interviewing the "actors in the scenes" you watched when observing. Try to understand the participant from his or

her point of view during observations. Look at their objects, actions, interactions, and emotions in various situations and write about them accurately. Focus on "trace measures," which are observations of existing objects, environmental elements, and processes that yield traces of evidence. Choose a single element to study, misunderstood signage, for example. Have you ever seen a sign taped up to clarify a misunderstood sign already in place at the location?
3. *Interview people in the environment.* Establish relationships during observations and recruit subjects for interviews. Make sure that you find the right people to interview, some who fit the entire spectrum of people in the environment. Interview the client's target audience members in their settings. Both videotape and write down their responses to gain non-verbal cues and have the option to further analyze answers. Take time to write thoughtful questions and offer time to respond, without answering the question for the subject. Be patient, listen, and look. These interviews can be with small groups or individuals.
4. *Analyze data to reveal themes and patterns.* The research should bear fruit in the form of information that reveals themes and patterns, which could lay foundation to design approaches and decisions. Take the data from the observations and the data from the interviews and log them into a table or spreadsheet for easier identifications.
5. *Generate personas.* After collection and analysis of observation and interviews, put the data into a more commercially useful form by using personas to synthesize observations into the form of description of what a typical person using this product or service would be like. A persona is a general description of a person's profile generated by primary field research (Martin and Hanington 2012) such as design ethnography. Persona data sets consist of highlighting the knowledge, activities, interests, behaviors, and backstory of a target audience member. It is an individual account that represents an identifiable receiver of a message or user of a product or service in an archetypical way.
6. *Generate scenarios based on data.* While the persona looks at the person, the scenario looks the place, purpose, and point of view and ultimately "brings personas to life" (Martin and Hanington 2012, 152) in the day-to-day life of a person in the target audience. A scenario is a story. It narrates problems and process of the consumer or user and outlines empathy needed to understand the human condition beyond simply designing to technical specifications. Looking at, seeing, thinking, hearing, feeling and doing, scenarios complement personas to offer vital foundation for communication design development.

4.5 Creating visual forms on paper

Sketching

In all types of marketing communications projects, thumbnails and sketches conceptualize layouts and establish composition within a document. Sketches create initial roadmaps for visual concepts. They are quickly executed freehand drawings using a multitude of overlapping lines. Sketches are not the same as illustrations, detailed drawings, or storyboards, which entail much more detail and require extended artistic abilities. Sketching should represent the visual elements within and exploratory composition and make use of the process as divergent in nature, thus enabling stronger compositions to emerge during the design process. Sketch on paper, preferably using a sketchpad instead of lined composition paper. Realistic forms, meaning life-like drawings, do not belong here per se. Geometric forms can also represent elements on the page. A line can represent a line of text. A very heavy line can represent a headline or subhead, and a rectangle, square or triangle can represent images and logos.

Figure 4.7a, b, and c From sketch to layout. Sketching to layout starts at thumbnail and ends with a "comp," which is short for composite artwork. A comp is a layout ready for review and proofing. Design by Kristen Crawford. Reproduced with kind permission of Kristen Crawford.

How to sketch quickly

1. *Use thumbnail sketches, which are small sketches, first.* The 10 × 10 square sketch method employs creating 10 × 10 rows of thumbnails. Art directors and designers use the technique to allow faster exploration of ideas due to their smaller size. Use a 3 × 3 grid on your sketch to help create a well-composed page that follows the rule of thirds and considers the design elements criteria of BANGPP.

2. *Generate thumbnails or full-page roughs before detailed sketches* to create and view many different compositions quickly, and allow for a "side-by-side" comparison of visual approaches. Using thumbnails helps determine which ideas warrant further development into more detailed sketches, which leads to determining which ideas make it to digital production. Use a 3 × 3 grid on your sketch to help create a well-composed page that follows the rule of thirds and considers the design elements criteria of BANGPP.
3. *Create full-page sketches to get a more refined look.* As concepts become concrete, art directors create detailed sketches to explore visual concepts. The more representative the sketch is, the more the client will understand the concept before digital production is undertaken.

Storyboards

Storyboards organize visual content into a sequence for a time-based project, such as a web site, motion graphics movie, animation, or video/film. Storyboards help designers and directors create work that has the proverbial "beginning, middle, and end," which ensures that the sequential content makes sense, and has an aesthetic flow.

How to storyboard
1. *Use boxes to show scenes or key frames in time.* The boxes represent frames, or moments in time. The storyboard should be set in a landscape view (wide) and placed in sequential rows. Sketch each

Figure 4.8 Storyboards show action. This storyboard screenshot from agency DDB Canada's website shows the makings of a product video for the Subaru WRX. The storyboard was integral to the video shoot as a planning tool, as well as a visual prop used to bypass live action filming issues, http://www.ddbcanada.com/#/Home/SubaruWRX.

point in time in a box, with each representing the changes that occur over time. You can also use photographic images to represent storyboards. The image placement has variations. Use images overlapped or presented as frames in sequence to illustrate moving concepts for commercials and videos, before starting production.

2. *Label action, sound, and special effects* for each frame when writing scripts to attach to storyboards. Use the abbreviations… SFX, ACT, and AUD to list what happens and when in the sequence of scenes.

Integrated sitemaps

In web projects and motion graphics work, rough sketches or comps in design application (Photoshop, Illustrator) can concept screens and then be integrated into sitemaps with flow to show interactions and links. The storyboard and site map can be very rough, as long as it is logical and labeled or quite detailed to present logical information flows. Used before creating an online prototype, the sitemap does not require an internet connection, just paper, which never loses bandwidth and crashes.

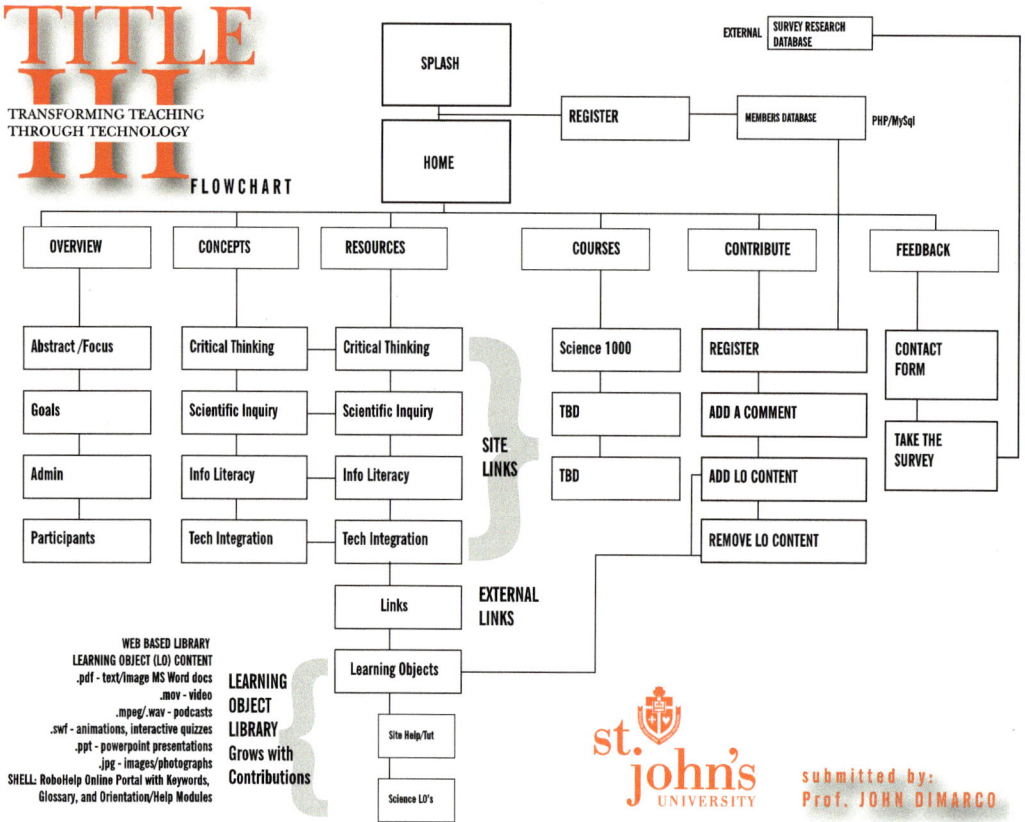

Figure 4.9 Mapping user pathways. Integrated sitemaps provide a vision of scope and flow for a user interface (UI) and user experience (UX) project.

How to create an integrated sitemap

1. *Use boxes and lines or page thumbnails to show entry pages and paths.* The boxes for the site map represent pages and should be set in a landscape view (wide) and placed in a linear structure, which shows non-linear connections through connecting lines. Each box, or page thumbnail represents a page and each line represents a link to that page. Add a dash—next to the page to highlight notable or critical content.
2. *Add a corporate logo and other branding elements.* Done well, the integrated site map takes the design of a website or any non-linear production and puts it into a print-based viewable format that can be used to sell the design in a meeting and inform the client on digital product flow.

4.6 Chapter exercises

Execute these exercises using Adobe Photoshop, Illustrator, InDesign, or Word. You may want to work with marker and paper first to develop ideas and then transfer them to the computer.

1. Visual research

    Role: Act as a communication designer developing an editorial graphic.
    Assignment: Pick an article from a news magazine such as *Time*, *Newsweek*, *Fortune*, or *The Economist* (or another of your choice). Using only type in Photoshop, Illustrator (preferably), or InDesign or Word, create an image that uses type and words to act as an illustration for the article. Design the graphic as the opening image for the article. Use words and phrases from the text as content.
    Include
    – Focus on typographic style that matches the tone and emotion of the article.
    – Use color, grayscale, or black and white in your palette.
    – Use an 8.5 × 11 inch space for the design and use the space any way you like.
    – Think about scale, position, and BANGPP in relationship to the live space for the design.
    – Illustrate with type. Use type strictly as shape, without traditional boundaries.
    Process
    Read a few articles from a magazine of your choice (preferably a news magazine). Then, choose one and illustrate an opening graphic based on the article. Use only type in your design.

Chapter references

Adler, Elizabeth. 1993. *Everyone's Guide to Successful Publications: How to Produce Powerful Brochures, Newsletters, Flyers, and Business Communications, Start to Finish.* Berkeley, CA: Peachpit.
Ausubel, David Paul. 1978. *Educational Psychology: A Cognitive View.* 2nd ed. New York: Holt, Rinehart and Winston.
Creswell, John W. 2003. *Research Design: Qualitative, Quantitative, and Mixed Methods Approaches.* 2nd ed. Los Angeles, CA: Sage.
Curedale, Robert. 2013. *Design Thinking Pocket Guide.* Los Angeles, CA: DDC.
Curtis, Hillman. 2002. *MTIV: Process, Inspiration and Practice for the New Media Designer.* 1st ed. Berkeley, CA: Peachpit.
DiMarco, John. 2010. *Digital Design for Print and Web: An Introduction to Theory, Principles, and Techniques.* 1st ed. Hoboken, NJ: John Wiley & Sons, Inc.

Drewniany, Bonnie L., and Jewler.A. Jerome 2011. *Creative Strategy in Advertising.* 10th ed. Boston, MA: Wadsworth Publishing Co.

Martin, Bella, and Bruce M. Hanington. 2012. *Universal Methods of Design.* Beverly, MA: Rockport Publishers.

Phillips, Jennifer Cole. 2011. *Graphic Design Thinking: Beyond Brainstorming.* Edited by Ellen Lupton. 1st ed. Baltimore, MD: Maryland Institute College of Art.

Wheeler, Alina. 2009. *Designing Brand Identity: An Essential Guide for the Whole Branding Team.* 3rd ed. Chichester: John Wiley & Sons, Ltd.

5

Design Tools

Present your message so that it will not be ignored. Lean and mean ... kick it out.

Hillman Curtis

Chapter objectives

After completing this chapter, you should be able to:

- identify and define industry-standard communication design tools and their uses in the creative domains.
- apply communication design concepts into creative projects.
- understand digital color.
- analyze file formats and basic digital design rules.
- create simple design pieces exhibiting visual, rhetorical, and technical focus.

5.1 Digital design tools for communication designers

To start, most designs are roughed out using paper and pencil, and then are produced using digital tools. Mastering digital tools is not required to be an art director, creative director, or even a graphic designer. However, the ability to solve problems and create solutions is golden in a world where information and communication technologies rule the networks. Being able to solve problems, write and create things, opens more opportunities to show off a strong technical skillset. Otherwise, you will need others to do the work for you. Later in your career, managing people is common, but if you are just starting out in communication design, you may want to strengthen your digital design software skills to become a more valuable professional early and an informed manager or director later in your career when you may be less likely to be doing the physical design.

Technology tools change and so do antiquated production processes and workflows. At work, you will use what software they put on your desktop computer ultimately. Below are some powerful, industry-standard design tools used for creating content and building marketing communications pieces across print, web, and mobile platforms. You will certainly encounter them in your career in communication design. You do not need to be an expert in all of these software packages, but you need to know what their usage is, and specialize somewhat in a few that are critically common in the marketing communications industry.

Page layout and word-processing

– Microsoft Word
– Adobe InDesign
– Quark Xpress (yes, still used in some companies)

Used across marketing communications print work, these programs allow you to create layouts using long and short-form text and placed graphics. These applications utilize frames and offer editorial and publishing tools (table of contents, indexes, style sheets, and master pages) for publication design. The value of these applications is typography control and the ability to import and place artwork consistently on pages with master pages, style sheets, libraries, and templates.

The difference between MS Word and professional page layout programs like InDesign and Quark are the ability to manage and output CMYK and spot color successfully. MS Word does not have color management tools, but more extensive text editing tools. For anything being printed on a desktop printer, where color accuracy is not crucial, Word is great. When a piece is being commercially printed on a printing press, InDesign or Quark must be used for multiple page, long form documents. Typically, text is typed and edited using Word. Next, the text is flowed into a layout in Adobe InDesign or Quark Xpress.

Page layout programs do have web page conversion features, but do not use them. Creating web pages and screen-based products is done best using raster tools like Photoshop and web authoring with programs such as Adobe Dreamweaver, pure hand coding with CSS/HTML, or a CMS/DIY web site creation online software tool like PortfolioVillage.com or Wordpress.

Presentations and e-learning

– PowerPoint
– ISpring
– Captivate

Used in presentations for many commercial and corporate purposes, and for online e-learning courses, these programs allow you to create screens in sequence that can contain multimedia components including text, graphics, animation, video, sound, and interactivity. They also allow for output of screens to video, instructional interface, PDF print document, and of course, a slide show. Most presentation and instructional designers start their work in PowerPoint. They either make screens in a program like Photoshop or layout the components (text, graphics, videos, animations, and buttons) directly in PowerPoint. After the pieces are placed in PowerPoint, the file can either be output from PowerPoint as a PPT presentation file or video. As a PPT presentation file, it can then be opened in Adobe Captivate, or enhanced within PowerPoint using ISpring Suite, which then allows rich interactions and e-learning components like quizzes and videos to be placed directly into the slide deck. The deck can then be output with instructional interfaces that include notes, highlight tools, module indexes, and instructor video and audio.

(a)

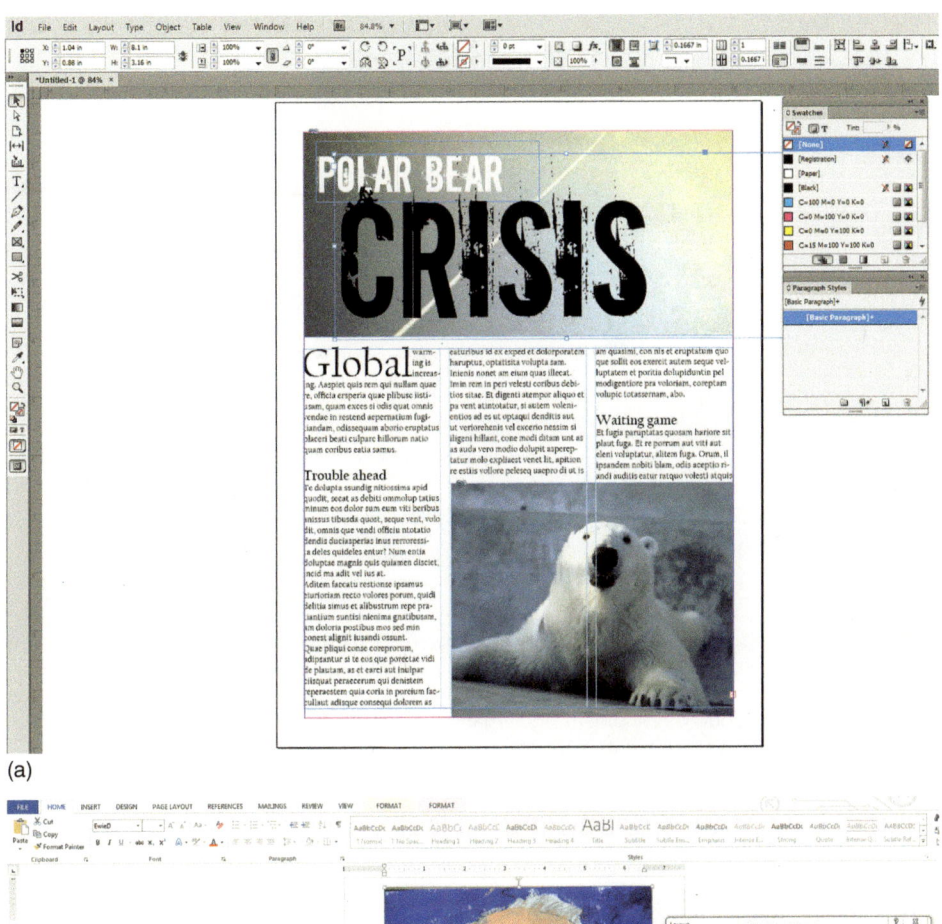

(b)

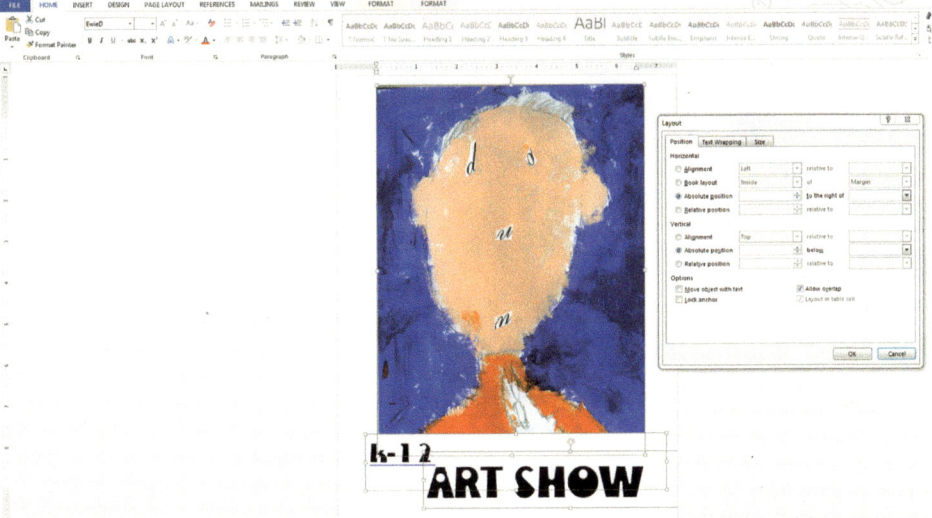

Figures 5.1a and b Box based layouts. Page layout programs use box based frames to place text and graphics on a digital page. Adobe InDesign (bear) is used for professional projects requiring press quality output and color management features. Microsoft Word (art), which uses inline text and box based layout tools also is used for word-processing, text editing, and layout of documents printed on desktop printers.

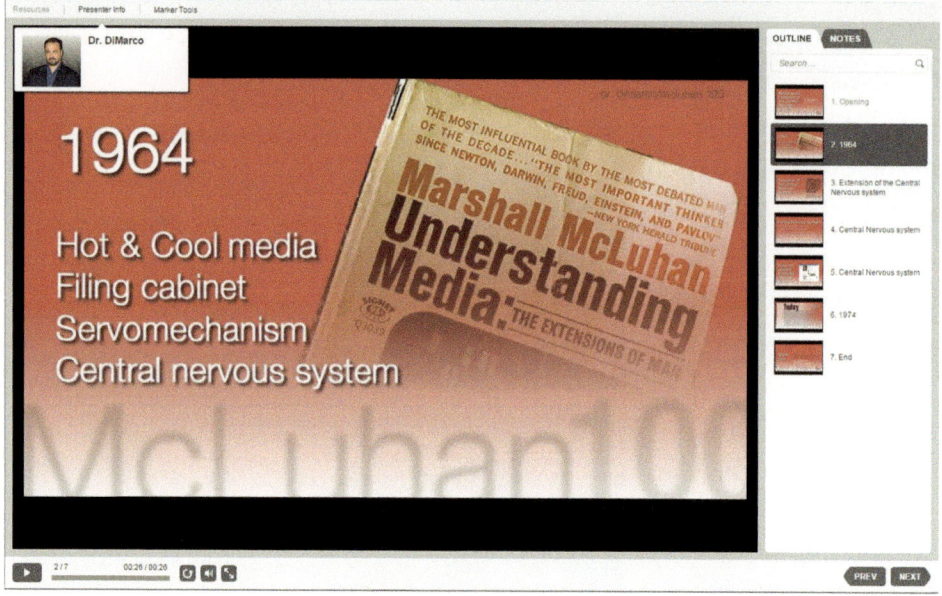

Figure 5.2 Slides to e-Learning. Presentation slides from PowerPoint can also be output into e-learning courses with interactive learning features and quizzes for product videos and training. Audio, controls, and interactivity tools create a new experience for the passive viewer, who now becomes the active user. This type of design is training based, which is used in product marketing, professional development, and organizational learning.

Digital imaging

Photoshop

The great thing about Adobe Photoshop is that is can be used for layouts, graphic manipulation, and drawing. A super-versatile raster-imaging tool, Photoshop allows you to do the following digital tasks:

– Retouching and image manipulation
– Page layout for print, web, broadcast, or film
– Digital drawing and painting
– Graphics creation
– Digital graphics output (export/save/print) to a wide variety of formats

The most common use for Photoshop is to create, retouch, and manipulate raster images, which in visual situations are typically photographs. Raster images are pixels. Pixels (short for picture elements) are bits of data mapped to a color and arranged in rows and columns. The small bits arranged together in a map create a bitmap, which can be opened and manipulated in digital imaging programs, the industry standard being Adobe Photoshop.

Designers and writers use digital imaging applications to create graphics for the screen and for print. The size of a digital image on screen, measured in ppi, is *pixels per inch*. When an image is printed, it is output at a dpi resolution, which is *dots per inch* (linear inch). For print resolution, you need 300 to 350 ppi to output at press quality resolution. This means if you design something in Photoshop to be printed, it should be 300–350 ppi at final size (100%) before it is printed. Otherwise,

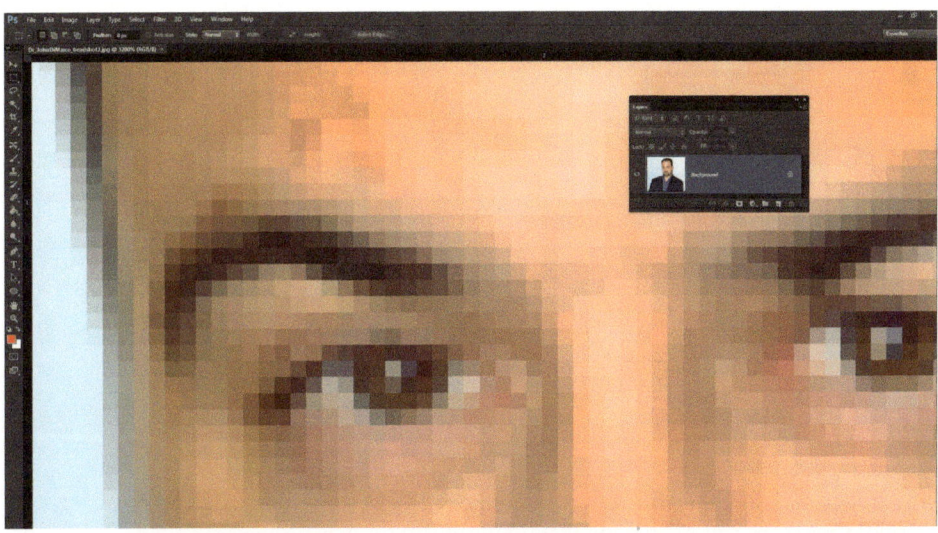

Figure 5.3a Pixels are picture elements. Raster images consist of pixels, which can be manipulated using programs like Adobe Photoshop. Zoomed in to 3200%, the pixels become clear.

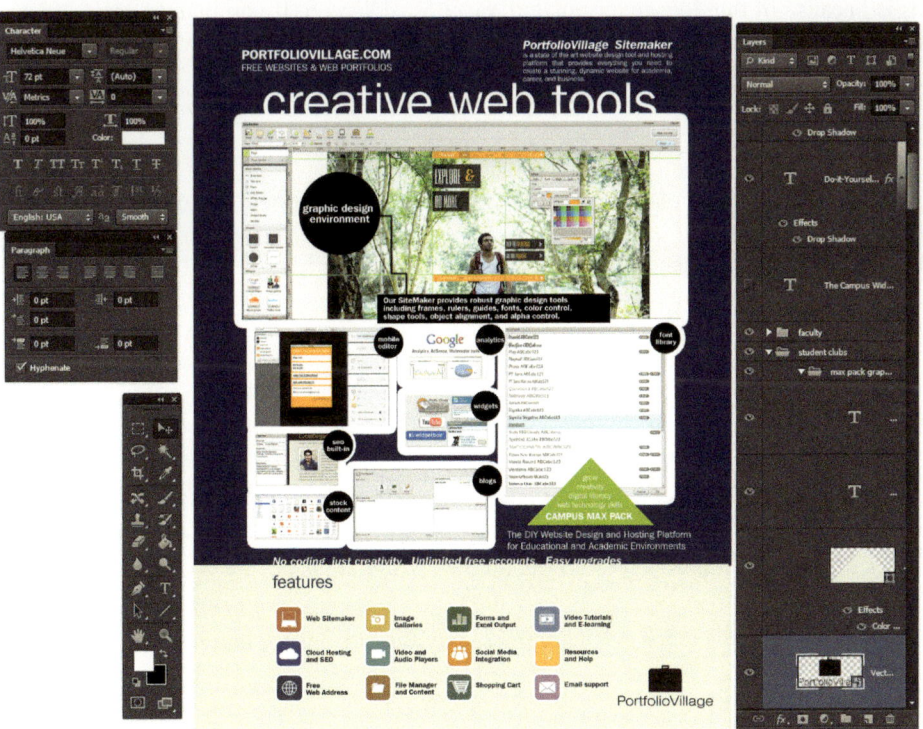

Figure 5.3b Photoshop for layouts. Programs like Adobe Photoshop also work well as layout tools for print and screen designs and for creating graphics that are imported into other applications.

Pen Tool Anatomy

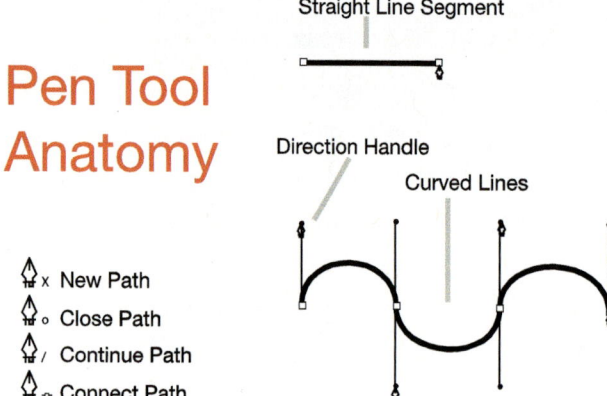

Figure 5.4a The mighty pen tool. Vector images are a series of anchor points and line segments, which are the heart of drawing and design with programs like Adobe Illustrator.

the quality of the image on the page will suffer. Remember PPI is pixels per inch, which is screen resolution. DPI is dots per inch. You need two pixels of input PPI for every line of output on a printing device, which is LPI, lines per inch. Most high-resolution output occurs at 150 LPI (or greater), which means files should be created in raster programs as 300 ppi or greater.

Use 72 ppi images at 100% size for creating graphics for a screen (web, gaming, video, television, film). This is because of the densely populated, pixel filled screen. If you plan to scale images for the screen, work with them at higher resolutions and then lower the resolution for the final output.

Remember these five critical industry rules for working with raster images for print or screen output:

1. Raster images are resolution dependent — you decide the resolution for new documents, measured on screen as PPI (pixels per inch).
2. Raster images for print projects need to be 300–350 ppi to scale for high-resolution output.
3. Raster images for screen projects need to be 72 dpi to scale.
4. Do not scale raster images above 100%–105% in page layout programs because resolution is lost and images are distorted.
5. Save raster images in Photoshop, as PSD files, to keep layers and edit ability.

Digital illustration

Use Adobe Illustrator for the highest resolution illustrations and graphics, as well as page layout. It is a vector graphics tool, which allows you to do the following digital tasks:

– Draw original artwork including logos, page graphics, and illustrations for marketing communications and editorial.
– Page layout for print or screen.
– Auto trace images to create illustrations.
– Develop high-resolution, flat graphics.
– Vector and raster output in single page (export/save/print) to a wide variety of formats.
– Output to a PostScript, .eps file format, for scalable artwork across platforms.

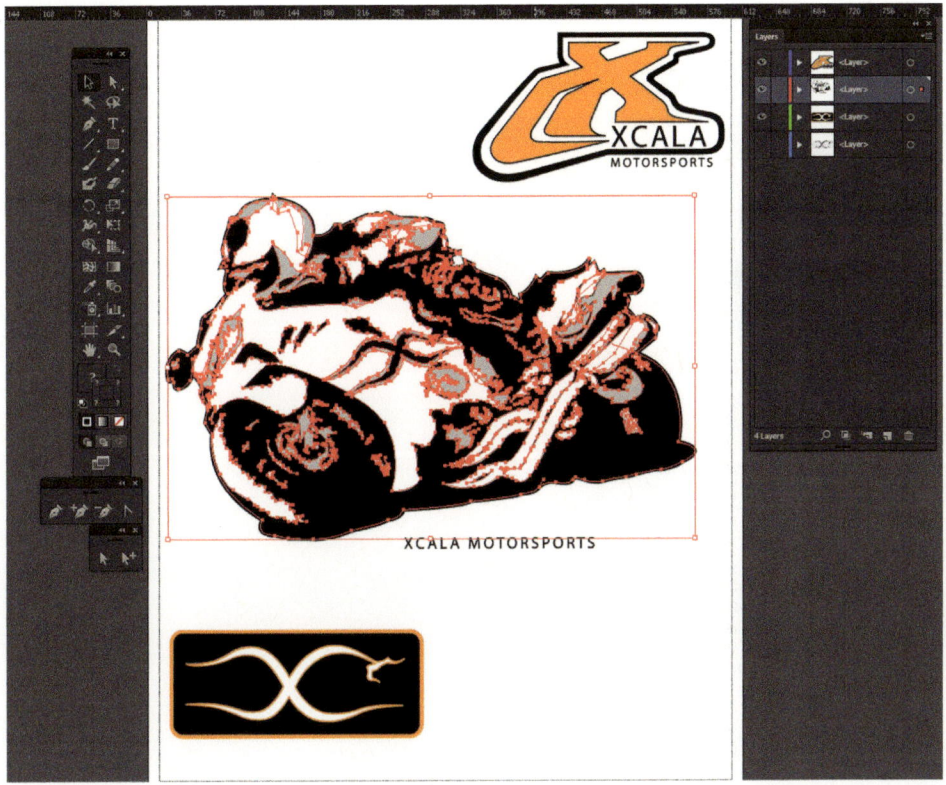

Figure 5.4b Branding elements come from vector graphics. Logotype and brandmarks are created using drawing and design techniques with vector programs like Adobe Illustrator. Design by Michael Calandra. Reproduced with kind permission of Michael Calandra.

The most common use for Illustrator is to create and manipulate vector images, which in visual situations are typically logos, line drawings, shapes, and illustrations. The formulas of French mathematician, Pierre Bezier, are the basis for Bezier curves, which are paths and points in Illustrator. Vector images are made up of anchor points and line segments that use Postscript Programming Language and mathematical formulas behind the scenes as the user interfaces with digital tools inside Illustrator including a pen, pencil, shapes, and eraser (to name only a few) to manipulate points and lines drawn between the points, which are known as paths. The lines are plotted to an invisible grid and arranged with the points, lines, color, and other attributes, which can be opened and manipulated in digital illustration programs, the industry standard being Adobe Illustrator.

Remember these five critical industry rules for working with vector images for print or screen output:

1. Vector images are resolution independent and are always 300 ppi at any scaled size. Logos and product packaging is created using Illustrator.
2. Vector images for print projects are 300 ppi and are capable of high-resolution output. Create outlines for all text before saving final files.
3. Vector images for screen projects need to be "rasterized" (exported or opened in Photoshop) to convert it to 72 dpi to scale.

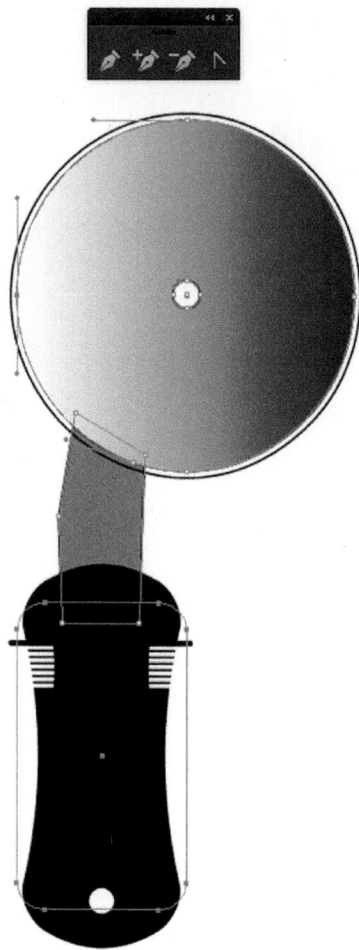

Figure 5.4c Illustration as an alternative to photos. Vector images can be created using shapes, type, or manually with the "Bezier" Pen tool. This product illustration in Illustrator shows an alternative image to a photograph, which may be more easily understood in an instruction guide. Illustration by John DiMarco.

4. Scale vector images freely and above 100% if needed in page layout programs.
5. Save vector images in Illustrator as .EPS file format, which allows for printing, placement in other applications, and editing from Illustrator.

5.2 Essential image production concepts

There are many, many techniques in the art of digital design. They span media and applications, which leads us to understand that we cannot master every tool, palette, and menu across the literally dozens of applications we encounter in our professional lives. The production concepts listed below are essential to understanding digital design techniques from their core basis. Opacity, selections, channels, and paths, layers, color and file formats all appear repeatedly in a wide range of visual approaches to design projects across persuasive communications. Understanding these essential concepts is a key to working as a professional in the marketing communications creative industry.

Figure 5.5a Lowering opacity. Using sliders in programs such as Adobe Photoshop provides an adjustment of pixel depth in images or text that allows show through or overlay create visual contrast and a "screened over" look. Notice how the display text lowered to 40% opacity, allows a see though effect and blending with the image.

Opacity

The ability to lower the opacity of an image in digital design programs is innate. It is a built in feature to the majority of applications that provide placement of images. Opacity is especially useful in all visual page or screen designs as it provides countless creative possibilities. The technical part of it is this: opaque is solid – 100%. Transparent is see-through at different opacity levels –1%–99%. Programs allow a 0–100 scale for lowering opacity (also called transparency in some programs). At the lowest levels (0–5) the image literally disappears. Lowering opacity is effective when overlapping images, to ghost an image, or to blend images together.

Selections, alpha channels, and paths

Selecting parts of an image is a critical technique used in digital media design across platforms. A selection can be done using bitmap (lasso, rectangular marquee) or vector tools (pen tool), depending on the final output. For print, the final selection is output in a file with a clipping path. For the

Figure 5.5b Type as image. Lowering opacity creates opportunities to develop type as image. Design by John DiMarco.

screen, the final selection output is a file with an alpha channel. What this means is that you can take an image, a photograph, for example, and use a selection tool to select a part of the image by either selecting the pixels or encompassing the part in a path that clips out the remaining part of the image. Look at any fashion magazine cover with a model standing in front of the publication masthead with type sprinkled around them. The subject was selected using the lasso tool, or clipped out using the pen tool and placed in a new file that eliminated any image parts outside of the selected areas. Selections are savable in the image as a clipping path for print output, or an alpha channel for screen output. Use the .EPS, .TIF, for print output and .PNG for screen output. This allows images to be placed with transparent backgrounds to create overlapping artwork that has depth and layered content.

Layers and compositing

Layers and compositing images are the most useful production feature available to designers. In the 1990s, digital layering and compositing were a gateway to the amazing digital production we have today. Items rest on layers (or tracks) and then become composited (assembled) to create a new design. Compositing allows all types of assets: text, images, moving clips, and sound to overlap in layers. Whether it is television, film, print, web, or mobile, layers and composite images create visual depth by using space and perspective to establish depth in a two-dimensional space.

Figures 5.6a and b
The power of selections. Selections in Photoshop allow you to clip out pixels in an image to select exactly the parts you want. You can drag pieces of images into other images to create new graphics and have control to overlap images and type.

(a)

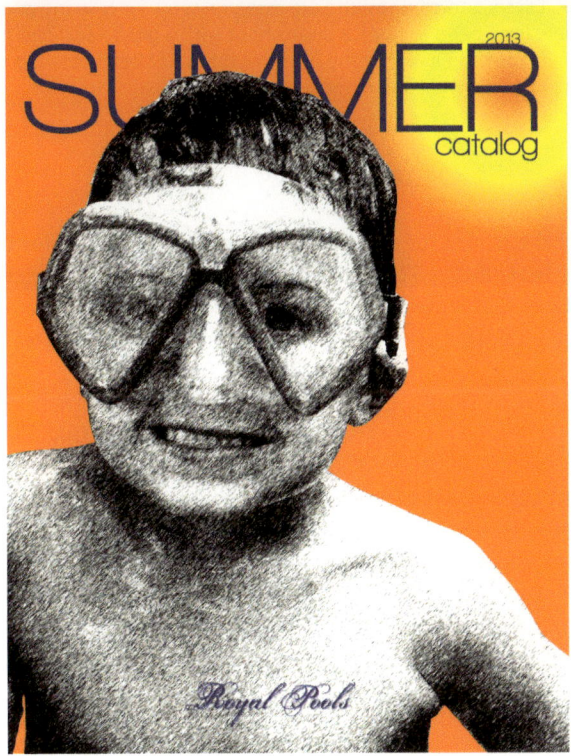

(b)

Figure 5.7 Compositing artwork. Layers and compositing are essential tools for creating photorealistic artwork in all types of advertising designs. There is no need to book a photoshoot with a giraffe and bird in an office hallway. Skillful assembly using layers, and then applying a blur to the background in Adobe Photoshop offers the perfect design solution. Design by Turnstyle. Reproduced with kind permission of Turnstyle.

5.3 Digital color spaces (RGB and CMYK)

Digital color is a monumental element for creating responsible computer files that will print or view on a screen accurately and beautifully. The most fundamental piece to digital color is the understanding of digital color space. Different from the artists' color wheel, which is a tool for sourcing color choices before going digital, the CMYK and RGB color spaces in digital design for both print and screen are heavily used.

The two-color spaces, RGB and CMYK, are connected. RGB : Red (r), green (g), and blue (b) wavelengths combined simulate a range of colors found in nature. Subtracting RGB wavelengths from white light creates cyan, magenta, and yellow (CMY). This is the subtractive color model. Taking the subtractive color model and applying it to printing, translucent cyan (c), magenta (m), and yellow (y), which are based on pigments, attract, absorb, and reflect light when on a printed page. Desktop printers and printing presses add a fourth color, black (k) to create a deep black for text and lines. CMYK, known as the process printing model, combines four ink colors, cyan, magenta, yellow, and black to create millions of printed colors.

Digital color rules

We use RGB for our preliminary designs because it allows the widest range of color options. Based on light, RGB provides a wider gamut (range) of color than CMYK, which is limited to the output of ink from a device.

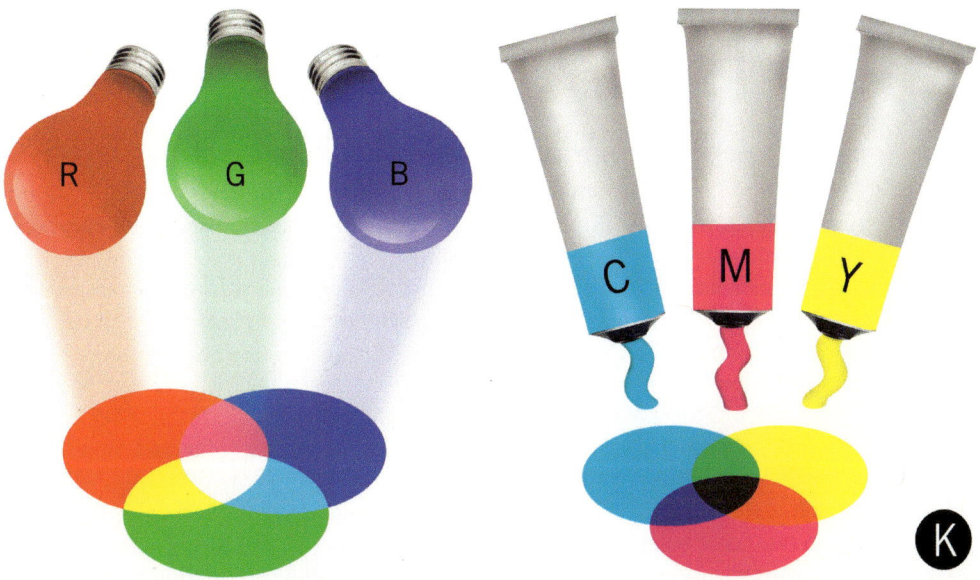

Figure 5.8 Color comes from light or pigment. The RGB color model is based on light. The CMYK color model is based on ink pigments. RGB is the color model used for communication design output to screen. CMYK is the color model used for communication design output to paper. Illustration by Kristen Crawford. Reproduced with kind permission of Kristen Crawford.

During a print project, begin the designs in RGB to have the most options available, and then convert to CMYK before outputting files to the printer or film image setter.

For paper (print) designs, start in RGB in Photoshop, and then convert to CMYK for final image output. All other programs (Illustrator, InDesign) use CMYK for print projects. Unless the piece is spot color, in that case you would be using CMYK and/or a Pantone ink color, which is an "off the shelf" color, consistent across printing outputs, used mostly for brand identity and logos.

If final output is on a screen in the medium of the Internet, film, gaming, mobile, or television, the outputted, final files will be RGB (DiMarco 2010). For screen (web, mobile, presentation, video, animation) designs, start and finish in RGB. Only use RGB in all programs. RGB is the color model for all screens.

Pantone swatch books

In digital design, we use CMYK and spot colors (Pantone inks) for output to paper or packaging substrate (paperboard, cardboard, film, metal, foil, or plastic). In commercially printed, trade level work (output resolutions above 1200 dpi), printers and prepress operators and designers understand that spot colors are solid inks that represent a single (ink off the shelf) color, while CMYK ink mixtures represent millions of colors.

Spot colors (Pantone) have two distinct purposes:

1. Using spot colors in one-color or two-color jobs saves money in printing costs when using traditional printing presses. With the advent of digital presses, that require no film or plates, cost savings for traditional two-color print jobs has mostly become obsolete.

116 *Communications Writing and Design*

2. Using Pantone inks and spot color as a guideline for color output and consistency of logos and brand color palettes is still a standard practice across print communication.

RGB vs. web safe color on screen

Designers use the RGB color model to create millions of visible colors, for the screen (web, TV, film, video). Monitors and video cards vary, just as printers and printing presses do. For screen graphics, when we need standard swatches for logos and brand colors, we have two main color palettes, the web safe color palette and the index color palette. These palettes use hexadecimal values for their names. The hexadecimal system, also known as *index color uses sixteen symbols to represent a color value.* The symbols 0–9 represent values zero to nine, and A, B, C, D, E, F represent values ten to fifteen. Color swatches using hexadecimal values are represented by six digits for each color. For instance, the color black is represented by #000000. The color white is #ffffff. The index color palette color represents the 256 colors available in the operating system of that particular computer (Mac and Windows). Generally, do not use the index color palette for page designs because it causes dithering, which is when colors adapt to the system palette colors for viewing of the image when the real color is absent. I suggest utilizing the web safe color palette. Use the web safe color palette for .GIF files (flat artwork) and color backgrounds in your web design projects. The web safe color palette contains 216 common colors (RGB) that appear the same across web browsers and computers (Windows, Mac, or UNIX based). Use web safe colors for background colors, web based text and lines, and for representing logos consistently on web pages. Use RGB based JPGs for photographic images. In Adobe Photoshop, you can convert these colors between palettes, but be sure to check matching as color may vary between color spaces.

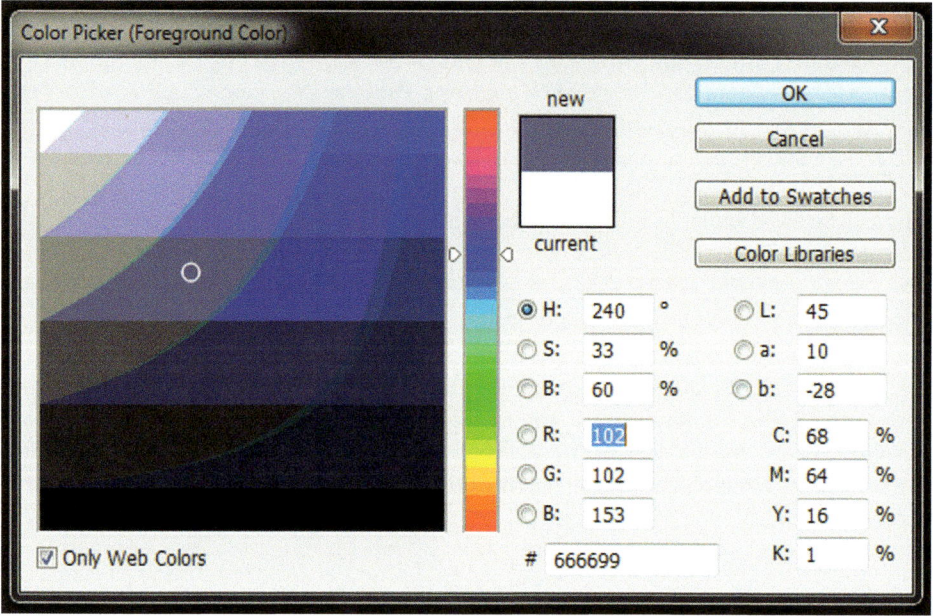

Figure 5.9 Web colors. The web safe color palette in Adobe Photoshop shows the 216 common colors across computer platforms and browsers.

Spot color vs. process color in print

Understanding print output beyond just the local desktop printer in your office is critical in communication design for print. Because CMYK colors mix to create millions of colors, color reproduction can vary because there are various types of output (printing) devices including inkjet printers, laser printers, digital copiers, and commercial printing presses with many different manufacturers. Although outputting soft proofs (digital) and hard proofs (film Matchprint) helps ensure consistency of color, process color reproduction is not exact in all cases. To solve this problem, designers and printers use spot colors, also known as Pantone inks, which are solid colors, premixed and coded for accuracy to a swatch book. The Pantone swatch books come in various sets with the Pantone coated and Pantone uncoated inks being the most widely used. The coated and uncoated refer to paper, as the swatch books present color chips that present small swatches of numbered color printed on coated and uncoated paper. By looking at the swatches, a designer can get an idea as to how the color will look when printed on coated or uncoated stock (paper). The finish of the paper affects the way the

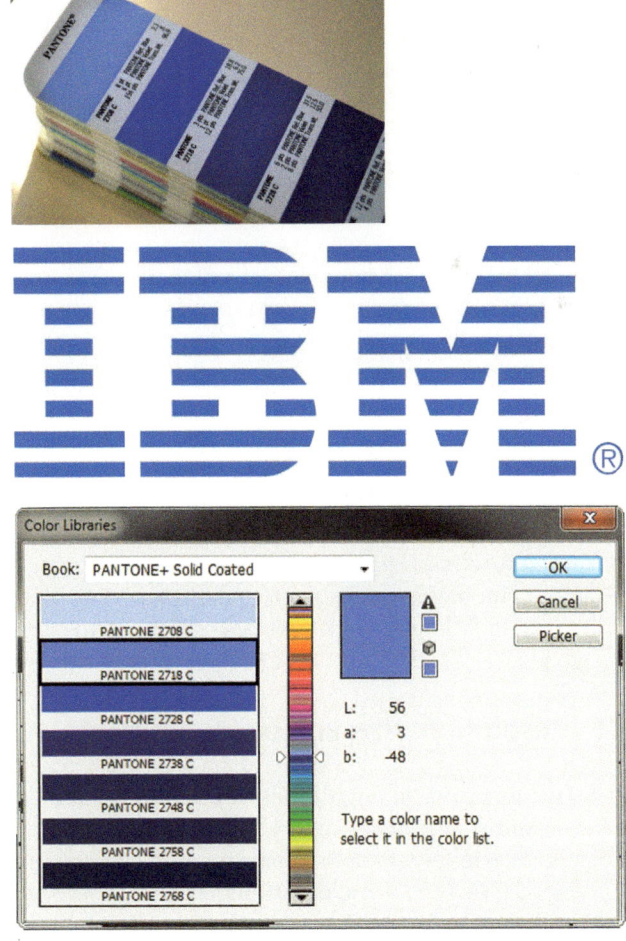

Figure 5.10 Pantone colors for the perfect match. Matching spot color requires using Pantone swatch books during conceptualization, then using the same electronic swatch book in Adobe Illustrator, Photoshop, or InDesign for outputting files. IBM officially requires Pantone equivalent 2718C. Pantones are spot color, or "premixed ink off the shelf," so they are consistent color on press. IBM and the IBM logo are trademarks of International Business Machines Corp., registered in many jurisdictions worldwide.

color looks when printed. Pantone colors are most widely used for one- and two-color print jobs and for logos. PMS stands for Pantone matching system. PMS is the print production industry's standard term for spot color.

The reason companies use Pantone inks when printing their logos is because it guarantees consistent color follows the brand and the corporate identity (business cards, letterhead, and brochures). Each company typically selects a Pantone color and records the values (RGB and CMYK) to ensure that color is the same across touch points. Two companies that provide solid examples are Coca-Cola and IBM. The trademark filing for Coca-Cola reveals the critical nature of spot color on brand identity. Notice the application for protection of the mark uses Pantone matching system colors PMS 484, PMS 8001, and PMS 116 as critical elements of the mark. IBM uses the Pantone 2718C ink when representing their respective logos. When a logo prints using PMS inks and appropriate paper stock, it will be the same from every print run. To ensure this, when ad agencies create a full-color print ad for a magazine placement, they often pay extra to have the ad printed using a fifth color. The fifth color is the Pantone ink required by the client. The five-color advertisement is then printed using the Pantone ink for the logo and whatever else needs the brand color. The four process colors, cyan, magenta, yellow and black are combined to create millions of colors for the photos and other line art, but the logo color and other brand elements using color must be exact, every time so mixing logo colors from CMYK inks is not preferred.

Three important takeaways on color

The basics of color become a tool to explore concepts, create mood, and communicate with vendors and colleagues. Three main things that you should know are:

1. *Concept*: The color wheel (ROYGBP) is the starting point for basic design using color in concept, not on a computer. When we are exploring color usage in design thinking, we use the color wheel to establish color schemes (color combinations) to use in our designs.
2. *Screen*: When we design for any type of screen, we need to end up with digital files in RGB color modes (or web safe color mode for flat mobile and web art). RGB uses the additive color model (RGB), which is based on light and used for output to a screen or monitor (web sites, video, television, mobile).
3. *Paper or other substrate* (surface): When we design printed pages, we need to end up with digital files in CMYK mode. The subtractive (CMY) and process (CMYK) color model are the basis for process printing on all types of printers and printing presses. CMYK is based on pigments (inks). The CMYK color model, used in printing on most substrates (the printed surface-paper is common), used in corporate communications, packaging, and advertising design, is a standard of digital print media. Spot colors, usually consisting of Pantone inks, are used for one- or two-color jobs and in full-color work to preserve identity color consistency.

5.4 Resolution, size, and output formats

Understanding how to output files to printing presses, websites, mobile phones, and large screens requires knowledge of resolution, image size, and resolution. The difference between successful projects and ones caught up with production issues is the knowledge of the designer to create responsible digital files. Different applications have their own native file format. Photoshop, for example uses .PSD as the native format. The native format is the most editable, but not necessarily the one needed for final output. For print projects, a Photoshop file starts out as an RGB, .PSD file, and may eventually be "saved as" a CMYK .EPS file @ 300 ppi for output to a printing press. That same file may be needed to be placed on a web page within a site. In this case, that .PSD file would be "saved as" an RGB .JPG file @ 72 ppi. Knowing those workflow outputs is a tremendous part of being considered a "professional" communication designer.

Prepress overview

After a designer creates and submits files for printing, they perform a process called prepress, alternatively known as preflight. The prepress process is a checklist used to ensure proper output of digital files to print output devices. Offset lithographic printing requires film negatives to be converted to metal or paper printing plates for use on a press. If the digital files have problems with resolution, fonts, color models, image nesting, or positioning, the film will also have those errors, so a thorough check is done by either the designer or a prepress specialist who is experienced in ensuring quality final files are delivered. Why is prepress so fragile and important? It is because there are serious technical considerations when creating files that are going to be printed on a press. Here is how it happens after we know that files are "prepress ready." Final files for high quality print output are sent

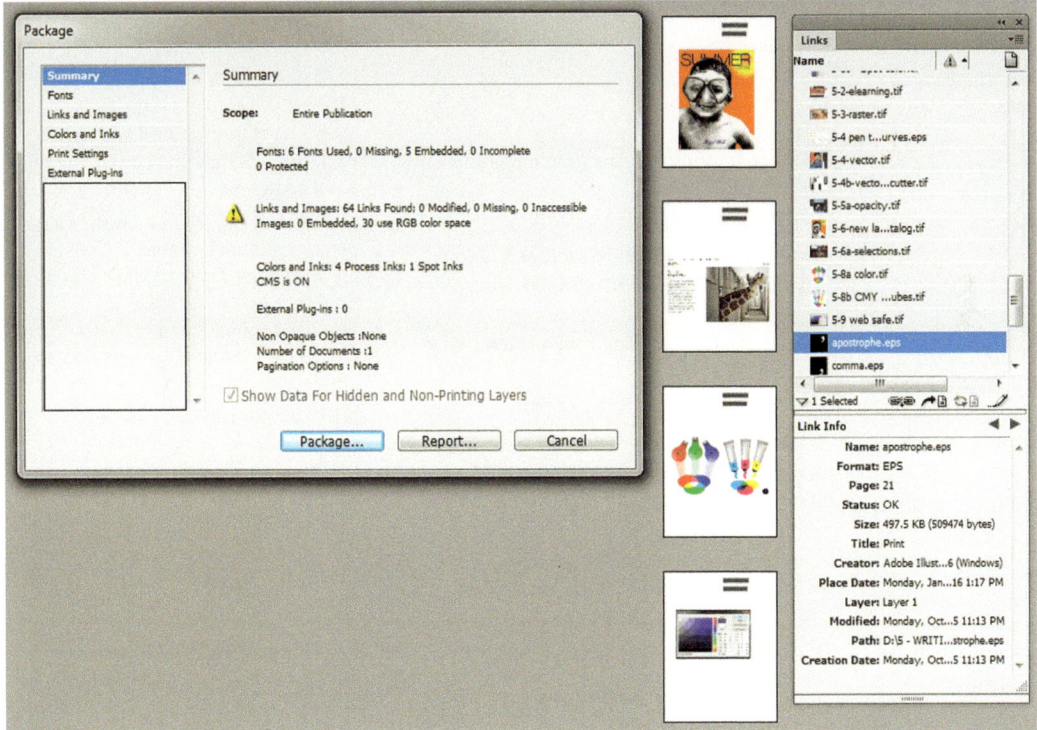

Figure 5.11 Packaging files for final output. The Package command in InDesign collects all the files needed for commercial output to a printing press and PostScript printer. It provides a "prepress checklist" that insures that fonts, image links, and color profiles are not missing or damaged before going to the device. The images and fonts are "called" by either the print server or the web server so that they can be ripped or uploaded accordingly. Regardless of the project, remember that all image files and fonts must be included in one location for print projects, motion, video, and web projects.

Adobe Photoshop **Raster graphics for print, web, and broadcast projects.**	**PRINT DESIGN** File Formats: .PSD for design .TIF for print .EPS for print .PDF for print or document management. *In Photoshop … Always save a .PSD with layers for future editing. Resolutions: Print projects: 300–350 ppi. Web and broadcast projects: 72 ppi. Always design to final output size.	RGB for initial design of print and web. CMYK for final output of print graphics (.TIF or .EPS). Convert all print documents to CMYK as a final step before saving or exporting as .TIF or .EPS. NEVER USE RGB for print graphics.
	WEB DESIGN File Formats: .JPG for web (photos or any graphics – you can use this for any image). .PNG for web (transparent backgrounds: logos, non rectangular images – you can use this for any image).	RGB for .JPG and .PNG. Web Safe Index color for .GIF and web backgrounds that must be the same in all browsers. NEVER USE CMYK for web graphics.
Adobe Illustrator **Vector graphics and layouts**	.AI for design .EPS for print. EXPORTS .TIF for print .JPG for web (photos or any graphics – you can use this for any image) .GIF for web (for flat graphics only). *Always save an .AI with editable text before creating outlines for future editing. Resolutions: Print projects: 300–350 ppi (high resolution is default in AI). Web and broadcast projects: 72 ppi. Always design to final output size. You can open .AI files and .EPS files in Photoshop and rasterize them into bitmap images for the web. Vector files cannot be placed in a webpage unless they are rasterized. You can export AI files as raster files also, which makes them web ready.	Export for web or TV: to RGB for .JPG, .PNG or other raster format. Web Safe Index for .GIF and web backgrounds that must be the same in all browsers. CMYK and PANTONE Swatches for print graphics (1–4 color). Convert all print documents to CMYK as a final step before saving as .EPS. Or Use PMS spot colors plus black for two-color work such as logos, cards, and letterheads. NEVER USE CMYK for web graphics. NEVER USE RGB for print graphics.
Adobe InDesign **Page layouts**	.IDD for design .IDD or .PDF for print Epub output. EXPORTS .TIF or .EPS for print .JPG for web (avoid exporting graphics from a page layout program). *Always save an .IDD with all fonts and graphics for future editing.	CMYK and PANTONE Make sure all type and placed graphics are CMYK or Pantone spot color before final output for print.

Figure 5.12 Guide to file formats for final output.

to an imagesetter, which is a high-resolution output device that can transfer electronic text and graphics directly to film, plates, or photo-sensitive paper. In process color printing, an imagesetter creates the separated output by "printing" the image four times — once each in cyan, magenta, yellow and black, which is the CMYK color space (Muir 2000). Imagesetters are high-resolution laser devices with dedicated raster image processors (RIP) to output the highest resolution PostScript file for the sharpest printed image possible. The resolution of a typical imagesetter is 1270 or 2540 dpi with a maximum dpi of 4000. This is vastly more coverage than the resolution of a home and office laser printer, which is typically between 300–600 dots per inch.

Knowing which file formats are proper for each application and final output to print and web media is critical to developing professional communication design files. The chart below provides a simple guide to using the correct format for final output.

5.5 Chapter exercises

Execute these exercises using Adobe Photoshop, Illustrator, InDesign, or Word. You may want to work with marker and paper first to develop ideas and then transfer them to the computer.

1. *Illustrating with type*

    Role: Act as a communication designer developing an editorial graphic.
    Assignment: Pick an article from a news magazine such as *Time, Newsweek, Fortune,* or *The Economist* (or another of your choice). Using only type in Photoshop, Illustrator (preferably), or InDesign or Word create an image that uses type and words to act as an illustration for the article. Design the graphic as the opening image for the article. Use words and phrases from the text as content.
    Include
    - Focus on typographic style that matches the tone and emotion of the article.
    - Use color, grayscale, or black and white in your palette.
    - Use an 8.5 × 11 inch space for the design and use the space any way you like.
    –
    - Think about scale, position, and BANGPP in relationship to the live space for the design.
    - Illustrate with type. Use type strictly as shape, without traditional boundaries.
    Process
    Read a few articles from a magazine of your choice (preferably a news magazine). Then, choose one and illustrate an opening graphic based on the article. Use only type in your design.

2. *Montage poster for a wildlife event*

    Role: Act as a communication designer developing a poster on a Word Wildlife Event that will raise awareness of a problem in the animal world. Undertake secondary source research to see what issues are prominent and choose one for direction. Then dive deeper into the topic by looking at direct data sources from government and environmental organizations.
    Assignment: Use stock images of animals and create an original poster that includes a montage of images and text that address one big problem for the animals you highlight. Pick photographs from domestic or exotic animals, or your own snapshots of animals you encounter. A short message (consisting of no more than 25 words) relating to the problem should be included.

Include
- Focus on image selections and developing a coherent theme that will support the message.
- Use color, grayscale, or black and white in your montage poster.
- Use an 8.5 × 11 or 11 × 17 inch page for the design and use only a few words.
- Think about simplicity and recognition of the animals and the problem you want to solve using this communication.

Process

Start with a receptacle (final) document at 11 × 8.5 (landscape). Next open one image at a time in Adobe Photoshop. Create a selection around the part of the image you want to use and drag it into the receptacle document. Repeat this for each image that you want in the montage. Each image will be on its own layer. Move the images around and position with the text to create an engaging design. Manipulate opacity when overlaying images for a blended look. Check the design against BANGPP to see if the poster follows the rule of thirds. Save the final design as a RGB PSD file in layers, then *save as* … CMYK TIF file for printing.

Chapter references

DiMarco, John. 2010. *Digital Design for Print and Web: An Introduction to Theory, Principles, and Techniques*. 1st ed. Chichester: John Wiley & Sons, Ltd.

Muir, Peter. 2000. *Preflight: Avoiding Costly Printout Problems through Proper File Preparation*. San Diego, CA: Windsor Professional Information.

6

Marketing Projects

6.1 Logotype and brandmark

Logotype and brandmark — defined

Brand identity consists of the visual elements that imprint a consistent, palatable image of the organization in the form of a word and a symbol, respectively called logotype and brandmark. Either or both of these may be respectively called a "logo," which is short for, you guessed it, logotype. When the logotype and brandmark combine in one design, they create the signature. Companies may have multiple signature combinations standardized and connected with multiple tag lines. The tagline is the short, punchy message under the logo. These variations move across different products, divisions, or business units in the corporation. ESPN, for example, has multiple signatures for the family of brands: ESPN, ESPN2, ESPN Classic, ESPN Magazine, ESPN Deportes, and ESPNU are a few of the ESPN brands that carry similar signatures, sharing the same logotype of ESPN, but with different brandmarks for each different segmentation.

Usage of the logotype and brandmark individually varies across different touchpoints with ads, products, collateral, stationery, websites, and other branded media items. Published usage guidelines come from the organization internally and externally to ensure a consistent look achieved across all media. Some brands have only logotype and some have only brandmarks. In recent times, companies have tried to move toward brandmarks in favor of logotypes and full signatures. Apple Computer, perennially represented the brand line with logotype, set in Garamond Condensed, combined with the distinctive Apple icon brandmark to create the signature. The company has moved toward using the Apple brandmark exclusively in many touchpoints.

Goal of the piece

The goal of the logotype and brandmark are to simplify the organization into a visual fabric that covers the essence of the organization, its products, people, and purpose. The piece is vital to establishing consistent brand identity, which connects the organization across marketing communications touchpoints.

Specifications and size

Logotype and brandmarks have followed an unwritten rule that they need to be highly legible at 1 inch ×1 inch. This idea comes from the need to place the logotype in the corner of an ad or on the face of a

Figure 6.1a The anatomy of a "logo." In this case, the design contains a brandmark and logotype, which can work individually to represent the brand and together within the full signature. Design by John DiMarco.

business card. In either case, scale matters. Test elements for clarity on screen and on paper to ensure acceptable quality at small sizes. Favicons, which are the icons seen in the browser address bar show how small brandmarks need to be in order to fill size requirements — they are 16 pixels × 16 pixels.

Research and conceptualization

It is important that you generate many ideas before settling on logotypes and brandmarks. This is critical to explore fully the creative process. Assuming that you have a name (naming is another step all together), you should:

- List the various signatures and tag lines needed for the corporate brand set.
- Research existing signatures in the industry and connected industries to look for visual patterns and styles.
- Examine websites from prominent design firms and aggregate sites such as logolounge.com to gain knowledge on logo trends and inspiration on creative approaches.
- Use ethnography to examine the organizational environment, people, and culture to establish visual themes for typography, color, and visual resonance.
- Brainstorm visual ideas using thumbnails and digital comps to generate multiple visual approaches.
- Think about different visual forms for the brandmark. Approaches that focus on literal illustrations, abstract forms, naturalistic motion, industrial strength, pictorial imagery, linear shapes, straight edged, angled, and negatively spaced, all have different visual essence and should be explored.
- Establish color guidelines — pick Pantone ink selections for spot color printing; choose RGB values for screen usage, and CMYK color values for full color printing.
- Narrow choices with stakeholders and designers.
- Create variations for multiple corporate applications.
- Test the logotype and brandmark against other major brands to see if it holds visual weight.
- Use brainstorming to create an initial name list and filter down to a short list of contending names.
- Use concentric circle exercise to establish words for tag line development.

Writing style

Tag lines and naming are the two most common writing assignments associated with logotype and brandmarks. Naming is a difficult task according to Shaw (2012) and Wheeler (2009), who both recommend developing a long list initially, generated by brainstorming. Once available, the long list receives examination, trimming, and discussion by the stakeholders and design team. Specific tasks in deciphering the potency of a name include positioning against other brand names, visual possibilities or limitations, availability within an industry (web address URL for example), and legal and regulatory issues such as trademarks and service marks, which protect the brand identity from others using the same name, description, and visual art in tandem, in commerce. Shaw (2012) recommends that after short list agreement, then an analysis of potential linguistic, historical, and issues are the focus including pitfalls such as possible misinterpretations of the name, double meanings that may arise, and spelling variations. Wheeler (2009) suggests contextual testing of the look, feel, and sound of the words in various organizational contexts such as voicemail, letterhead, business cards, headlines, and web pages.

Tag lines are short bursts of persuasion that cement the identity of the organization with a slogan that sticks to the logotype, brandmark, and signature. Written as headlines of sorts, but are reliant on direct, clear communication, tag lines require a tremendous amount of patience and attention to insure they position the brand correctly. Word count for tag lines should be targeted at five words or less, with three-word tags being a particularly effective and magical number for such text: "I'm lovin it" — MacDonalds, "Finger Lickin Good" — KFC, "Just Do it" — Nike, and "be all you can be" — US Army, are some notable examples of masterfully written tag lines that stuck with consumers.

Logotype, brandmark, and signature design format

When creating a brand identity, remember that the design entails the creation of one to three visual elements. The logotype and the brandmark get married in the signature. This means that the design process needs segmentation so that each element gets its creative due.

For the logotype, be brave and explore different typefaces, styles like bold, italic, and black, and color and shade combinations. Experiment with serif and san serif typefaces to match the style of the organization and the font, looking for connections with serif styled naturalistic lines and curves or san serif pronounced industrial thickness and sharp edges. Mix typefaces to create visual contrast or use one face with different styles or shades to create a more subtle offset. Consider color and size relative to the brandmark and overall signature.

For brandmarks, experiment with different variations including: crests, shadows, hubs, lines, dots, swirls, blurs, gradients, hubs, overlaps, transparencies, and rubber bands. Explore halves, overlaps, dots, and other existing visual themes such as animals, fruits, flowers, leaves, and ribbons. Consider color and size relative to the logotype and overall signature.

Logotype, brandmark, and signature checklist

- Did you *create a logotype that stands up to competing brands?*
- Did you *include a clear logotype that is recognizable, readable, and fluid across mediums?*
- Did you *test sizes against the 1 × 1 inch print rule for logotype and the 16 pixel × 16 pixel favicon test for brandmarks?*
- Did you *keep color unique and related to the brand for quick recognition?*
- Did you *specify spot (PMS), RGB, and CMYK values for the logotype and brandmark?*
- Did you *test the logo visually and contextually across critical brand touchpoints?*
- Did you *print a proof to view color and image consistency?*

Figure 6.1b The variety of marks. Line, text, and image create unlimited possibilities when it comes to logotypes and brandmarks. Design by Paula Scher, DJ Stout, Natasha Jen, and Michael Gericke, Pentagram. Reproduced with kind permission of Pentagram.

Figure 6.1c, d, e, and f Touchpoints across a brand. This non-profit brand identity shows the different usages developed incorporating logotype, brandmark, and full signatures with taglines clearly communicating purpose and requisite brand division. Design is the bond that visually and functionally ties the different media together. "The branding is built around a friendly and accessible mark that is designed to appeal to everyone from park visitors to policy makers." Design by Michael Bierut, Pentagram. Reproduced with kind permission of Pentagram.

Figure 6.1g and h Iconic and indexical mark. The millennial leaning update for Microsoft Windows 8 marries logotype and brandmark with exquisite clarity, simplicity, and friendly functionality. Design by Paula Scher, Pentagram. Reproduced with kind permission of Pentagram.

(g)

(h)

Creative assignment

The identity creation game

This game allows you to "sprint" through various names, taglines, logotypes, brandmarks, and signatures.

How to play

Each person in a class or group acts as a designer and copywriter working on an original name and brand identity consisting of logotype, brandmark, signature, and tagline.

Using the words in the word bank, create five logotype and brandmark designs. Each design must use the words from the bank in the name of the company only. The tagline is purely creative and can be from one to five words.

Use any design software you like including Illustrator or Photoshop. Illustrator is the best tool for logotypes and brandmarks because it allows creation of resolution independent, scalable, vector artwork. Nevertheless, this is practice, so use what you have available, even if it is only Microsoft Word.

Once created, the identities are submitted and posted on a wall. Comment on the weakest designs using concept, design, and execution as criteria and then choose the strongest work in categories including:

- the most inviting logotype
- the most memorable brandmark
- the proudest looking signature
- the most creative name
- the punchiest tagline

Everyone votes for each category. Tally the votes for each category and crown winners. Most importantly, learn from the experience for future identity projects.

Be sure to include:

1. *The created names*
   Using the word bank only, create company names to use in your spec brand identity designs. Use any number of words, but remember they need to be represented in the logotype and brandmark effectively.
2. *Use one image for the brandmark*
   Illustration of many sorts (see above) can be the mark. Keep it simple and you will see results.
3. *Logotype*
   Choose the right typeface. Keep it to one font if design possible, two fonts maximum. Remember the brand voice and audience appeal of the logotype and use color that reflects that relationship.
4. *The signature*
   Put it all together to make the full graphic signature.
5. *The tagline*
   Make it memorable and not more than five words. Test five word tags first and then filter them down by removing words and scrambling different words to create new meanings. You can create any tag lines you want.

Word bank

lion	diamond	shop	paper	dog	list	beauty
garden	book	lock	bird	king	light	sharp
mail	onion	tree	wise	ball	box	town

6.2 Business card, letterhead, envelope — company stationery

Company stationery defined

Brand identity transcends through touchpoints. As discussed throughout the text, there are almost endless touchpoints, traditional and undiscovered, but two of the most important to corporate identity are the business card and letterhead. The logotype, brandmark, and signature, in both screen and print versions, see natural usage on the business card, letterhead, and mailing envelope.

Goal of the piece

The goal of company stationery is to be a mini marketing billboard for frequent communications from the organization. The business card, letterhead, and envelope have a long and thriving tenure in marketing communications, used for many critical functions including face-to-face networking, correspondence, invoices, employee communication, legal letters, media kits, and press releases. These pieces are informational in nature, before integration and population of other content, on a letterhead, for example. This means that they contain core organizational information that brings the organization to the public.

Specifications and size

The letterhead is 8.5 × 11 inches and the business card is 3.5 × 2 inches. Letterheads are always portrait. Business cards are either wide or tall with either portrait or landscape orientation being used by companies today. Envelopes are varied sizes, with the #10, business envelope being standard at 4.125 × 9.5 inches. Cards, letterheads, and envelopes can have bleeds, which show the image extending to the perimeter edge of the page.

Research and conceptualization

Research for design and creation of letterhead and business cards involves exploring visual composition, paper choices, ancillary artwork (a photo on a business card for example), and technical specifications for color (PMS vs. CMYK).

- Contact the printer before designing to discuss print processes, resolution and color guidelines, and pricing for different print runs. Get competitive quotes and go with the vendor who you feel most comfortable with, which is not always the lowest cost.
- Research existing cards and letterheads in the industry and connected industries to look for visual patterns and styles.
- Examine websites from prominent design firms to gain knowledge and inspiration on creative approaches to designing stationery.
- Painstakingly gather, verify, names/spellings, titles, telephone numbers, email addresses, social media handles, and physical address for accuracy. Get sign-offs from people named on documents to ensure all is correct with spellings. Once printed, mistakes incur additional costs, waste time, and make you look bad.
- Brainstorm visual ideas using thumbnails and digital comps to generate multiple visual approaches to placements, scale, and typefaces.
- Establish standard design guidelines for cards, letterheads, and envelopes across the organization. If other divisions need varied stationery, be sure to gather their information and represent it in a consistent way with other divisions.
- Narrow choices with stakeholders and clients.

Writing style

The writing on a business card and letterhead is minimal, and typically consists of the logotype, brandmark, and vital contact information. This information can have a variety of styles, but it is best to commit to a standard style to ensure consistency across documents. Keep these facts grouped in either one or two batches so that the reader seeks and finds vital information quickly.

This is typical:

Name
Title
Address
Tel #
Cel #
Email
Web URL
Social media handle

Stationery design format

When creating stationery, remember that the design usually requires the logotype, and the brandmark possibly, or a full signature. Designers use different approaches to what they represent on company stationery. You can too, but the most important thing is that the vital information is represented on the card or letterhead.

Once you establish what goes in, then the design problem is tackled, with the solution a challenge of balance, alignment, negative space, grouping, proximity, and perimeter edge (BANGPP).

For business cards, use different alignment styles (right, left, centered) to explore legibility of the information sets. Think about bleeds and margins. Does the image go to the edge of the page, or is there white space for a margin? How will this look? Make certain the logotype and/or the brandmark are the strong silent base of the design. Use the front side card of the card as a billboard, with a bleed photograph, or a tagline — some cards also employ the logo only front, with information on the back. Then place the contact information on the back. There are many options for designing business cards, but keeping an eye on basic design techniques. A 3 × 3 grid will help position elements proportionally on the page, while using type from 7 pt. to 11 pt. max for body copy will allow a less cluttered look — unless the design calls for large type to create a specific visual theme. Use reverse text, which is white text on black or color background, only with san serif faces 8pt. or above for best clarity.

For letterheads, use space in different ways to conceptualize design. Place block of information, logotype, and brandmarks in different places on the page to get various visual possibilities. Before you complete the design, place an actual letter on the page and design around it to see how elements and page text will get along in various instances. Use alignment and proximity to establish rough layout and formal composition. Keep the letterhead and business cards consistent in visual attributes including fonts, sizes, alignments, colors, and styles.

Figure 6.2a Popping with color. The stationery set for this power company shows a clear, engaging brand identity through color and consistent placement of elements throughout the card, letterhead, envelope, and folder. Design by Natasha Jen, Pentagram. Reproduced with kind permission of Pentagram.

Figure 6.2b Iconic identity uses shape and color to define the identity. This design uses an environmental palette with different earth tone papers and organic images to transcend nature through the stationery set. Design by Turnstyle. Reproduced with kind permission of Turnstyle.

Figure 6.2c White space as design element. Clean and crisp, and keeping printing costs low, this design uses white space as an effective design element in the stationery, plus a branded writing instrument. Design Natasha Jen, Pentagram. Reproduced with kind permission of Pentagram.

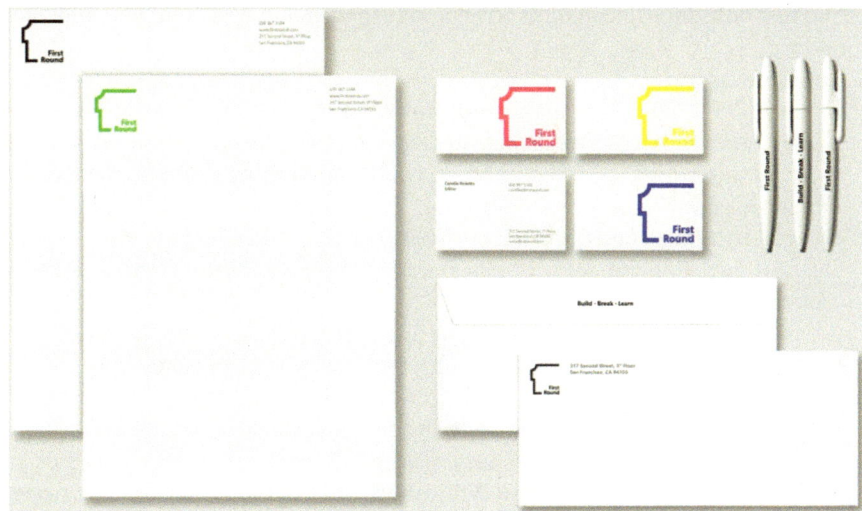

For envelopes, bleeds are fine, but expensive. Use a simple layout of the signature on the upper right. Research postal guidelines before final printing, but generally, the rule is to leave at least 60% of the space open on the left side for a mailing address and postal stamp.

Business card and letterhead checklist

- Did you *create a card that acts as an information billboard for the brand?*
- Did you *create a letterhead that can be multi-purpose, with adequate space for text of letters, invoices, and other company correspondence in the framework?*
- Did you *include a clear logotype that is recognizable, readable, and clear at 1 inch × 1 inch?*
- Did you *keep color usage for text and ancillary images other than the signature related to the brand for quick recognition?*
- Did you *specify spot (PMS), RGB, and CMYK values for the information text, logotype, and brandmark on the cards and letterhead?*
- Did you *test the card and letterhead with target audiences to insure recognition, legibility, and understanding of information quickly?*
- Did you *print a proof to view color and image consistency?*
- Did you *get sign-offs from clients, bosses, stakeholders, and anyone else in the process?*

Creative assignment

Create a business card and letterhead using your own original logotype

You are a marketing communications specialist who plans to head out and work as a freelancer for various companies. These organizations work by appointment only and require a letter of interest and a business card for consideration. You must create a personal logotype and use it in a layout for a business card and letterhead with your information on it.

Be sure to include:

1. *The logotype*
   Use text only and choose fonts wisely. This text should represent you and your name with clarity and dignity.
2. *The business card*
   Create a 3.5 × 2 inch business card prototype. Include name, school address, email, telephone number, and social handles or website. Fit everything nicely on one side with the logotype. Create a second side with a full bleed photo of you, or something to show what you do.
3. *The letterhead*
   Create a letterhead design on a letter size page (8.5 × 11). Include the same information from the business card. Experiment with placement of type and image to find a clear visual solution.
4. *The envelope*
   Create an envelope design adhering to postal regulations. Keep the envelope consistent with the letterhead and card in color, typography, and logotype placement.
5. *The comps*
   Comp is short for composite which is a print consisting of assembled design pieces. Now critique, filter, and revise. Reprint comps until perfect. Once the designs are perfect, output the final files as .PDF, TIF, or native InDesign, Photoshop, or Illustrator. These files can be sent to a commercial printer for professional high quality press output. Make sure you include graphics, font, and document files with the submission.

6.3 Product packaging

Product packaging defined

Marketing brings product to market, and packaging design requires industrial design, graphic design, photography and typography at the highest level as brand experience through packaging is an integral part of a product launch. Packaging contains product offerings. The package has more than just a logotype and brandmark that markets the product, but it is a sales and marketing vehicle with technical writing and promotional copy.

Goal of the piece

The goal of the package is to draw attention on the shelf, in the catalog, or on the web site store so that consumers are interested. There are many products on shelves in retail environments. Many are similar in quality and utility, but those with the most enigmatic package win eyeballs first. The package is also a tool for point of sale to give out product data, but also a sales management tool with UPC barcodes for sales tracking, product identification, and categorization.

Specifications and size

Package design varies from product to product and may be customized for individual products by flexographic, lithographic, and roto gravure print houses that specialize in making and printing on boxes, plastic molds, tags, bags, labels, cartons, bottles, tubes, jars, shrink wraps, and wrappers for any item you may see on a shelf. Work with printers and their industrial engineering partners to explore footprint size, material choices, durability, and tamper and theft security parameters. Packaging companies have "stock" size templates that they can offer customization for at much lower costs than custom dies, or new applications. Ask about previous projects that the print house has undertaken in the same product area to get ideas.

Research and conceptualization

Research for design and creation of packaging requires:

- Research existing package designs to see competitive packaging and historical industry examples.
- Conduct research with target market focus groups to determine usability needs and wishes for the package, opinions on previous package designs, and language that satisfies brand and market communication requirements.
- Execute a GACMIST brief to identify goals, audience, concept, message, images, style, and theme for the package project.
- Research all legal requirements that must be included on the package or in the product literature. The package may need instructions or warnings inside with the product.
- Contact the printer before designing to discuss functional, technical, and cost options and specifications.
- Brainstorm multiple rough visual approaches using supplied print house templates or custom die templates, which are two-dimensional flat versions of the package design that can be edited in Adobe Illustrator, InDesign, and Photoshop.

Writing style

Packaging educates customers. The package is an information tool, which carries short chunks of data, sometimes not much, but each is key as space is minimal and all text and graphics are highly prevalent on package designs. Clarity is paramount and clutter can confuse the consumer and cloud the brand identity. Extended promotional copy is sometimes included on the back of packages espousing product history, company philanthropy, or contribution to culture on the back of the package. Warnings, legal disclaimers, nutrition language, and brand histories are all parts of the package requiring a skilled copywriter.

Some critical elements seen on package designs are:

- Product name
- FAB (features, advantages, benefits)
- Distributed by (who distributes the product to retail sales outlets)
- Manufactured in (country of manufacture)
- Sold by (Who sells the item? Is it exclusive to?)
- List of contents (What's in the package)
- Nutrition data (fiber, sugar, carbs, calories)
- Warnings (flammable, shock, vapor)
- Facts (drug or nutrition)
- Instructions for use (quick setup, step-by-step)
- Other products (product family promotion)
- Brand or product history (think Bachmann pretzels story on the back of the bag)
- UPC barcode (for point of sale and inventory)
- Environmental information (recycling, disposal, deposit and return)
- Mice copy (trademark, rights, customer service)
- Company name, web URL, social media handles and addresses

Packaging design format

Packaging design requires a panel approach, which means that each section on the package is a panel; each panel has content area filled, or, remains as white (negative) space. The placement of text and graphics depends on panel structures and space on the package structure. Use bold, dominant graphics and appropriately sized text in front and back panel layouts — think readability. Artwork might include logotypes and brandmarks, as well as different brand or informational icons, so be prepared to manage graphic scale and live area thoughtfully. Keep watch on panel dominance, with front and back being the most visible and spines and edges holding less important messages and information. Keep typefaces consistent and experiment with one font family, with bold, condensed, and italic faces, rather than multiple fonts (more than two is asking for muddled design), which may hurt the visual continuity. Focus on alignment and hierarchy of text in information rich elements like nutrition tables and warnings so that legibility is clear.

Package design checklist

- Did you *create a package that evokes intrigue, appeal, and attention?*
- Did you *focus on critical requirements for legal, security, safety, and information content?*

Figure 6.3a, b, and c Illustration in package design. This packaging shows incredible use of illustration (rather than photography), color, and typography to provide important nutritional and product information for a kid focused mac and cheese brand. Design by Turnstyle. Reproduced with kind permission of Turnstyle.

(a)

(b)

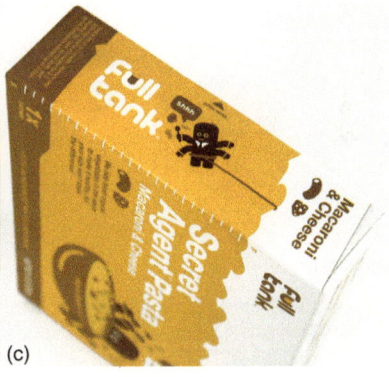

(c)

Figure 6.3d Culture in content. This food package marries cultural identity with a comic book like graphics in small multiples to establish a brand experience that engages you, rather than just providing a way to transport Chinese fast food takeout. Design by DJ Stout, Pentagram. Reproduced with kind permission of Pentagram.

Figure 6.3e Clarity through negative space. Sheik, smooth, sultry, and stylish is the only way to feel about this hair product line, Seven. Notice how negative space is vital to the modern design. Design by Turnstyle. Reproduced with kind permission of Turnstyle.

- Did you *include a clear logotype and product brandmark that is recognizable, readable, and clear at 1 inch × 1 inch on the package?*
- Did you *keep color usage related for brand and product type recognition?*
- Did you *specify spot (PMS), RGB, and CMYK values for the information text, logotype and brandmark on the package?*
- Did you *print a proof to view color and image consistency?*
- Did you *get sign-offs from clients, bosses, stakeholders, and anyone else in the process?*

Creative assignment

Create a package from an existing package
You are a marketing product manager working with a package designer tasked with redesigning the package for an existing product. Choose an industry and product package. Use the existing product package as a template to mock up a new design for the package based on your own new ideas. Redesign using your own approaches to color, graphics, typography, and layout. Keep all the vital existing information, but change layout and typography and add new artwork. Use the existing package as the base and add printed work over the existing artwork to create a three-dimensional prototype, or use the structure as a template, scan the flat box or label, or photograph the bottle or bag to make a two-dimensional mock-up.

6.4 Collateral brochures

Collateral brochures defined

Collateral communication, in the form of brochures, flyers, newsletters, and broadsheets of all kinds, help inform, educate, entertain, and persuade readers, consumers, and corporate buyers. Strong collateral communication delivers precise information that has value to the reader in an instance of inquiry: such as learning features and benefits of a product before deciding to buy, understanding the steps to stopping your child's bedwetting before seeing a doctor, or evaluating the mission statement and goals before contributing to a charity. In many cases, collateral entertains, educates, and informs the reader as with the program guides at professional sports games, circuses, plays, and events.

Goal of the piece

Collateral material is also known as sales and marketing material, which points to the primary goal of collateral, which is to make it easier to sell, explain, and bring someone to action. Brochures help bring products to market yielding importance before sales calls and as leave behinds after sales calls. They are available at the point of sale to cement buying decisions and then act as a tool to support the product, with instructions, questions and answers, or tips. Collateral brochures also show the product and its virtues visually, with photographs, exploded views, and illustrations offering different highlights and feature sets.

Specifications and size

Collateral can be a single brochure or flyer, or a series of pages in a presentation folder. Sizes can be any dimensions, as printers are able to print many variations of size, but in most cases, brochures are common sheet sizes:

8.5 × 11 inches
8.5 × 14 inches
11 × 17 inches

Paper choice is important. Finish, price, quality are all factors when choosing paper stock. Make sure you get paper samples to evaluate coated and uncoated stocks, transparency (see through), and final costs for different print runs. Shorter runs cost more per piece.

Finishing includes bindery, which involves cutting, folding and binding. Cutting is used to create bleeds, and die cuts. Different fold types include single fold, tri-fold, accordion fold, and gatefold. Bindery combines multiple pages using staple stitching, perfect binding, spiral binding, velo binding, and comb binding. Talk to the print vendor to get pricing and options on size and digital specifications for the project.

Research and conceptualization

Research for design, writing, and creation of collateral brochures requires:

- Research existing brochures to see what has been done, what is usage now, and then analyze competitors' collateral and pieces from other industries.
- Interview stakeholders, clients, and employees to get first-person quotes, testimonials, and perspectives.

- Conduct research with target market focus groups to determine audience expectations and needs for the piece. Will it inform, educate, entertain, or persuade?
- Execute a GACMIST brief to identify goals, audience, concept, message, images, style, and theme for the collateral project.
- Research all contact, follow-up, and legal text requirements that must be included in the brochures.
- Outline copy needs, with section heads (What are the main headings?) that show the flow of information in the brochure.
- Contact the printer before designing to discuss functional, technical, and cost options and specifications.
- Brainstorm multiple rough visual approaches using thumbnails and rough drafts to establish design parameters before final prototypes are created.

Writing style

Brochure writing requires a skilled copywriter who understands the brand language, which incorporates brand words, language style, and tone of voice. Each of these items becomes a thrust of copy in the brochure. Brand words include specific words that characterize and relate to the brand in any context. "Refreshing," for example is a brand word for soft drinks. Language style refers to the portrayal of writing stylistically, with approaches varying from formal, relaxed, technical, regal, or universally simple. Keep the product level, cost, and benefits forefront when addressing audiences through brand language.

Choose the correct voice. Will it be first person (I, we), second person (You, your), or third person (he, she, or it) as you communicate directly with the reader? Making it formal, third person works best. With relaxed tone and persuasive copy, the second person "You" viewpoint works well. For narrative storytelling, first-person usage in quotes and dialogue is effective. Always strive to write actively.

Think about features, advantages, and the benefits (FAB), and unique selling proposition (USP) delivered. Create a table showing these elements and use them in the brochure copy as chunks.

Here are ten tips on writing better brochures (with some adapted tips from Bly 2005, 173–199)

1. *Know the role of the brochure* in the sales and decision-making process.
2. *Establish the use of the brochure* — is it a set or campaign, or is it a standalone piece.
3. *Add a strong sales pitch on the cover* to draw in the reader.
4. *Provide accurate, complete information* and provide web page sites or downloads for extended data and content.
5. *Use sections* as a guide for organization and flow.
6. *Write in chunks and small multiples*, which are short snippets of information that are easy to read and visually jump from one to another.
7. *Highlight headings* to guide the reader.
8. *Provide visuals* with captions or call outs wherever you can. Images grab attention, clarify meaning, and foster vivid memory, so use them if you have them.
9. *Keep it simple*. Make the writing easy to digest, and get to the point.
10. *Ask for action* and lead toward the next step of the buying process.

Use the WWCCRR editing process: **w**rite, **w**alk away, **c**omeback, **c**ut, **r**ead aloud, **r**ewrite.

Collateral design format

Designing brochures and other collateral requires typography considerations including use of columns, type size, leading, headline sizes, color, and the typographic system used. For layouts, determine copy amounts in words to see how to fit all the text needed. Brochures have front and back covers. If creating a collateral series, develop a system of brochure styles using a standard design that changes images and copy with different usages, but keeps the overall design across pieces.

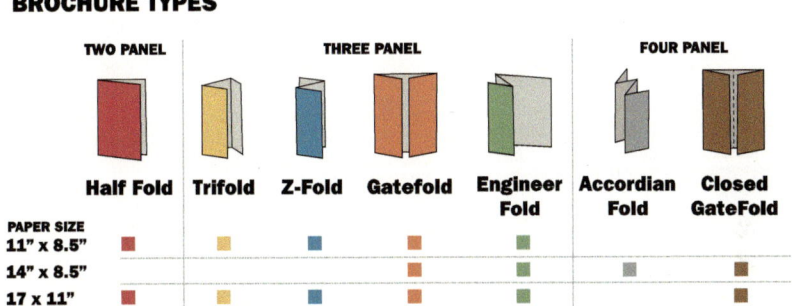

Figure 6.4a Make a dummy first. Design with folding in mind. Mock up brochures on blank paper, which helps you panel out content before using the computer.

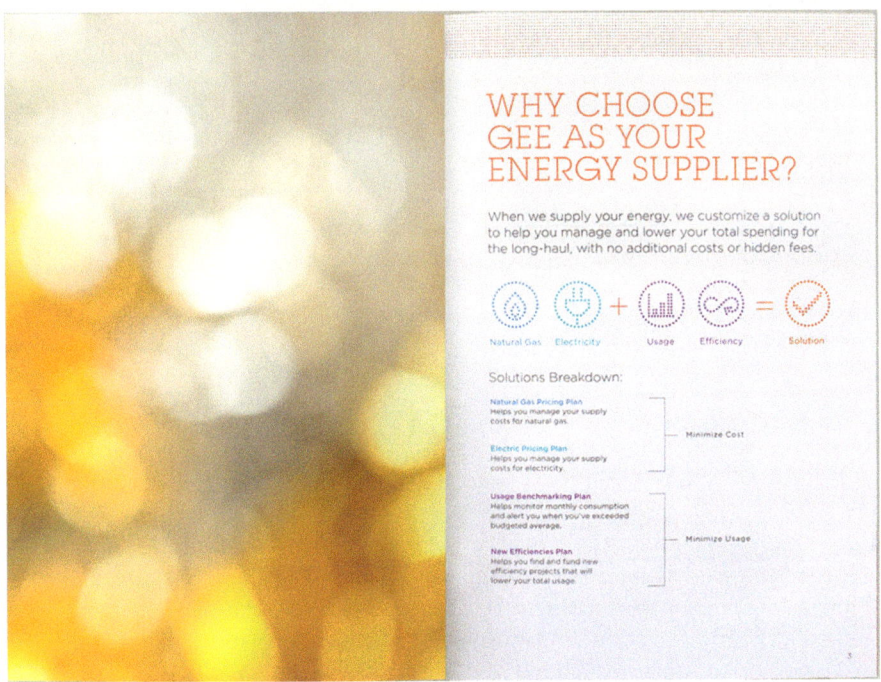

Figure 6.4b Open with a question, and then explain the solution. This brochure opens with a headline that asks a question and then flows to a subhead with the solution. Body copy and illustrations weave in visual and contextual cues introducing features and benefits. These features and benefits support the unique selling proposition, the solution of the lower costs over time, which sets the company apart from competitors. Design Natasha Jen, Pentagram. Reproduced with kind permission of Pentagram.

Communications Writing and Design

(c)

(d)

Figure 6.4c and d Ask for action. This non-profit brochure highlights facts and focuses chunked copy on academics, essentials, and advocacy. Notice the call to "get involved today" in the "action" panel. The brochure copy voice is third person and the response form is first person. Design by Turnstyle. Reproduced with kind permission of Turnstyle.

Create a standard typographic system for the brochure, using one or two typefaces maximum and recording type specifications for leading, kerning, tracking, and sizes of body copy, heads, subheads, drop caps, and pull quotes. These attributes can be set up as a style sheet to ensure consistency throughout the document and series. In addition, record color specifications and use in style sheets whenever possible to keep color accurate throughout.

Before you start on a computer, make a paper dummy. This is a plain white sheet of paper, folded or bound in the same manner as the final piece. It can be a smaller sample if the final piece is oversized, but true to scale is the best way, so get paper samples from the printer to use for making larger dummies or ask the printer to make one for you. The dummy allows you to map out the content and view where it sits in the finished format.

Figure 6.4e and f Newsletters, the news and promotion vehicle. Newsletters act as collateral also. They are brochures that mix newswriting, persuasive copywriting, and technical writing into an organizationally branded publication. This piece marries the brand identity and brand language into sections that illuminate the core activities, announces events, and espouses the virtues of giving. Design by Turnstyle. Reproduced with kind permission of Turnstyle.

(e)

(f)

(g)

(h)

Figure 6.4g and h The interactivity of print brochures. Interactivity is not just for the screen. This accordion fold brochure offers perforated postcards to send or put on a bulletin board to remind the reader to "Take Travel Back." The copy uses repetition in the opening sentence of each text block, "This isn't about," solidifies the meaning of the message and its purpose. Design by Turnstyle. Reproduced with kind permission of Turnstyle.

Brochure design checklist

— Did you *create a dummy piece to evaluate space, positioning, and finishing?*
— Did you *create a cover that invites intrigue and attention?*
— Did you *focus on FAB and USP visually and typographically selling the product or idea?*
— Did you *include a clear logotype, product brandmark, or signature that is recognizable, readable, and consistently used?*
— Did you *keep color usage related brand recognition and brochure system sets?*
— Did you *check type sizes and attributes to ensure style sheet consistency?*
— Did you *specify spot (PMS) and/or CMYK values for the information text, logotype, and brandmark on the package?*
— Did you *read, edit, reread, and reedit the brochure copy to eliminate useless words, tighten grammar, and revise sentences?*
— Did you *print a proof to view color and image consistency?*
— Did you *get sign-offs from clients, bosses, stakeholders, and anyone else in the process?*

Creative assignment

Create a single fold brochure

You are a marketing product manager working with fruit manufacturer to promote their fresh fruit lines of oranges, apples, peaches, and pears. You job is to create a brochure, 8.5 × 11 folded to 5.5 × 8.5 inches (two sided) that promotes the fruit's taste virtues to the public. There is to be no mention of the manufacturer. The star is fruit. Use this tag line across the brochures: "Nature's tasty treat." Alternatively, create your own three-word tagline. The target audience is the supermarket shopper who wants a delicious snack that is a treat to eat.

Research facts of one fruit and compile at least 5–10 facts about the fruit before writing copy. Use the data to generate headlines and subheads. Expand with body copy.

Create a brochure system for each fruit line as a point of sale information piece to be distributed at the supermarket's fruits and vegetable display tables. Picture a produce table filled with peaches. Next to it is a holder with a brochure that illuminates why one should eat more peaches.

Print the brochures on a desktop printer (letter size) and fold (to half size) to create a soft proof and prototype.

Think about:

– Consistent usage of scale, typography, word counts, layouts, and alignments for the brochure system.
– Creating stylized color palettes for each brochure.
– Shooting your own photos of fruit, stock images, or illustrations.
– Using the same grid for each brochure in the set.
– Writing an outline for copy chunks.
– Focus copy on FAB — use features to lead to the benefit for audience member.
– Developing smart, meaningful headings and subheads.
– Keeping copy lean and use a lowest common denominator tone.
– Making a dummy brochure that shows what you will put on each page.
– Making sketches of potential layouts.
– Creating a killer cover that draws the reader in.
– Using the inner spread for the FAB and make the pitch to eat more fruit.
– Using the back cover to seek more information and move people to act.

Chapter references

Bly, Robert W. 2005. *The Copywriter's Handbook: A Step-by-Step Guide to Writing Copy That Sells*. New York: Henry Holt.
Shaw, Mark. 2012. *Copywriting Successful Writing for Design, Advertising, and Marketing*. 2nd ed. London: Laurence King.
Wheeler, Alina. 2009. *Designing Brand Identity: An Essential Guide for the Whole Branding Team*. 3rd ed. Chichester: John Wiley & Sons, Inc.

7

Advertising Projects

7.1 The Ayers No. 1 ad defined

Described as "the simplest, most transparent form to give an advertising message" by White (2007, 116), the Ayers No.1 is a staple form of ad creation because of its presentation is invisible and allows the readers to cut through structure and bite into content. The formula for the Ayers No.1 advertisement is a logical structure containing an image, the headline, subhead, body copy, and logo, all in a descending order. The Ayers No.1 has literally become a standard for full-page ads. If you want to see many examples of the Ayers No. 1 in action, open up any high circulation magazine such as *GQ*, *Cosmo*, *Rolling Stone*, or *Time*, and you will notice that most ads follow the No.1 format, but many find their own visual space by using variations of the design style.

Goal of the piece

The goal of the Ayers No.1 ad is to persuade the reader to believe and buy or act. The important elements of the piece are both image and text. However, many ads are light on copy and allow the image to speak the message with some support from a headline (or not) and logo (most always). Remember the goal of advertising is to sell, so make that the focus as you develop visual assets. Your mission is to create a "big idea" that can break through to your target audience and resonate an actionable message.

Specifications and size

The Ayers No. 1 ad, typically designed as an 8.5 × 11 inch portrait document in practice, has various final trim sizes for print publications like magazines and newspapers. See the advertising rate card specifications for exact size before you create the ad. You may need to create the ad a bit larger to accommodate for an image bleed on the page. Ads can be black and white or color, depending on the publication. You will see terms like "live area," which is where the art and copy goes. The bleed is the extension of artwork to get the "off the page" look. The trim is where the page cuts, so anything beyond it is lost.

Research and conceptualization

Developing advertising goes beyond simply just ads. Sometimes ads can be one-offs, which is when one ad is the extent of the work. These are different from campaigns, which are multi-faceted, with a wide variety of communication pieces across various media. Messages transcend across media, so

Communications Writing and Design: The Integrated Manual for Marketing, Advertising, and Public Relations,
First Edition. John DiMarco.
© 2017 John DiMarco. Published 2017 by John Wiley & Sons, Ltd.

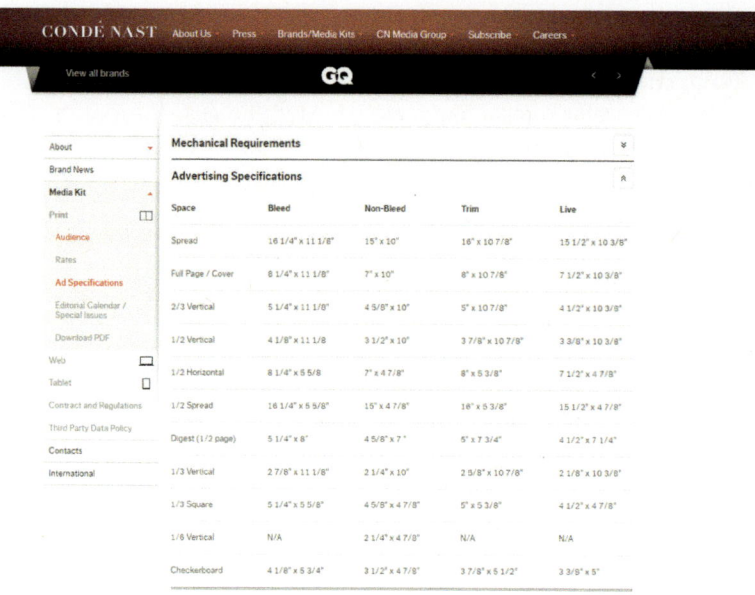

Figure 7.1a Check the specs before you start to design. The *GQ* magazine advertising specs offer agencies and designers clear guidelines for print and digital media. Make sure you contact the advertiser in advance of producing your digital artwork, regardless of online or print delivery. This helps ensure that the design meets critical specifications.

their development is key to a successful outcome, regardless of campaign length. Research for an ad can take different routes. In many cases product focus groups are executed to establish keywords to pursue and themes to explore in message development. It is important that you have only **one idea per ad.**

Try following these research and conceptualization steps in developing a creative ad:

Identify audience, problem, and communication goals. "We need to create brand awareness for the widget," for example. Create a client creative brief during this stage.

Research the audience by using focus groups, interviews, and observations to create a persona, which is a descriptive list of attributes and behaviors connected to a particular target audience. Develop a list of keywords from the research data that are frequently seen in responses to questions.

Target using the keywords. Find a unique emotional center that connects deeply with the audience. Use design research methods such as concentric circles and mind mapping to isolate concrete directions for concepts development. You should have the written makings of the "big idea" at this stage. Complete the GACMIST design brief to list the specific goals, audience target, concept, messages, images that will be used, the style (visual approach-retro, modern, historical, revolutionary), and the theme of the piece, which is the essentially the story that the ad is telling in simple terms.

Conceptualize by writing the copy first (see writing style below) in most cases and then move toward developing visual pieces through thumbnailing and sketching. Then, create a series of rough layouts that offer variations of the ad with different twists (cut off image bleeds, juxtaposed text and images, textures and visual anomalies.

Create mockups, proofs, prototypes, and treatments that exhibit the ad direction. Show the client.

Revise work to filter content and build agreement with client on final design choices.

Evaluate the work with target audience focus groups to establish the final design.

Writing style

The two main written parts to the ad, if it contains text, are the headline and the body copy. The headline is focused on grabbing attention, but it also has value in giving the reader a hint of what he or she can expect to get from a product or service being advertised. Advertising is not only a vehicle for persuasion, but also provides information, which in turn should persuade the reader to buy the item being advertised.

Headlines should be as short as possible, usually less than ten words. There needs to be a connection between the image and text, and if there is only text, it must have a message that satiates the brain, with action words doing the heavy communicating. These are display type so they should be more dominant than other type.

Subheads should act as a bridge between headlines and body copy. Keep subheads to a line with a two-line maximum. Make the subhead illuminate the headline and build anticipation for the body copy.

Body copy should be in the active voice, using the "you" viewpoint whenever possible. Think about stating the features and selling the benefits of how the product can help. Use the USP (unique selling proposition) to further inform the reader on how the product or service offers a better solution. The USP is what sets the product apart from competitors. The USP is the brand's promise to help solve a problem.

Ayers No. 1 design format

The visual design of the ad can vary. There are two main approaches, the standard, approach, which is an image with headline, body copy, and logo in descending order. Another way is to create an inverted Ayers ad, which positions headlines on top of the ad with body copy underneath. Headline type is typically 24 point or greater, with subheads from 14–16 point and body copy at 8–11 point size.

Here are some quick tips for a better ad:

- Choose a photograph or illustration that is arresting or thought-provoking.
- Use a 3 × 3 grid to arrange artwork and text in a BANGPP positive layout.
- Keep messages and visual elements simple for quick recognition.
- Use color to attract, isolate, or enhance the visuals.
- Use size to clarify meaning of products and messages.
- Use familiar themes to connect with the audience.

Ayers No 1. advertisement checklist

- Did you *follow the standard or inverted Ayers design format?*
- Did you *include a headline that grabs attention and builds interest?*
- Did you *subhead bridge the headline and body copy (if you have one)?*
- Did you *provide body copy that connects the USP (unique selling proposition) to the reader (if you have it)?*
- Did you *add the logo at correct size and proportion?*
- Did you *ask for action?*
- Did you *check all the correct names, telephone numbers, web addresses, and locations for accuracy?*

Figure 7.1b The marriage of copy writing, image, and layout using small multiples. This clever ad uses the Ayers No. 1 format with a unique selling proposition of "improving intelligence." Design by Milton Glaser. Reproduced with kind permission of Milton Glaser.

Figure 7.1c The power of visual dominance. This Ayers No. 1 format ad creates an emotional connection to the reader and humankind using only a headline. Design by Milton Glaser. Reproduced with kind permission of Milton Glaser.

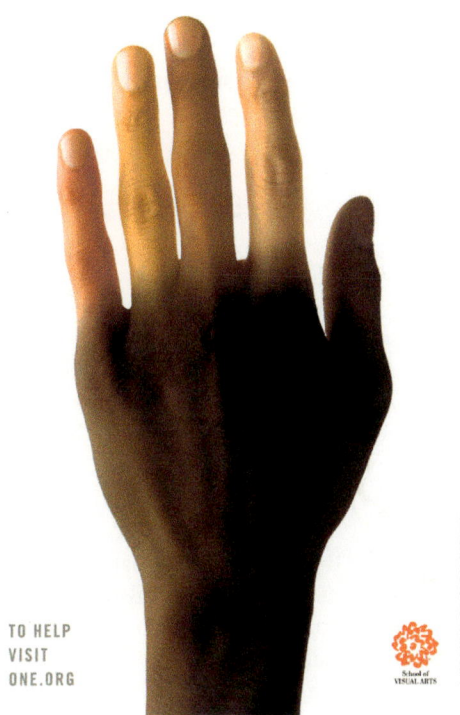

– Did you *reread, edit, and reread again to catch any spelling, grammar, and image errors?*
  [yes or no]
– Did you *print a proof to view color and image consistency?*
  [yes or no]
– Did you *create a final file for submission at 300–350 dpi at final trim size (with bleed)?*

Creative assignment

Create a mock Ayers No. 1 Ad to save an endangered animal
Pretend you are working as a freelance designer and you are tasked with creating ads for a wildlife organization (choose one). The project requires research, conceptualization, and final design. You must come up with a big idea that will have usage in a two-ad campaign to save the _____. The animal you choose fills in the blank. Only one idea per ad is permitted, so each ad has the same look and feel, but a different image and copy. Be sure to include:

1. *Headline*
   Generate a headline that has magnetic intelligence and resonates with readers.
2. *Subhead or body copy*
   Write a chunk of subhead or body copy or both. Use this as a bridge to the action.
3. *The artwork*
   Use a photograph or illustration. One or two images maximum plus a logo.

Create a GACMIST brief before you start to design. Then with the copy created and the images sourced, create thumbnails of possible layouts using simple sketching symbols. After you have some thumbnails, choose two layouts and begin to design your ad in InDesign, Photoshop, or MS Word. Print. Critique with others and revise.

Concentrate on using one image as a dominant image and the other image (a logo) as the supporting image.

7.2 Posters and billboards

Posters and billboards defined

Persuasion and information pieces by nature, the poster and billboard are large-format advertising vehicles that can also act as signage or display. The use of large-format work is vital to brand engagement on buildings, in-store, and at events like trade shows and launches. Posters and billboards are advertisements used for distribution in public spaces, instead of placement in a publication or online.

Goal of the piece

The goal of the poster or billboard is to attract attention and deliver a clear message. The writing must be short and punchy, but also be consistent in a reinforcement role for the image, which is what the viewer is initially attracted to, and then the text completes the story. Posters may have more copy, as they are smaller than billboards and people can get close up to them, rather than billboards which are seen cruising down a highway or on the side of a structure. The time, space, and distance curtail the use of text in billboards.

Specifications and size

Posters fit a variety of sizes and can be:

> 11 × 17, 17 × 22, 24 × 36, 36 × 48 inches or larger. Billboards span several or many feet and are dependent on the structure they sit on including inner and outer building walls, signs, and displays.

Research and conceptualization

It is important that you have only *one idea per poster or billboard.*

- Use the steps for research and conceptualization of an ad, shown in section 7.1, to execute the seven-step design process.
- To help, look at other posters and billboards around in various spaces. Examine images presented in the medium. Get insight on colors and type that has resonance visually at large sizes.
- Use ethnography to examine spaces, structures, and environments to get ideas on how and where to add created posters and billboards.

Writing style

Writing poster and billboards is primarily headline writing, with some supporting body in the form of a subhead or a few lines. Posters may have more written components or be only text. That is fine as long as the design supports the content, meaning that all words are readable and have impact in the piece.

Try to connect the image and copy with puns or clever slogans that are easy to understand and hard to forget. Think of the NYC posters and billboards to combat terrorist incidents using civilian vigilance, "if you see something, say something," reinforced with a photo of a backpack sitting unattended in a subway car. Think about clever delivery and emotional messaging or offer a literal call to action. In either instance, avoid cluttering your message with too much text.

Poster and billboard design format

The visual design of the poster is like any good ad, illustrating one big idea. The idea needs support from elements that help establish the theme of the piece and visual components such as color, rhythm, layout, and typography to give the poster appeal. Headline type is typically 72 point or greater, with subheads from 24–36 point and body copy at 8–11 point size. Keep the body copy to a minimum. Use mostly headlines and subheads to get to the point. Remember to use a 3 × 3 grid to arrange artwork and text in a BANGPP positive layout. Billboard designs are quite often only an image and a logo, sometimes with some supporting text. The importance of the image is critical. Type can be used as an image, but make sure it is attention-grabbing and has unique visual power using color, type, scale, and proximity.

Poster and billboard checklist

- Did you use a *thought-provoking image, type as image, or a visual pun as a main element?*
- Did you *include a headline that grabs attention or use type as image?*
- Did you *make sure text is large enough and has contrast for easy viewing?*
- Did you *keep messages and visual elements simple for quick recognition?*
- Did you *add the logo at correct size and proportion?*
- Did you *check all the correct names, telephone numbers, web addresses, and location for accuracy?*
- Did you *reread, edit, and reread again to catch any spelling, grammar, and image errors?*
  [yes or no]
- Did you *print a proof to view color and image consistency?*
  [yes or no]

Creative assignment

Create a persuasive environmental poster

Create a poster that focuses in on one environmental fact that you find alarming or encouraging. Then, write and design a poster (11 × 17, landscape or portrait) that illustrates and communicates your point clearly and persuasively. Use a strong fact as the central piece of the design and incorporate a photo, type as image, or illustration that visualizes the point for the reader. Make the poster using any page layout or digital design program. Use a 3 × 3 grid to place text and graphics.

Be sure to include:

Use one image
Take a photo or create an original image using other found content as source materials. Make sure the image is thought-provoking and has resonance with the audience.

Figure 7.2a Experiment with art elements and principles. This poster uses text, color, shape, juxtaposition, and negative space to create intriguing poster that grabs the viewer. Design by Paula Scher, Pentagram. Reproduced with kind permission of Pentagram.

Figure 7.2b Tell the story. This billboard uses though-provoking images to attract viewers. Design by Paula Scher, Pentagram. Reproduced with kind permission of Pentagram.

Subhead or body copy
Write a chunk of subhead or body copy or both. Use this as a bridge to the action.

The artwork
Use a photograph or illustration. One or two images maximum plus a logo.

Create a GACMIST brief before you start to design. Then with the copy created and the images sourced, create thumbnails of possible layouts using simple sketching symbols. After you have some thumbnails, choose two layouts and begin to design your ad in InDesign, Photoshop, or MS Word. Print, critique with others, and revise.

Figure 7.2c "This is a poster," poster. This poster shows the elegance of simplicity and the enigmatic power of headlines. No image is needed to draw in your curiosity here. Design by Angus Hyland and Fabian Herrmann, Pentagram. Reproduced with kind permission of Pentagram.

7.3 Ad specialties

Advertising specialties defined

Not all advertising is comes in the form of an ad. Many ad campaigns and companies use advertising specialty items that go beyond traditional print and online media. These items include calendars, invitations, bags, apparel, rubber bracelets, and other "merch" (merchandise). Each piece proudly displays the logo and other brand identity elements of the organization, such as product marks and tag lines.

Goal of the piece

The goal of advertising specialty items is to spread the brand through different channels and provide the consumer a take-home item that keeps the brand name in their sight and on their mind. These items are an expression of brand identity, which creates a visual personality that connects with consumers, employees, and media. Do you remember the Livestrong campaign? The centerpiece to the incredibly successful attention was an ad specialty item, a yellow rubber bracelet.

Specifications and size

Item sizes can vary greatly, but logo size on the items is usually consistent with some prescribed guidelines from the design department. Size, color, and placement are certainly important to know.

Logos typically must adhere to the color specifications exactly. Use of Pantone colors helps match logo colors exactly, so be sure to use them when preparing artwork in Photoshop, Illustrator, and InDesign. Keep logo sizes the same across items with regard to scale. Have a standard, minimum size logo and then a guideline on how much a logo can be enlarged to as a percentage for use on an ad specialty item.

Research and conceptualization

- Build a knowledge of available items by looking at catalogs and contacting vendors who print the items.
- Ask for samples to evaluate textures, actual sizes, and quality before you design and order bulk.
- Ask about file size and digital color requirements and then ensure that your files meet specs.
- Look at specialty items based on price, usability, and value for the customer.

Writing style

Writing for specialty items depends on the work. Invitations require a clear presentation of vital 5w information (who, what, where, when, and why). Other items like bags, tee-shirts, flash drives, pens, mugs, and vehicle wraps may have some text in the form of a tag line or some other slogan or statement that has meaning. Typically short and punchy, advertising specialty copy is kept to a minimum.

Advertising specialty design format

The visual design of advertising specialties can vary. The simplest design requires you to look at the product and decide where to place the logo and any other text or graphics. This instance requires you to evaluate the space on the surface and how the colors will interact with the printed substrate. In other cases, the specialty item is created as a custom item, such as a pop-up or custom-sized printed piece. In these cases, there needs to be a much higher level of design knowledge and expertise. Keep artwork and text within a color scheme and do not over design, as it will create a crowded look that does not help the brand.

Ad specialty checklist

- Did you use a *thought-provoking image, type as image, or a visual pun as a main element?*
- Did you *get a sample of the item(s) before you create the design?*
- Did you *include a tag line or text? If so, does it have value in message or attention?*
- Did you *make sure text is large enough on the item and has contrast for easy viewing?*
- Did you *keep logos and artwork at specifications on the placement instructions?*
- Did you *add the logo at correct size and proportion?*
- Did you *check all the correct names, telephone numbers, web addresses, and location for accuracy?*
- Did you *reread, edit, and reread again to catch any spelling, grammar, and image errors?* [yes or no]
- Did you *request a flat proof to view color and image consistency?* [yes or no]
- Did you *create a high-resolution file for final submission at 300–350 dpi at final trim size?*

Figure 7.3a Using design to promote. This self-promotion kit shows off the firm's design skills while contributing to their brand presence in the lives of clients. Design by Turnstyle. Reproduced with kind permission of Turnstyle.

Figure 7.3b Invitation design with practical purpose. This design firm's anniversary Halloween party invitation acts as an ad specialty item offering a few masks to help invitees get in the mood. Design by Turnstyle. Reproduced with kind permission of Turnstyle.

Creative assignment

Create an advertising specialty pitch sheet

You are the new agency for a brand (pick one or create a mock one). You job is to propose an ad specialty program that incorporates three items. Take photographs or collect images from stock art or online of household items such as pencils, bags, boxes, mugs, hats, soda cans, and tee-shirts, or find generic prototypes of items online. Take the images of the objects and open in Photoshop. Then

Figure 7.3c Keep it simple. Size, placement, substrate, and color are critical decisions when designing advertising specialty items. Design by Natasha Jen, Pentagram. Reproduced with kind permission of Pentagram.

using layers, ad a logo (make your own or use an existing logo from www.Brandsoftheworld.com) on the layer on top the objects. Use the free transform tool, hold CTRL or Apple key to manipulate perspective on the logo and position it onto the object in a natural looking way. Then add a tagline that offers a NEW BIG IDEA that the brand can leverage. Arrange the ad specialty images into a one-page layout to pitch a client on your BIG idea. Explain in one paragraph on the pitch sheet why this ad specialty campaign will promote the brand and extend customer loyalty.

7.4 Postcards

Postcards defined

Postcards are iconic print advertising pieces. They represent an advertising medium that blossomed with the industrial revolution and advances in printing technology. Their smaller size, short messages, vivid images, and engaging nature made them the tweets and posts of the times during the early 1900s ('The Postcard Age' 2013). Today, postcards continue as a staple persuasion tool across industries.

The postcard offers a small billboard to advertise your ideas and in some cases a collection piece for the recipient to savor. This military postcard shows the prowess of this United States Air Force base.

Goal of the piece

The goal of the postcard is to announce and sell events, products, services, and causes. The postcard is a money-saving piece as it gets special postal rates, is less bulky to be shipped, and can be produced quite cheaply in small or large print runs. Postcards can also be digital, in the form of e-cards that are directly emailed to people rather than snail mailed or handed out.

Specifications and size

Postcard sizes for print are standard. Three by five, 4 × 6, 5 × 7, and 5.5 × 8.5 inches make up typical sizes, usually landscape orientation. The cards can be black and white or full color, or both, with different paper stocks being part of the production decision. Coated or uncoated stock is used

Figure 7.4a The postcard offers a small billboard to advertise your ideas and in some cases a collection piece for the recipient to savor. This military postcard shows the prowess of this United States Air Force base.

depending on the look and feel desired and the image content. Many designers will place a color photograph, graphic, or illustration on the front of the postcard and use a coated finish for that and a matte finish for the back of the card, which houses the address label and mostly text.

Research and conceptualization

Postcards carry messages. Messages require conceptualization and copywriting. This means that research of specific data elements (audience, product or event, and conceptual keywords) need to be collected to build a direction for the big idea and the message that delivers it.

- Create a GACMIST brief that identifies message and design content.
- Use both qualitative and quantitative methods to establish data sets that are meaningful and relevant to moving someone to act.
- Pull one meaningful data point out and use it to reinforce the message by offering evidence.

Writing style

Writing for postcards is short, chunked, and headline driven on the front side. This is the mini-billboard section of the postcard. Keep texts on this side to a minimum, with long paragraphs being extended to a website via a URL or link in an e-card. The backside is the address side for printed pieces. Make sure that you leave at least 40% of the back blank for a mailing label and postage placement. The other 60% can have message or image, but make sure you keep the sides clearly separate. Otherwise, the post office may not be able to process the mailing.

Postcard design format

Postcard design has a few common features. Most cards are printed landscape and contain an image (or type as image) on the front and text and the mailing area on the back. A thought-provoking, attention-grabbing photograph is a typical approach for events or product postcards. Some cards that are handed out, such as in nightclubs or in-store may have full color front and back, with collage-like images and messages scattered across the piece. Postcards can have image bleeds, which

Figure 7.4b and c Postcard designs should sell. The postcard should offer something of value to the consumer. When writing copy, ask questions and highlight features, and insert the USP. Stay true to design specifications, especially if mailing the piece. This postcard for training and professional development abides by the 60/40 rule and leaves ample space for label, postage, and USPS processing marks.

(b)

(c)

allow the postcard to have a dynamic look by eliminating margins on the front side. The backside needs margins being mailed so that it conforms to postal specifications. E-cards are designed at 72 dpi and are set to pixel sizes while print postcards are measured in inches or centimeters.

Postcard checklist

– Did you use a *thought-provoking image, type as image, or a visual pun as a front side?*
– Did you *use the 60/40 or 50/50 space ratio on the backside if mailing?*
– Did you *check with the Post Office before final printing to get approval if using bulk mail?*

- Did you *include a tag line or text? If so, does it have value in message or attention?*
- Did you *create a bleed in the design? If so, is an image bleed in digital file?*
- Did you *keep logos and artwork at specifications on the placement instructions?*
- Did you *add the logo at correct size and proportion?*
- Did you *check all the correct names, telephone numbers, web addresses, and location for accuracy?*
- Did you *reread, edit, and reread again to catch any spelling, grammar, and image errors?* [yes or no]
- Did you *request a flat proof to view color and image consistency?* [yes or no]
- Did you *create a high-resolution file for final submission at 300–350 dpi at final trim size for print and a 72 dpi file for e-cards?*

Creative assignment

Create a postcard series for a sneaker company

You are the new art director and copywriter for a fictitious retail sneaker company called Soul Sneaker Experience (SSX). The new retailer needs a postcard set to hand out at upcoming trade shows. You have to write and design three postcards that have a unique theme, which that unites the cards as a set. Use photos of sneakers, people, culture, or philosophy to get sneaker buyers to visit the store's booth at sneaker shows. Think about the USP (unique selling proposition), and how you can differentiate your store and company from other sneaker sellers. The cards can have important information, advertise a particular shoe, or be a useful information tool — you decide. Use any digital design program you like. Make the postcards jumbo size at 5.5 × 8.5 inches. Use both sides, as these will be handouts not mailers.

7.5 Banner ads

Banner ads defined

Banner ads are digital advertising pieces embedded into mobile and computer websites and act as display advertisements online. Web banners are commonplace on a majority of sites and are used for third party and in-house advertising. They sit atop, alongside, and in-page and have linkable interactivity that is triggered by static or moving images with persuasive messages.

Goal of the piece

The goal of web banners is to induce action from the user. The banners contain hyperlinks that move the user to completing a sale or getting additional information that moves him or her toward a sale. That sale could be an actual product or service buy, or signing of a petition, or donating to a charity. The banner must present a persuasive message that gains attention using type and image.

Specifications and size

Banner ad sizes are dictated by the website that publishes them. File and physical size specifications can be found with print advertising specs on the rate card. Typical sizes are 728 × 90 pixels and 1000 × 90 pixels for leaderboard ads, 300 × 250 pixels for in-page display ads. Other sizes can vary depending on web page dimensions and content, but most ad buyers buy the leaderboard and display ads for a homepage, so that concept linked ads are seen as the user scrolls down.

Research and conceptualization

Banner ads are typically included in a print and digital campaign. The ad concepts in these projects are woven together and spread across a variety of different-sized paper and electronic spaces.

- Use surveys to gain initial thoughts and patterns and then focus groups to test messaging and image approaches.
- Develop a variety of ad ideas that feed off the main concept, but can fit into a variety of sizes on paper and screen.
- Organize these ideas to make a mind map to help branch out individual ad ideas from the main concept and show how they fit into available media sources.
- Create a GACMIST brief to isolate design and message directions.
- Perform a usability test to insure that users know how to engage the banner ad to take action and click.

Writing style

Writing banner ads is much like writing display ads for print, but the banner involves motion graphics and very limited space so economy and rhythm of words is critical. Use short direct messages, puns, and questions that engage the viewer. Remember, you are fighting for eyeballs on the web page, which is a lot more challenging to grab attention than a single page ad on its own. Be aware of word count and avoid going beyond a single line in leaderboard and a few lines in banner display ads. Relate to the reader by identifying and using the "you" viewpoint in the banner concept.

Banner ad design format

Banner ads are 72 dpi for use on the screen. You can create banner ads in Photoshop as individual static layers and then create motion by bringing the layered files into After Effects or Flash. The design of a banner is challenging due to the size. Images need to be clear, the correct resolution (72 dpi) and scaled to banner size, otherwise, performance will suffer and the advertiser may not accept your digital files due to heft. Type should be sized correctly and high contrast for legibility and be visually appealing plus intriguing for readability. Use one idea per ad and if multiple images are used, be careful of image alignments, placements, consistency, and negative (white) space. If you use motion, keep it clean and fluid. Use key framed animation sequences with product or simple fades, dissolves, and smooth linear motion paths with type and image. Finish the banner ad with a logo and a call to action such as button to learn more or to "buy now."

Banner ad checklist

- Did you use a *clear product image or text element that grabs interest?*
- Did you *include only one idea per ad?*
- Did you *make sure all images are 72 ppi and scaled to the size of the banner?*
- Did you *include a strong message that offers a USP or FAB via the "you" viewpoint?*
- Did you *ask for action and end with the brand logo?*

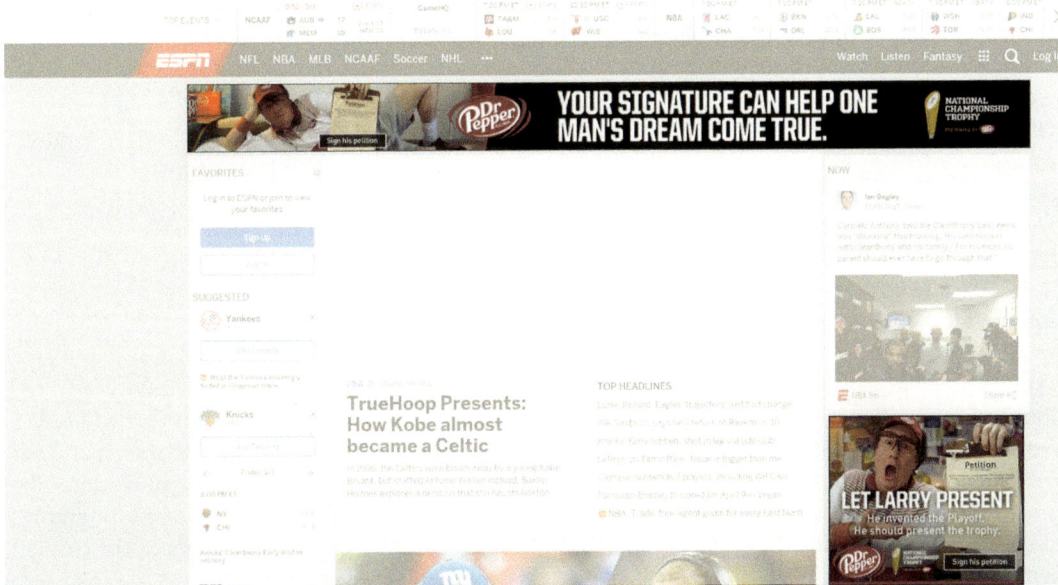

Figure 7.5a Banner campaigns calling for action. This Dr. Pepper banner ad campaign invites you to support Larry as a playoff trophy presenter. The action is for you to "sign the petition," which creates a digital connection to the brand. Notice the 1000 × 90 and 300 × 250 banners sit together on one web page with a consistent creative focus.

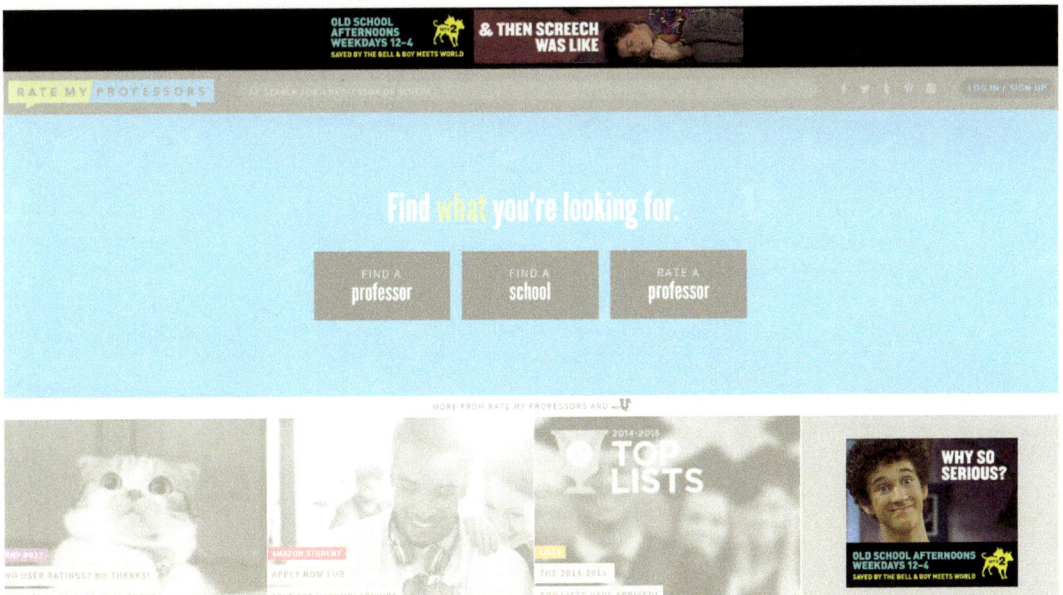

Figure 7.5b Banner campaigns inviting old school viewers. This MTV2 banner ad campaign on a college rating site invites you to watch *Saved by the Bell*, just like when you were a kid. Notice the campaign banners in this impression set focus on one memorable character. Notice the 728 × 90 and 300 × 250 banners sit together on one web page and share one message.

- Did you *keep logos and artwork at specifications on the placement instructions?*
- Did you *check web links and locations for accuracy?*
- Did you *reread, edit, and reread again to catch any spelling, grammar, and image errors?*
  [yes or no]
- Did you *proof on various browsers and computers, tablets, and phones to view color and image consistency?*
  [yes or no]
- Did you *create a 72 ppi file that meets physical digital file size specs for the publisher?*
- [yes or no]

Creative assignment

Create a banner ad campaign design for non-profit

Choose a non-profit organization and create a banner ad campaign. Create a concept that will feed a 728 × 90 leaderboard and a 300 × 250 display ad. The ads must carry a common creative style and sell the same idea. The goal of the piece is to get users to click to learn more about the organization. The banners should contain a strong image, a clear message, and brand identity in logo, color typography, and theme. Create the ad concepts as files in Photoshop by using layers for each stage of the banner. Then import the layered file into After Effects to add motion and interactive links.

Chapter references

Hunt, Kevin. 2012. "Early Advertising with Postcards." November 26. Accessed December 30, 2015. http://www.blog.generalmills.com/2012/11/early-advertising-with-postcards/

"The Postcard Age." 2013. April 14. Accessed December 30, 2015. http://www.mfa.org/exhibitions/postcard-age.

White, Alex W. 2007. *Advertising Design and Typography*. New York: Allworth Press.

8
Public Relations Projects

8.1 Public relations / News release

The news release defined

The granddaddy of all PR pieces, the news release is a news story prepared by an organization and distributed to the media. It is written for newspapers and print media using news-writing style (AP) with the purpose of publicizing the entire organization, including its people products, services, and activities (Bly 2005). The news release is non-fiction (factual), with a news-writing approach to delivering information succinctly and smoothly so that an editor or reporter can grab the facts and news value with a quick read. A staple of journalism sources, the news release remains a critical tool in the practice of public relations. A PR writer, marketing specialist, or corporate communications staffer typically writes the release, but in some cases, a business owner or entrepreneur handles their own media relations.

Three critical elements must be part of the press release; publicity, angle, and story. Publicity requires you to present the information in a clear, newsworthy way to facilitate understanding and action from gatekeepers, who filter news to their audiences. This means tight leads and concise, hi-fidelity writing. Angle is the direction the story goes in to make a point. If we were publicizing a walkathon our company was sponsoring, an angle might be, "Annual walkathon by XYZ CO raises $50,000 help the Palm community," or, "XYZ raises $50,000 for community enrichment." The piece is news because it has local appeal and it provides publicity that positions the company as a community partner and philanthropic leader. Story is the fabric that engages the readers to the piece by human emotion, wonder, or intimate connection. For example, a story element might be, "This year's XYZ CO walkathon honors Katie Smith, taken by the disease in 2011." Accomplish creating the "story" in releases by character, quotes, setting, chronology, motive, and process (Clark 2006). The release is essentially a report, which contains elements of a story. Creating a combination of report and story is an important part to writing great releases.

Goal of the piece

The goal of the news release is to get publicity and to publish news. Publicity is different from advertising in that it comes from a third-party endorsement is ultimately uncontrollable. Editors and other gatekeepers in the media use news releases daily to create news stories, product reviews, and other news media items. Releases come directly to editors from agents, corporate communications departments, business owners, and wire services. The editor strips down the release and either weaves in to a new story or news snippet, or it may become one part of many sources collected for a larger story. The news release must have a news angle, which is a story direction that connects readers with the local and relatable aspects of the article. The editor, producer, or reporter may contact the person listed on the release to get more information or secure a segment or interview.

Specifications and size

News releases are 8.5 × 11 inches (letter-size paper) — typically one page in length for paper, sometimes two or three. They are also placed on web pages in the company pressroom or as a PDF download. The writing and formats differ for news releases sent to print, broadcast, on radio and television. Newspaper and magazine releases tend to be longer, with television releases shorter, and radio releases being the shortest with a few paragraphs at most (Haynes and Newsom 2005). Exceed one page with caution; most editors will not read on past a single page release unless the subject has national interest and extensive details.

Research and conceptualization

Researching a news release could involve a number of different methods depending on the news. The announcement of a newly hired executive could require the writer to interview the new person and other decision-makers or colleagues involved. Primary research makes a direct connection to the subjects and stories must be attained using observations or interviews. A news release might require ethnography studies, where the writer goes to a location to observe the atmosphere, collect quotes, and report on the happenings, such as in an event for example. This approach yields data necessary for constructing a storied release with salient quotes. Secondary research adds to build the facts in a story, so expect instances where you are citing company reports, government statistics, or referencing third parties. Be open to multiple research methods when writing news releases. This allows access to plenty of facts and information, which can be valuable in finding a strong angle or help generate other valuable angles for future news.

Writing style

The essence of the news release is the lead, which sits in the first paragraph and contains who, what, where, when, why, and occasionally, how. This is known as the "5 ws and the h approach" to lead writing, which is a borrowed practice from journalism. The inverted pyramid is utilized in every release, which dictates the news-writing approach by placing the most important facts first (the lead) and the less important facts filing in the body of the story.

You can subtlety weave in important messages later on, but make your leads tight. Try to think like a journalist when writing your release and leads because it helps the media absorb and inject your words and ideas into their own stories and news cycle. Research diligently and use hard numbers and facts in your storytelling, as a journalist would. Get a quote that makes sense and is relevant to your story. The second paragraph after the lead or later on down the piece typically houses one or two pertinent quotes. The quote can be "invented" with approval of the source, providing leeway for you to honestly, subtly manipulate the words of the speaker (Bivins 2011). Other, less important information filters down the piece into the third and/or fourth paragraphs. Here, you will offer the background details and shape your message further by filling in the blanks behind the news such as history, involvement, significance, collaboration, impact, and future goals or current progress.

The final paragraph contains the boilerplate, which provides a standard summary of the company for consistent branding purposes. This stays the same for all releases company-wide to ensure that the media does not interpret what your company does and can understand it if it is technical. For example, look at the IBM Security boilerplate in Figure 6.1. If you asked most people what IBM does, they would say make computers. When you read the boilerplate, you see that is not what this division of the company does. Companies typically have various boilers for each division of the organization.

News release design

The visual design of the news release is similar to a company letterhead. An organization's logo and contact information make up the bulk of the design. The headline, release date, date of news origin, and contact information need to be at the top. For an online release, the navigation bar serves as the header logo. Whether the release is for print or online, be sure to keep the logo consistent with the brand guidelines. It should not be so large or obtrusive that it diverts attention away from the headline or the story. Watch your logo sizes and resolution. 300 dpi for print and 72 dpi for digital. Make sure to scale the logo correctly and proof to ensure the image is not blurry.

News release writing checklist

– Did you develop a clear headline that sums up your story in seven to ten critical words? [A]
– Did you *create a strong, newsworthy lead paragraph with the five ws and the how?* [B]
– Did you *provide both the release date (immediate or not) and the date of origin for the news?* [C]
– Did you *establish an angle that makes the story newsworthy and localized to the audience?* [D]
– Did you *add a relevant quote to the second paragraph or beyond?* [E]
– Did you *use active, concrete, short sentences and paragraphs that provide common words?* [F]
– Did you *check all the correct names, telephone numbers, and emails for further information?* [G]
– Did you *include the boilerplate, providing a summary of the organization or division?* [H]
– Did you *end the release with either a ### symbol, or - 30 -, or more if there are additional pages?* [I]
– Did you *eliminate superlatives and complimentary adjectives to keep it unbiased?* [yes or no]
– Did you *reread, edit, and reread again to catch any spelling, grammar, and AP style errors?* [yes or no]

Creative assignment

Write and design a fictitious news release

The high school you attended is sponsoring a presentation on the dangers of texting and driving. The event is titled: _____ (make a name up). The goal is to eliminate texting and driving in the community. The first objective is to get parents and students together, talking about the subject openly in order to teach them how to communicate better with each other about the dangers of texting and driving. The second objective is help build support between parents and kids in promising never to text while driving. Last year the school sponsored the same event and the turnout was very weak. Accidents from texting and driving in the state are recorded and were at a ___% (find this data if you can) level reported by local or state police.

Write and design a news release for local print media outlets as a PDF that announces the school event and provides persuasive evidence that will motivate community members to attend.

IBM Named a Leader in Gartner Magic Quadrant for Security Information and Event Management

Select a topic or year

↓ News release ↓ Contact(s) information
↓ Related XML feeds

ARMONK, N.Y. - 01 Jul 2014: IBM (NYSE: IBM) today announced that Gartner, Inc. has positioned IBM Security Systems as a leader in providing Security Information and Event Management software in the newly published Gartner Magic Quadrant for SIEM Technology. [1] This report follows the recent recognition of IBM moving up Gartner's worldwide security software rankings to the number three spot.

"We believe Gartner's recognition helps validate IBM's approach to security that focuses on helping customers benefit from security intelligence and analytics, and overcome challenges created by fragmented point solutions," said Brendan Hannigan, General Manager, IBM Security Systems. "Our IBM Security QRadar SIEM solution is also part of a broader integrated Threat Protection System that goes far beyond the traditional approaches of protection. We can now disrupt advanced persistent threats, prevent data breaches and anticipate behavioral changes in applications regardless of whether they are from known or unknown threats."

Among the 15 vendors evaluated in the report, IBM was placed furthest on the completeness of vision and highest on the ability to execute axes. With regard to completeness of vision, Gartner analysts evaluated market understanding among seven other evaluation criteria which is the "Ability of the vendor to understand buyers' wants and needs and to translate those into products and services. Vendors that show the highest degree of vision listen to and understand buyers' wants and needs, and can shape or enhance those with their added vision."

With regard to ability to execute, seven criteria are evaluated including customer experience. "Customer experience is an evaluation of product function or service within production environments. The evaluation includes ease of deployment, operation, administration, stability, scalability and vendor support capabilities. This criterion is assessed by conducting qualitative interviews of vendor-provided reference customers in combination with feedback from Gartner clients that are using or have completed competitive evaluations of the SIEM offering."

IBM Security QRadar conducts behavioral analysis of an organization's business processes and applications to help determine if potential security-related events are simple anomalies or potential threats -- all with small rates of false positives limiting the need for Chief Information Security Officer (CISO) teams to deploy unnecessary resources.

Unlike traditional SIEM, IBM Security QRadar also provides log management, anomaly detection, incident forensics, configuration and vulnerability management capabilities. It also fully integrates with IBM's Big Data and Analytics platform.

Gartner estimates, "SIEMis a $1.5 billion market that grew 16% during 2013 — with an expected growth rate of 12.4% during 2014." In the overall security software market, IBM has experienced six straight quarters of double digit growth fueled by a significant investment in organic development and the acquisition of companies, including Q1 Labs, Trusteer, Guardium, Ounce Labs, Watchfire and Fiberlink/MaaS360.

To view the full report, visit: http://ibm.co/1x5MxpW

To read a blog post on the report and its implications to the market, visit: http://ibm.co/1pQe9Lr

About IBM Security

IBM's security portfolio provides the security intelligence to help organizations holistically protect their people, data, applications and infrastructure. IBM offers solutions for identity and access management, security information and event management, database security, application development, risk management, endpoint management, next-generation intrusion protection and more. IBM operates one of the world's broadest security research and development, and delivery organizations. IBM monitors 15 billion security events per day in more than 130 countries and holds more than 3,000 security patents. For more information, please visit www.ibm.com/security, follow @IBMSecurity on Twitter or visit the IBM Security Intelligence blog.

Disclaimer: Gartner does not endorse any vendor, product or service depicted in its research publications, and does not advise technology users to select only those vendors with the highest ratings. Gartner research publications consist of the opinions of Gartner's research organization and should not be construed as statements of fact. Gartner disclaims all warranties, expressed or implied, with respect to this research, including any warranties of merchantability or fitness for a particular purpose.

###

[1] Gartner "Magic Quadrant for Security Information and Event Management" by Kelly M. Kavanagh, Mark Nicolett, Oliver Rochford, June 25, 2014

Contact(s) information
Michael Rowinski
IBM Media Relations, Security
1 (720) 395-8497
rowinski@us.ibm.com

Figure 8.1a Facts drive the news release. A digital news release from the pressroom of International Business Machines, Inc., describes hard data that reporters and consumers can ingest as relevant news. IBM and the IBM logo are trademarks of International Business Machines Corp., registered in many jurisdictions worldwide.

FOR RELEASE 2/4/13 0600EST
<<Logo Image Available>>

electrofreeze.com

Media Contact:
Mark Holden
MHolden@electrofreeze.com
309-755-4553
Website: www.electrofreeze.com

NEW ELECTRO FREEZE® LOGO AND WEBSITE INTRODUCED TO ENHANCE BRAND RECOGNITION AND HONOR HERITAGE

East Moline, IL February 4, 2013 – Electro Freeze®, a division of H.C. Duke and Son, LLC (Duke), introduced their new Electro Freeze® logo and website today, making the most dramatic change to its visual identity since 1969. "The most profound change to the logo is the EF Cone icon," said Tom Hotard, President. "Electro Freeze® is known for its premium soft serve dispensing equipment and for developing the first twist soft serve machine in 1958, a concept that revolutionized the soft serve industry. A cone image was displayed on the arch at the top of our machines in the '30s and '40s, but was never really a part of the logo." The updated corporate identity reflects the Company's history of providing soft serve frozen dessert and beverage dispensing solutions and is released in conjunction with the launch of the Company's new website. "This new site brings our solutions-based strategies to customers 24/7," continued Hotard, "and is focused on optimizing the equipment, product and customer connection for business success."

"Electro Freeze® is known for leading soft serve equipment development and we created the site to present the equipment from more of an application basis with the soft serve products," noted Penny Klingler, V.P Sales. "We partner with our customers, providing them with equipment and education enabling them to produce profit-generating menu items that will drive their success." Electro Freeze® equipment is sold and serviced through a solid distributor network of trained professionals across the United States and in 32 foreign countries.

"Our dedication to helping provide profitable solutions for customers is evidenced by our 2011-12 soft serve machine rollout with Checkers® and Rally's®," continued Klingler. "The successful rollout of their Cold Creations menu contributed significantly to the brands' category-leading sales growth over the last two years. Moreover, during the rollout, we also identified a need for an optimized shake program. Now, Checkers and Rally's are introducing our new labor-saving CS705 shake machine to both their current and new restaurants throughout their quickly growing chain."

2116 Eighth Avenue, East Moline, IL 61244 • 309.755.4553 • FAX 309.755.9858 • SALES AND SERVICE 1.800.755.4545

Figure 8.1b The news release design. This news release from the pressroom of Electro Freeze, a division of H.C. Duke and Son, LLC, offers great looking design and an engaging story. It also boasts a clean and clear with a boilerplate at the end. One possible edit is to delete the quote in the lead. In most cases, avoid putting quotes in the lead, unless the quote is the thrust of the news.

Design a print layout and a digital design for a news release template page using Microsoft Word or Adobe InDesign. Place the logo and contact information on the page. Make sure to leave plenty of room for the text. Be economical in your use of space and font size. Headlines can be 14–16 pt. Subheads should be 12–13 pt. and the body copy should be 10–11 pt.

Specs:

- One or two pages maximum with school logo, contact information, immediate release date
- Include two fictitious quotes
- Include a boilerplate about the school

Think ahead, archive your work

- Print three copies for use as interview writing samples
- Convert to PDF for your insertion into a print portfolio book and as a JPG or PNG for an online web portfolio
- Backup your native files

8.2 Public relations / Fact sheet

The fact sheet defined

The most basic PR piece is the fact sheet, which provides a chunked summary of key facts about an organization, issue, product, service, or event. Fact sheets are rich in facts and typically include statistics and hard data used as a "hook" to capture the reader's and reporter's attention.

Goal of the piece

The goal of the fact sheet is to provide a quick read for consumers and journalists alike in an effort to inform and elicit "hmm" that is interesting, which may lead to a purchase, membership to a cause, or a story idea for a journalist. Provocative facts can create buzz and attract a reporter or editor to build a story around the entire data piece. Distribute fact sheets at events such as presentations, trade shows, interviews, and press conferences. They also act as a source of background information for other marketing communications projects within the organization. They can help sell a pitch by offering additional information relevant to the audience. The editor, producer, or reporter may contact the person listed on the fact sheet to get more information or secure a segment or interview, so make sure contact information is included. In the case of an event, make sure the date, location, and time are prominent.

Specifications and size

The fact sheet can take multiple forms, with bullets, narrative paragraphs, or questions and answers (Q&A). Fact sheets are 8.5 × 11 inches (letter-size paper) — typically one page in length, sometimes two or three — or posted on a web page. Fact sheets created for print, as a PDF, are downloaded from an online pressroom, or from an event site connected to a web site. Fact sheet deployment includes direct mailings to clients and media, as well as inclusion into media kits.

Research and conceptualization

Research to develop a fact sheet involves gathering hard data that can be translated into understandable facts for the consumer, press, or internal staff. Perform secondary research to gain a reliable source group before writing facts. For companies, use government or institutional data for public issues and historical data for company information. For individuals, use verifiable information such as industry accomplishments, educational background, business highlights, and personal plateaus. Sources for research include public databases such as BLS.gov (Labor and industry statistics), Gallup.com (Gallup Polling data on politics and culture). Another source is people. People sources include experts and representing groups, which can be quantitatively researched using polling and surveys and qualitatively researched using focus groups, interviews, and observations. Build data in headings to gain a clear path to explaining the facts. For example, facts sheets use a wide variety of headings, but a few notable ones include: "Key Personnel," "Corporate Structure," "Mission," and "Products and Services" (Zappala and Carden 2010, 133).

Writing style

There are three main writing styles for fact sheets. They are bulleted list, narrative form, and Q&A (questions and answers). Each one uses essentially the same writing style, which is third person, active voice, short sentences, and devoid of hyperbole. Three critical elements must be part of the fact sheet: research, truth, and news ability, or "hook value" of the facts. It is critical to collect information on stakeholders, publics, and communication channels (Tucker, Derelian, and Rouner 1996) in order to develop strong fact sheets, regardless of the type or purpose. Once the facts are collected, assemble them by headings or sections.

Fact sheet design

The visual design of the fact sheet is similar to a company letterhead. An organization's logo and contact information make up the bulk of the design. For an online fact sheet, the navigation bar serves as the header logo. Whether the facts sheet is for print or online, keep the logo consistent with the brand guidelines. Watch your logo sizes and resolution. 300 dpi for print and 72 dpi for digital. Make sure the logo is scaled correctly and is not blurry.

Fact sheet writing checklist

- Did you *write the word facts or fact sheet somewhere on the piece?* [A]
- Did you *write strong, newsworthy facts based on credible evidence?* [B]
- Did you *provide headings that offer structure to the information?* [C]
- Did you *offer hard data that is verifiable?* [D]
- Did you *use active, concrete, short sentences and paragraphs that provide common words?* [E]
- Did you *check all the correct names, telephone numbers, and emails for further information?* [F]
- Did you *use the correct logo and placement to be consistent with the brand?* [H]
- Did you *include all dates, times, and locations for event fact sheets?* [yes or no]
- Did you *eliminate superlatives and complimentary adjectives to keep it unbiased?* [yes or no]
- Did you *reread, edit, and reread again to catch any spelling, grammar, and AP style errors?* [yes or no]

Fact Sheet
SOCIAL SECURITY

2015 SOCIAL SECURITY CHANGES

o **Cost-of-Living Adjustment (COLA):**

Based on the increase in the Consumer Price Index (CPI-W) from the third quarter of 2013 through the third quarter of 2014, Social Security and Supplemental Security Income (SSI) beneficiaries will receive a 1.7 percent COLA for 2015. Other important 2015 Social Security information is as follows:

o **Tax Rate:**

	2014	2015
Employee	7.65%	7.65%
Self-Employed	15.30%	15.30%

NOTE: The 7.65% tax rate is the combined rate for Social Security and Medicare. The Social Security portion (OASDI) is 6.20% on earnings up to the applicable taxable maximum amount (see below). The Medicare portion (HI) is 1.45% on all earnings. Also, as of January 2013, individuals with earned income of more than $200,000 ($250,000 for married couples filing jointly) pay an additional 0.9 percent in Medicare taxes. The tax rates shown above do not include the 0.9 percent.

o **Maximum Taxable Earnings:**

Social Security (OASDI only)	$117,000	$118,500
Medicare (HI only)	No Limit	

o **Quarter of Coverage:**

	$1,200	$1,220

o **Retirement Earnings Test Exempt Amounts:**

Under full retirement age	$15,480/yr. ($1,290/mo.)	$15,720/yr. ($1,310/mo.)

NOTE: One dollar in benefits will be withheld for every $2 in earnings above the limit

The year an individual reaches full retirement age	$41,400/yr. ($3,450/mo.)	$41,880/yr. ($3,490/mo.)

NOTE: Applies only to earnings for months prior to attaining full retirement age. One dollar in benefits will be withheld for every $3 in earnings above the limit. There is no limit on earnings beginning the month an individual attains full retirement age.

SSA Press Office 440 Altmeyer Building 6401 Security Blvd. Baltimore, MD 21235 410-965-8904 FAX 410-966-9973

Figure 8.2a Bulleted fact sheets offer a quick read. The Social Security Administration Fact Sheet that provides clear information to citizens and journalists.

Social Narratives
Fact Sheet

Brief Description

Social narratives (SN) are interventions that describe social situations in some detail by highlighting relevant cues and offering examples of appropriate responding. They are aimed at helping learners adjust to changes in routine and adapt their behaviors based on the social and physical cues of a situation, or to teach specific social skills or behaviors. Social narratives are individualized according to learner needs and typically are quite short, perhaps including pictures or other visual aids. Usually written in first person from the perspective of the learner, social narratives include sentences that detail the situation, provide suggestions for appropriate learner responses, and describe the thoughts and feelings of other people involved in the situation.

Qualifying Evidence

SN meets evidence-based criteria with 17 single case design studies.

Ages

According to the evidence-based studies, this intervention has been effective for preschoolers (3-5 years) to high school-age learners (15-18 years) with ASD.

Outcomes

SN can be used effectively to address social, communication, behavior, joint attention, play, school-readiness, academic, and adaptive skills.

Research Studies Poviding Evidence

Barry, L. M., & Burlew, S. B. (2004). Using social stories to teach choice and play skills to children with autism. *Focus on Autism and Other Developmental Disabilities, 19*(1), 45-51. doi: 10.1177/10883576040190010601

Bock, M. A. (2007). The impact of social-behavioral learning strategy training on the social interaction skills of four students with Asperger syndrome. *Focus on Autism and Other Developmental Disabilities, 22*(2), 88-95. doi: 10.1177/10883576070220020901

Campbell, A., & Tincani, M. (2011). The power card strategy: Strength-based intervention to increase direction following of children with autism spectrum disorder. *Journal of Positive Behavior Interventions, 13*(4), 240-249. doi: 10.1177/1098300711400608

Chan, J. M., & O'Reilly, M. F. (2008). A Social Stories™ intervention package for students with autism in inclusive classroom settings. *Journal of Applied Behavior Analysis, 41*(3), 405-409. doi: 10.1901/jaba.2008.41-405

Figure 8.2b Narrative fact sheets tell the story. A narrative based fact sheet provides paragraphs, rather than bullets. This example uses the narrative form to explain a practice used in helping children with autism.

Ebola Q&A for the public
October 2015

Questions about Ebola symptoms, treatment and contact tracing

What is Ebola?
Ebola virus disease (previously known as Ebola haemorrhagic fever) is a rare but severe disease that is caused by Ebola virus. It can result in uncontrolled bleeding, causing damage to the patient's vital organs. It was first recognised in 1976 and has caused sporadic outbreaks since in several African countries.

The virus is initially transmitted to people from wild animals and spreads in the human population through human-to-human transmission through contact with blood and body fluids.

What are the symptoms?
An infected person will typically develop a fever, headache, joint and muscle pain, sore throat, and intense muscle weakness. These symptoms start suddenly, between two and 21 days after becoming infected. Diarrhoea, vomiting, a rash, stomach pain and impaired kidney and liver function follow. The patient then bleeds internally and may also bleed from the ears, eyes, nose or mouth. Ebola virus disease is fatal in 50-90% of cases. The sooner people are given care, the better the chances that they will survive.

Who is at risk?
Anyone who cares for infected people or handles their blood or fluid samples is at risk of becoming infected. Hospital workers, laboratory workers and family members are at greatest risk. Strict infection control procedures and wearing protective clothing minimises this risk.

Can you catch Ebola by touching the skin of someone who was symptomatic?
Even with a symptomatic person, direct contact with blood or body fluids is the only way Ebola is transmitted. If the person has a fever but no other symptoms, then the level of virus is very low and unlikely to pose a risk of transmission. In later stages, all body fluids such as blood, urine, faeces, vomit, saliva and semen are infectious, with blood, faeces and vomit the most infectious. Ebola virus disease is **not** spread through ordinary social contact, such as shaking hands, travelling on public transport or sitting beside someone who is infected but who does not have any symptoms.

Figure 8.2c Q&A fact sheets. The question-and-answer-based fact sheet offers answers to direct questions that are central to an issue, product, or person. Start with a clear explanation and move toward specific instances of concern or interest.

Creative assignment

Research, write and design a fact sheet

Choose a classmate or friend and interview them to develop a list of facts for a fact sheet about them. Develop a list of questions that you feel will help build basic background information based on their life and what information they can reveal during the interview. The facts should be positive, not negative and the interviewee can decide not to answer an interview question if it is too private in nature. Once the interview is over, switch and now the interviewer becomes the client. Once the facts are collected, write up a bulleted facts sheet that lists five to seven clear, "hookable" facts. Add a little more learning to this assignment and spend one minute presenting this person to the group as if you were their PR representative via video (5 point bonus).

Specs:

- One page maximum with client (student interviewee) name, date, and the words: fact sheet at the top of the page.
- Include five to seven relevant facts in bullet form.
- Have fun creating a text-based personal logo for the top of the page.

8.3 Public relations / Backgrounder

The backgrounder defined

The backgrounder is an information piece, which provides a more detailed explanation of a subject, typically two or more pages in length and written in the style of an article, in paragraph form, as a year-by-year chronology, or as a "Q&A" structure (Zappala and Carden 2010). As the name implies, backgrounders offer background information, and they are in many cases used in conjunction with news releases in media kits to fill in gaps and offer solid research sources (Bivins 2011).

Goal of the piece

The goal of the backgrounder is to expand on a subject with concise, neutral, and factual writing. The document answers potential questions and is used to report on current issues in the organization, as part of a report to a board or shareholders, to offer a biographical sketch of someone, or to describe an internal or external situation (Tucker, Derelian, and Rouner 1996). In addition, these pieces can have value as a tool to present an organization's history with a chronological account or a description of the evolution of a person, product, or brand.

Specifications and size

The backgrounder is typically two to five pages and 8.5 × 11 inches (letter-size paper). Content dictates length, but keep it as lean as possible, with concise paragraphs and subheads if the information is better served in sections. Deployment includes direct mailings to clients and media, as well as inclusion into media kits or distribution at events such as trade shows.

Research and conceptualization

Writing a backgrounder requires multiple methods of research. Use secondary sources including old articles, brochures, news releases, and reports from inside the organization as well as external sources including media placements and personal interviews. Build the source list before writing and then look for the elements (facts, anecdotes, quotes, and first-hand accounts from interviews) that will provide you with the "meat" of the piece. Create an outline of topics with subtopics and use it to structure your account of the subject. The outline should place items in chronological order with main topics as headings and subtopics that add the information underneath.

Writing style

Backgrounder styles vary. They come in the form of articles, chronologies, or as a question and answer format, but in all cases, they begin with a concise issue statement, which describes why the issue needs addressing (Bivens 2011). In the case of a backgrounder for a person, the piece starts with a lead paragraph that sets the story direction with an introduction that typically highlights an event or accomplishment and then funnels into more extensions of the person's life, career, and impact. The backgrounder is not a product of news-writing, but it is more like technical writing, in that the structure is based on thorough explanation, rather than reporting the five ws and the h. This means that you do not use the inverted pyramid. The backgrounder should not be advertising copywriting either, but should offer a complimentary piece of information that explains or acts as a connection with a media release about something (a new product, service, event, person, or issue). It can lead the reader to action through answering questions, but cannot be a blatant sales pitch; otherwise, it loses credibility with gate-keeping media and industry folks and impact with media-literate consumers.

1. Start with a short issue statement that has resonance by identifying a problem or highlighting a situation. Briefly, state who your organization is in the context of the issue or product, what is happening, and how people and organizations are affected.
2. Present a historical overview that clearly maps the origins up to the current state of the problem or situation. Reference external sources here to build your case and offer your sources in text ("The national Child Safety Group in 1995 cited 500 accidents last year that could have been prevented with …").
3. Use subheads to break up paragraphs and structure the flow of information. One idea per paragraph and a subhead guides readers seamlessly through complex explanations and more lengthy documents beyond a page or two.
4. Discuss the issue status and prominent concerns for the future.

Backgrounder design

The visual design of the backgrounder is in report form, with a cover page and a titled, subheaded document. An organization's logo and contact information make up the cover and title pages. Keep the branding (logos and company marks) less prominent as the backgrounder should be and look like a serious report, rather than an attention-grabbing advertisement.

Backgrounder writing checklist

- Did you *open with an issue explanation?*
- Did you *base your writing on credible research and secondary evidence?*
- Did you *provide headings that offer structure to the information?*
- Did you *offer hard data that is verifiable with sources identified in text?*
- Did you *trace the history and milestones enough to provide a clear timeline?*
- Did you *check all the correct names, telephone numbers, and emails for authorship and further information?*
- Did you *use the correct logo and placement to be consistent with the brand?*   [yes or no]
- Did you *reread, edit, and reread again to catch any spelling, grammar, and AP style errors?* [yes or no]

Malaria kills. Send a net. Save a life.

CAMPAIGN BACKGROUNDER

Nothing But Nets

Nothing But Nets is a global grassroots campaign to save lives by preventing malaria, a leading killer of children in Africa. Inspired by ESPN columnist Rick Reilly, thousands of people have joined the campaign that was created by the United Nations Foundation in 2006. Founding campaign partners include the National Basketball Association's NBA Cares, The People of the United Methodist Church and *Sports Illustrated*. Other partners include AOL Black Voices, ExxonMobil, Junior Chamber International, Malaria No More, the Mark J. Gordon Foundation, Major League Soccer's MLS W.O.R.K.S., the National Basketball Association's WNBA Cares, Orkin, Rotarians' Action Group on Malaria, Time Inc. Home Entertainment, Union For Reform Judaism, Unwired Appeal, VH1 and the Wasserman Foundation.

Malaria Kills

Malaria is preventable, but infects nearly 500 million people each year and kills more than 1 million of those who become infected. Ninety percent of deaths caused by malaria occur in Africa, where the disease is a leading killer of children. Every 30 seconds a child dies from malaria. Children who are able to survive the disease are faced with physical and mental impairments, such as poor growth and development.

Moreover, every day 25 million pregnant African women risk severe illness and harm to their unborn children from a malaria infection. Malaria contributes to low birth weight among newborn infants, one of the leading risk factors for infant mortality.

Malaria incapacitates people and keeps them from working while they recover or take care of sick children. Malaria keeps countries poor. In addition to the burden on the health system, malaria illness and death cost Africa $12 billion a year in lost productivity.

Send a Net

Every $10 donation to *Nothing But Nets* goes directly toward the purchase, distribution and education about the proper use of a long-lasting insecticide-treated bed net. Bed nets work in two ways: They stop mosquitoes from biting during the night and spreading the disease, and the insecticide on the net kills the mosquitoes when they land on it, stopping them from flying on to find their next victim. Bed nets can prevent malaria transmission by 50 percent and up to 90 percent in areas with high-coverage rates. They are distributed through the Measles Initiative—a partnership led by the United Nations Foundation, the American Red Cross, U.S. Centers for Disease Control and Prevention, the World Health Organization and UNICEF. Working closely with national governments and local communities, the Measles Initiative has reached more than 500 million children in nearly 60 countries.

Save a Life

With your help, we can stop this deadly disease. Please visit www.NothingButNets.net to send a net and save a life.

Figure 8.3a The narrative backgrounder. This concise narrative backgrounder tells the story of how people and organizations are working to fight malaria. It identifies the organizations involved, highlights facts about the disease and its causes, proposes a solution, and creates urgency for action. Notice the header design, which reinforces the message.

Answers to Tough Questions
Talking Points for Community Officials

Working with media, local and State officials, and property owners, you need to be armed with answers to a variety of questions before and after a flood. The following frequently asked questions address the tough issues that are often asked, with preapproved responses to assist with your outreach efforts.

Before a Flood

"Since I don't live in a flood zone, I don't need flood insurance, right?"

Wrong. Everyone is at risk for flooding. Floods can happen anywhere, at any time. Residents who live in and outside of a high-risk area, also known as Special Flood Hazard Areas (SFHAs), should know their risk and consider protection. More than 20 percent of all flood claims are filed by people outside of mapped high-risk areas.

If you live outside of a high-risk area, you might be eligible for the low-cost Preferred Risk Policy (PRP), which includes coverage for your building and its contents.

"I have flood insurance, but after a recent flood, my personal belongings weren't covered. Why?"

Flood insurance is available for building only, contents only, and building and contents. A standard flood policy for a building will cover structural, furnace, water heater, and air-conditioner damage; flood debris cleanup; and floor surface damage, such as to carpeting and tile.

However, unless you also purchase contents coverage, items such as furniture, collectibles, clothing, jewelry, and artwork will not be covered. You should talk to your insurance agent to make sure your flood policy adequately protects your home and belongings in the event of a flood.

"Why should I purchase a flood insurance policy if the Federal Emergency Management Agency (FEMA) makes disaster assistance available after a flood?"

Disaster assistance is only available if the President declares a Federal disaster. If you qualify for disaster assistance funds, it will most likely be a loan that must be repaid, with interest. Flood insurance claims are paid even if a disaster is not declared by the President. A flood insurance policy is also more cost-effective than relying on disaster assistance. The average cost of a residential policy in 2014 was $630 annually.

"Why can't I get flood insurance if I live in a Special Flood Hazard Area (SFHA)?"

You can and should get flood insurance if you live in an SFHA. These areas are considered at high risk for flooding, and the National Flood Insurance Program (NFIP) encourages every homeowner, renter, and business owner whose building is in an SFHA to invest in flood insurance protection. Flood coverage also is available to anyone who lives in one of more than 21,800 NFIP-participating communities across the country (to find out if you live in an NFIP-participating community, visit **fema.gov/national-flood-insurance-program/national-flood-insurance-program-community-status-book**). You can call your insurance agent for more information, or visit **FloodSmart.gov** to find an agent in your area.

JUNE 2015

Figure 8.3b The talking points backgrounder. This internal FEMA backgrounder provides questions with "pre-approved" answers to assist public officials fielding tough questions during a crisis and persuade homeowners in flood hazard areas to purchase flood insurance. This document, providing background information for common questions, helps local government officials to stay on message with media and community groups.

Creative assignment

Write a historical backgrounder and Q&A backgrounder on a president

You are the PR writer for a former president who plans to go on a speaking tour. Their media kit requires a backgrounder in both narrative and Q&A formats. Choose one president and research their life and political and personal milestones. Next, build an outline of salient facts to weave together into a chronological story. Start by writing with an outline. Write the historical backgrounder in two or three pages and cite all the sources you use in MLA format. Next, extract the items that you think most relevant items the media will inquire about and develop a Q&A backgrounder that presents four to five questions about the ex-president. Offer short, acceptable answers to those questions.

8.4 Public relations / Annual report

The annual report defined

The annual report to shareholders is a document used by most public companies to disclose corporate information. It is usually a state-of-the-company report, including an opening letter from the Chief Executive Officer, financial data, operations, market segment information, new product plans, subsidiary activities, and research and development activities on future programs. There are essentially two annual reports: the 10-K annual report, which the SEC requires, and the "financially shorter" annual report that we can call it the "corporate" version), which the SEC allows companies to produce and distribute. The annual report on Form 10-K, which must be filed with the SEC, may contain more detailed information about the company's financial condition than the company's annual report and will include the annual financial statements of the company. In many cases the company annual report is a visual and promotional extension to the 10-K. The annual report should be reflective of the organization's vison and values while offering a factual, straightforward, and compelling story of the state of the company financially and functionally spotlighting the direction it is going. Although not required, many non-profit organizations develop and distribute annual reports.

Goal of the piece

The goal of the annual report is to inform and persuade the shareholder, potential shareholder, and the financial community that the organization is healthy and meeting its mission. The document is primarily an internal piece, and typically glosses over bad news and focuses on positive outcomes and directions (Bivens 2011). The financial piece of the annual report, required by law, is only a portion of the company-wide report, typically called the Shareholder Report for public corporations. The annual report is essentially a publicity tool first in that it yields great value due to its all-encompassing nature and the freedom for creativity in design and presentation.

Specifications and size

The annual report takes many visual forms, but is typically 8.5 × 11 portrait in final trim size. The forms include color or greyscale photos, or simply just black-and-white text. Annual reports mainly find distribution to shareholders, and prospects. Reporting companies must send annual reports to their shareholders when they hold annual meetings to elect directors. The document also posts to the organization website for shareholders, media, and others in the financial world.

Research and conceptualization

Writing an annual report requires extensive research on financial, historical, and public policy issues within the organization, especially their growth or impact during the past five years. Remember, the annual report is also a social tool, providing a public relations platform to illustrate commitment to a group, cause, or philosophy that is innate and drives the organization. The public relations department works with the finance, law, and executive staff to compile data for the report.

Bivens (2011, 228–229) outlined standard elements to the corporate annual report:

- Company description, name, address, company headquarters and divisions, the overall business and a summary of operations that usually take a narrative and numerical form.
- President's letter to shareholders that offers a description of annual achievements, a diagnosis of industry environments and markets, and an evaluation of future business strategies and next directions.
- Full financial review using SEC guidelines including:

    Certified financial statements for two years
    Explanation of accounting differences
    Summary of management analysis for five years
    Identification of company directors and occupations
    Stock and dividend data for two years
    Description of business and product lines
    Differences in accounting principles and financial statements
    Supplementary inflation accounting

- A narrative report on any aspect of the company

Writing style

The two main parts to the annual report that require the skills of a writer are the president's letter and the narrative report. Most of the document is devoted to tables, figures, charts, photographs, which require a designer's hand with the assistance of a writer to provide snippets, important stats, and captions.

Both the president's letter and the narrative use numerical data to make the case and provide the meat of the message to readers. However, there is an opportunity in both pieces to craft highly engaging communication that espouses truth, ethics, and credibility for the organization. Here are a few approaches to consider when executing annual report writing:

1. President's letters can weave statistics with messages that create an honest, straightforward entry by the president of the organization's current state. They can also be number-free and offer a more visionary focus, rather than a business-environment approach as many do.
2. Narrative reports (under MD&A) should encompass the entire organization, its people, products, and philosophies coordinated with each other to offer a cohesive story of the company over the past year and previous years in which past plans have now come to fruition.
3. Write in a style that the average person can understand. Use data to support narrative elements by stating an idea and then using a statistic to support the concept. Think about the shareholder who wants to learn about the company.
4. Eliminate jargon and hyperbole so that the presented data is without confusion and spin.

Annual report design format

The visual design of the annual report can be conservative, moderate, or liberal. Reports are ouput to PDF files for web downloads, which allows the publication to maintain design integrity from print to the online platform. Design styles depend on the organization, but the sections are typical. The Inc.com encyclopedia ("Annual Reports" 2004) describes the order of sections at a minimum:

Company description
List products and markets served and provide a basic understanding of what the company does.

The letter
This may be called a number of things including: Letter to Shareholders, Chairman's Message, President's Letter, CEO Letter, or Executive Letter.

Management's discussion and analysis (MD&A)
The narrative driven overview of the company's financial performance in the language of business: sales, profit margins, operating income, and net income, capital expenditures, cash flow, changes in working capital, and items under examination. It also offers a forward-looking display of future opportunity for the company.

Financial summary
Provides key data from the statements of income, financial position, and cash flow for a number of years.

Management/directors
Clear lists the management of the company and its board of directors, including their backgrounds and business experience.

Investor information
Company's address and phone number, the stock transfer agent, dividend and stock price information, and the next annual meeting date.

How to start the design
If you need a starting point for a layout, create three columns in Word or InDesign. Close the box down so that it fills only half a page and leaving a healthy portion of white space above for headings and images that relate to each section of the report. Then add text to the text box and carefully decide on placement of section headings and images.

Annual report checklist

- Did you *follow the standard annual report design format?*
- Did you *include SEC required financial data?*
- Did you *provide headings that offer structure to the information?*
- Did you *offer hard data that is verifiable with sources identified in the text?*
- Did you *trace the accomplishments, issues, and milestones?*
- Did you *check photos for quality and rights clearance?*
- Did you *check all the correct names, telephone numbers, web addresses, and location for accuracy?*
- Did you *use the correct logo and placement to be consistent with the brand?* [yes or no]
- Did you *reread, edit, and reread again to catch any spelling, grammar, and data errors?* [yes or no]

Figure 8.4a A striking promotional and information tool. This hip annual report offers plenty of data beautifully integrated with engaging design. Design by Paula Scher, Pentagram. Reproduced with kind permission of Pentagram.

Figure 8.4b Show the strengths in the report. This annual report highlights the most important parts of the university, students and faculty, with the theme of learning evident. Design by Turnstyle. Reproduced with kind permission of Turnstyle.

Creative assignment

Create a mock annual report design for your favorite sports team

Pretend you are the PR writer for a sports team that is going to go public. Your job is to research the accomplishments of this team and gather data, both numerical and narrative, to use in an original mock four-to-eight-page annual report design. You will complete the first three sections of the report to illustrate your design and writing abilities.

1. *Company description*
   List products and markets served and provide a basic understanding of what the company does.
2. *The letter*
   Write a president's letter from the team owner based on data. Write about the past, current, and future forward visions and how they offer a bright future.
3. *The MD&A*
   Write and design one to two narrative spreads (MD&A) that offer a glimpse into the successes (or failures) of the team, stadium stats, player milestones, and stadium/building information (capacity, history, championships). Do this in small multiples of facts and chunk form, with short paragraphs that are packed with information explaining data and its relevance (see the Public Theater example above).
4. Add any other sections you want (company information or achievements).
5. Package the writing with images pulled from the team website or media sources.
6. Final output: develop a cover (with team logo), letter page design, and interior MD&A design and package together, then print and bind with spiral or comb binding.

8.5 Public relations / Infographic

The infographic defined

The infographic (short for information graphics) is a visually driven graphic that displays data. Built on statistical data mainly, the communication piece is invaluable in making pertinent connections when used to make a "visual argument." The infographic must contain visual components and cannot be literally all text. Visualizations are infographics also as they are visual representations of data sets. As a standalone piece or displayed in a social media site post, web page, guide, manual, or annual report, the infographic creates a potent tool for persuasive, fact-driven communication in a visually thirsty society.

Goal of the piece

The goal of the infographic is to inform and persuade with factual data, without being overly subjective. It fits as a public relations piece because it makes a case for something and tries to use the power of text and image to relay the information and hidden persuasive message. It must be informative and provide credible information backed by citations of sources.

Specifications and size

The infographic is not a typical page size in many cases. On paper, working more like a poster of sorts, the infographic can be as small as 8.5 × 11 and as long as 24 inches in length, sometimes more.

Most infographics see digital distribution on a web site or social media platforms. In this case, there are also some limits to sizes. Patel (2015) recommends a manageable length and size of infographics with limits at around 8000 pixels or so. However, he notes that longer infographics degrade the user's attention span, but also cites infographics at over 24,000 pixels in length as seeming to be too long. The idea is to offer the most valuable information in a flowing layout that brings essential information points into one cohesive form.

Research and conceptualization

Writing the infographic requires the same diligence in research as a backgrounder or fact sheet. It incorporates facts that derive from relevant, credible sources including government data, published academic and scientific findings, industry reporting, and institutional studies.

1. The ideas for developing an infographic should first start with the question: "What is the issue and what critical data points need highlighting in the piece?" Investigate a topic with exploratory research to find the big chunks of data connected to the issue.
2. Once you have an idea of the issue's big components (these become the headings), list each in a column. Go back and research the smaller more detailed elements (stats and other data pieces) that make up the larger issue. Use secondary sources to build fact bases.
3. Below each main component, create a numbered list of the detailed facts for each column. This allows you to create a flow of facts for each important element, which will become the facts in each section of the infographic.

Writing style

The two main parts to the infographic are the information and the graphic, which both need writing and design. Writing consists of short paragraphs and bylines that serve as rhetoric on the argument. This is in the form of bulleted text. Next to the images that house statistics and data visualizations, the writing is in chunks, which are small nuggets of information from one to six lines or so, without long prose. These snippets get right to the point and describe the highlighted fact in an active way, with clear explanation. Typography contained in infographics consists of numbers and textual data chunks, which need precision and care in their interpretation and assembly. The text should have connective visual tissue in the form of graphics that support the ideas behind the text and numbers. Tell the story in each chunk and paragraph with care, not wasting words or obscuring true meanings.

Infographic design format

The infographic design is a patching together of small visualizations for each data point, within one, two, or three columns; the more prominent facts take up more room. It is primarily show, rather than just tell with infographics, demanding the creator to focus on how the information visualizes and flows through the design. Infographic designs can differ, but a typical approach is a top-down structure consisting of a headline and a variety of grid layouts. The visual principles of BANGPP (balance, alignment, negative space, grouping, proximity, perimeter edge) are a good way to analyze the design and improve its visual impact. Look at a variety of infographics to determine a design or use an online DIY template application to provide the design elements. The designs of the infographics you see on the web are created using Adobe InDesign, Illustrator, and Adobe Photoshop. They can even be created using PowerPoint or Word, but the design flexibility is a little limited compared to the Adobe applications for creating artwork. Use what you are comfortable with and focus on the

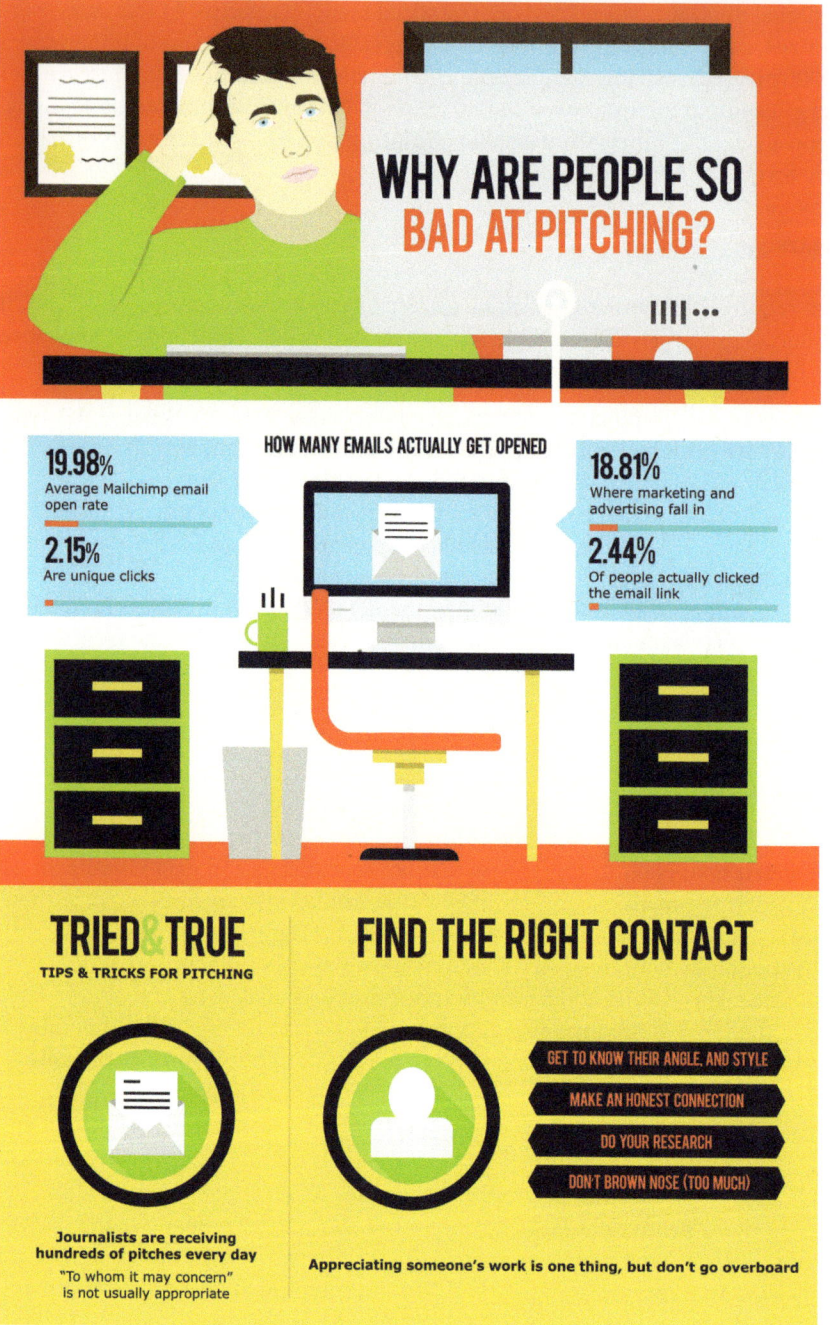

Figure 8.5a
Infographics should deliver and explain information so that it has context and meaning. This infographic educates uses a variety of qualitative and quantitative data and information to explain how to pitch the media. Design by Nowsourcing.com. Courtesy Brian Wallace. Reproduced with kind permission of Brian Wallace.

Figure 8.5a (Continued)

quality of the design and accuracy and clarity of the writing. The infographic is traditionally long, with a letter-size print page or average web page wide (8.5 × 11 inches or around 800–1000 pixels) of information length being too short in most cases. The physical specs can vary as mentioned, but it is a good exercise to start with 8.5 × 14 inches for print and 1000 × 5000 pixels for online infographics. Ultimately, content will dictate length, but having a defined space may help you filter out facts less important to the argument. The design should have flow and move the viewer through the thought process (2015), rather than just a barrage of data and information that obscures the main point.

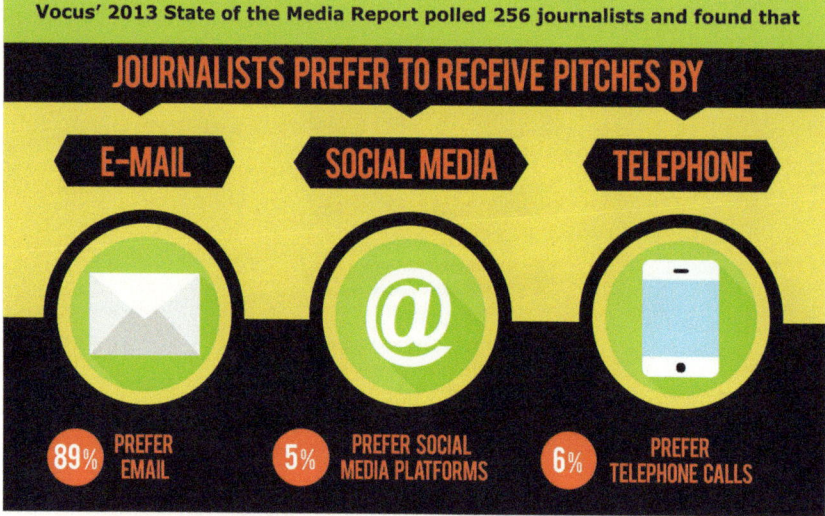

Figure 8.5a
(Continued)

Infographic checklist

– Did you *compile facts that are relevant to the issue and the argument of the piece?*
– Did you *include a host of data representations that connects the issue?*
– Did you *follow BANGPP design checklist to review the layout?*
– Did you *include a prominent, attention-grabbing headline?*
– Did you *check the facts, their accuracy, and sources?*
– Did you *cite the sources of the statistics?*
– Did you *present the argument and data with a flow with each section having a headline?*
– Did you *check all the numbers, names, telephone numbers, web addresses, and locations for accuracy?*
– Did you *use the correct logo and placement to be consistent with the brand?* [yes or no]
– Did you *reread, edit, and reread again to catch any spelling, grammar, and data errors?* [yes or no]

Figure 8.5a
(Continued)

Figure 8.5a
(Continued)

Creative assignment

Create an infographic on your favorite public charity
Pretend you are the communications manager for a public charity in any country. Your job is to research the accomplishments of the charity and gather data, both numerical and narrative, to use in an original infographic design. Your goal is to show how the charity is helping people and what financial factors are vital to continued success.

1. *Choose a charity and research*
   Perform multiple research methods to build a data set for the project. You need more information than can fit in the graphic so gather as many statistical and representative elements as possible.
2. *Organize the facts*
   Outline headings and list facts with sources for each data "snippet" that occupies the infographic.
3. *Design format and layout*
   Use a print format (8.5 × 14 inches) and convert to PDF or JPG for online distribution. Look at other infographics online to get inspiration and design ideas. Do not take the design verbatim, but use the visual concepts in your own design, utilizing your own approaches to type and color, in addition to the unique data.
4. *Add identity*
   Brand it with the organization logo. Add the line "Designed by _____." (With your name)
5. *Add references and credits*
   List all sources in a common bibliographic format as well as give credit to illustrators, photographers, writers, and designers.

Chapter references

"Annual Reports." 2004. Inc.com. http://www.inc.com/encyclopedia/annual-reports.html (last accessed November 12, 2016).

Bivins, Thomas H. 2011. *Public Relations Writing: The Essentials of Style and Format.* Boston, MA: McGraw-Hill.

Bly, Robert W. 2005. *The Copywriter's Handbook: A Step-by-Step Guide to Writing Copy That Sells.* New York: Holt, Henry & Company.

Clark, Roy Peter. 2006. *Writing Tools: 50 Essential Strategies for Every Writer.* 1st ed. New York: Little, Brown.

Haynes, Jim, and Doug, Newsom. 2014. *Exercise Workbook for Newsom/Haynes' Public Relations Writing: Form and Style.* 10th ed. Boston, MA: Wadsworth Publishing Company.

Patel, Neil. "12 Infographic Tips That You Wish You Knew Years Ago." Accessed December 8, 2015. https://blog.kissmetrics.com/12-infographic-tips/.

Tucker, Kerry, Doris Derelian, and Donna Rouner. 1996. *Public Relations Writing: An Issue-Driven Behavioral Approach.* 2nd ed. Upper Saddle River, NJ: Prentice Hall.

Zappala, Joseph M., and Ann R. Carden. 2010. *Public Relations Writing Worktext: A Practical Guide for the Profession.* 3rd ed. New York: Routledge.

9

Social Media for Marketing, Advertising, and Public Relations
Kara Alaimo Ph.D.

Chapter objectives

After completing this chapter, you should be able to:

- understand social media concepts in marketing, advertising and public relations.
- analyze how research, writing, and design drive social media.
- evaluate content for social media communication.
- create social media content across multiple platforms.

9.1 Social media defined

Merriam-Webster (2016) defines social media as "forms of electronic communication (as web sites for social networking and microblogging) through which users create online communities to share information, ideas, personal messages, and other content (as videos)." Social media is used in marketing, advertising, and public relations to communicate directly with target audiences.

From a public relations perspective, the beauty of social media is that it is unfiltered: In contrast to the traditional press, your messages are not translated through the lenses of reporters and you do not necessarily need to pay for advertising. From a marketing and advertising perspective, social media is valuable because it allows you to "nanotarget" individuals based upon highly defined criteria such as their jobs, interests, employers, marital status, education, gender, and age. Kerpen (2011, 25) describes nanotargeting as "a concept similar to hypertargeting but with search criteria so narrow that you can target one individual among hundreds of millions." (He once took out an ad targeted specifically to one person: his wife!)

The other characteristic that makes social media unique is that audiences talk back. This makes social media a powerful tool for building relationships with key constituencies — but also allows crises and criticism of your organization to spread like wildfire.

Some of the most important social media platforms include:

Facebook: Users of the world's largest social network create profiles and post text, images, videos, and links (Statista 2015). Content can be marked as public or viewable only by friends with whom they connect. Facebook's users are the oldest among the eight largest non-Chinese social networks (Mander 2014).

Twitter: Users create a Twitter handle (which starts with a @) and "tweet" content. Posts must be 140 characters or less. Tweets are publicly available and show up in the feeds of anyone who follows a particular user's Twitter handle.

Instagram: Users share photos and videos, using special filters to design attractive images.

Snapchat: This platform's youthful users share "stories" that their friends can view for 24 hours and send one another text, picture, and/or video messages called "snaps" which disappear after a few seconds.

YouTube: YouTube has a billion monthly active users — in other words, one in seven people on Earth use the platform monthly to watch videos (Billboard 2015). Anyone can create a YouTube channel and post videos.

LinkedIn: This social media platform is used primarily for professional networking. Users create profiles listing their resumes and can post blogs on LinkedIn Pulse. This is a great way of establishing your organization and its executives as thought leaders in your field and reaching prospective employees.

Yelp: Users post publicly-available and often very influential reviews of organizations.

9.2 Research for social media

The first step in using social media for marketing, advertising, and public relations is identifying your target audience(s). Marketers often develop "personas" to help them identify with the people they are targeting. As Alaimo (2017) writes:

> Pam Didner [...], a global content marketing strategist based in the U.S., explains that [...] a persona is a semi-fictional representation of your ideal audience member based upon research and real data about your existing customers or supporters. Be specific about your persona. For example, simply thinking of millennials is not specific enough; your persona might be a four-year college student in the U.S. named Kelly. [...] It is not uncommon for a global organization to have ten or more personas!

Once you know who you wish to reach, gather as much information as you can find about them online. For example, what are their habits? What do they seem to like? What do they dislike? According to Alaimo (2017),

> Michael Leis [...], Senior Vice President of Social Strategy at Digitas Health Lifebrands, [...] recommends getting to know subcultures on social media "through the kind of artifacts they leave behind," such as their profile photos, how users are connected to one another, what they are talking about beyond your subject matter, and how they are using technology.

This will give you a sense of the type of content that will appeal to them. However, you will need to experiment. Keep careful track of how your followers respond to particular types of content, mediums, and channels.

9.3 Writing for social media

Be pithy. Even if you are not working under Twitter's character restraints, attention spans on social media are limited. Brevity is key. When including a hyperlink in a Tweet, take advantage of the website www.bit.ly, which will create a shorter version of the link for you — leaving more room for your own characters.

Don't bombard your followers or be overly promotional. People go on social media to engage and have fun. If you are overly promotional, you will turn people off and they will stop following you. The top two reasons people "unlike" a brand on Facebook are because the company posts too frequently and because users' walls become too crowded with marketing posts (ExactTarget 2011, 13).

Create diverse content. The third most common reason people "unlike" a brand on Facebook is because "the content became repetitive or boring over time" (ExactTarget 2011, 13). Have some fun. Make your posts humorous, unexpected, interesting, and helpful.

Be interactive. Social media is about engaging in dialogue and building relationships with your followers. Encourage two-way communication by asking questions of your audiences. Kerpen (2011, 120) notes that asking questions creates marketing value in these four ways:

1. Helping you guide the social media conversation without appearing forceful
2. Allowing you to become consumer-centric marketers rather than brand-centered marketers
3. Demonstrating that you value openness, honesty, and feedback (three values customers and prospects universally hold in high regard).
4. Showing that you care about what your customers have to say.

Get your users to create content for you. Consider running contests in which you ask audiences to post photos or stories. This gets others to do your work for you and can help you acquire compelling content. It can also drive purchasing. A study of contests run by a Canadian loyalty program called AirMiles which asked social media users to post content in exchange for the chance to win prizes found that people who posted spent more money — not just immediately, but also over time (Malthouse, Vandenbosch, and Kim 2014).

9.4 Social media design

Be visual. Compelling images get 94 percent more views than content that does not contain visuals, while posting videos can double users' engagement (Cohen 2013; Signore 2013). As Walter and Gioglio (2014, 15) note, "research indicates that consumer interest in visual content isn't necessarily just a preference; it's actually easier and faster for humans to process. The right picture can go further than just telling your story visually; it can make you feel emotions, evoke memories, and even make you act differently."

There are many different ways of being visual. Walter and Gioglio (2014, 24) note that your options include

- Photography
- Graphs and drawings
- User-generated images
- Collages
- Images with text overlays: captions, quotes, and stats
- Word photos
- Memes
- Postcards and e-card

Use infographics (also known as data visualizations) to display written content in visual form. This can often make complicated topics easier to understand. Websites such as Infogr.am, InfoActive,

Easel.ly, Piktochart, Visual.ly, and iCharts can help you create them (Walter and Gioglio 2014, 165).

Use GIFs. Walter and Gioglio (2014, 33) explain that "GIFs, or pictures in the Graphics Interchange Format, allow users to store multiple images or still frames from a video in an image file, bringing the image to life with animation."

9.5 Social media checklist

Post regularly. One study found that, in order to be perceived as credible and trustworthy, brands must keep their social media pages active (Fussell Sisco and McCorkindale 2013).

Curate content. Didner recommends not only creating content but also sharing content created by others with your followers. Doing so "shows that you care for your target audience, not just [about] sharing your own point of view" (Alaimo 2015).

Respond to criticism in real time. Garcia (2012, 117) explains that, when organizations experience a crisis, they must respond within 45 minutes in order to have the opportunity to define the situation for themselves. Otherwise, "given the proliferation of social networking and citizen journalism, the likelihood is that more and more people will hear very quickly about the issue, with critics, adversaries, commentators, and others defining the issue, your motives, and your actions." Be sure to have responses at the ready for the types of crises that could befall your organization so that you can post immediately.

Show who is posting on behalf of an organization. As Rybalko and Seltzer (2010, 339) explain, this facilitates two-way communication and engagement because "it is no longer some faceless public relations department or corporate entity communicating with the publics but an actual person."

Post your social media policies. As Kerpen (2011, 77) explains, "the do-not-delete (DND) rule states that "unless a comment is obscene, profane, bigoted, or contains someone's personal and private information, never delete it from a social network." Having your policy posted will make it easier to justify any criticism that results if you do need to take down a post.

Partner with content creators. In addition to creating content for your brand, you can pay individuals who have large followings on social media to create and/or share your content. Companies such as FameBit, Grapevine and Reelio help match brands with content creators.

9.6 Social media examples

Social media for marketing

Fiestagram

To promote the innovative technology on the Ford Fiesta, the automaker launched its "Fiestagram" campaign on social media. Each week for six weeks, the company announced a new hashtag related to the car's features, such as #entry and #hidden. Social media users were invited to post photos on Instagram with the hashtag of the week and #Fiestagram for a chance to win prizes including the car itself. Klamm (2012) notes that Ford gained over 120,000 new Facebook followers as a result of the campaign and that "importantly, Ford successfully attracted the attention of its target demographic: fashion, style and technology trendsetters."

Figure 9.1 Using multiple platforms to build buzz. Fiestagram, on Facebook, promoted the Ford Fiesta to fans and leveraged Instagram to continue the social media connection.

Social media for advertising

Send your Facebook profile to Cape Town

When Cape Town Tourism hired Ogilvy & Mather to promote the city of Cape Town, South Africa as a tourism destination, Ogilvy & Mather created a social media campaign to send people's Facebook profiles to South Africa. The campaign allowed users to create their own itineraries for their trips. Users received boarding passes and individually tailored content in their Facebook timelines, including photos, videos, and status updates which they could "like" and share with their friends. At the end of the campaign, participants received personalized videos of their vacations; users also received gifts in the mail from places their profiles had visited. According to Ogilvy & Mather (2016):

> Over 350 thousand people engaged with the campaign. Over 44 000 friends were invited to send their Facebook profiles to Cape Town. Table Mountain [a major tourist attraction] received its highest volume of visitors in 83 years. Cape Town received a 4% increase in Tourism over the festive season. Next year's bookings for holidays in Cape Town are up by 118%.

Social media for public relations

Airbnb's #OneLessStranger campaign

To promote its company which asks people to open their homes to strangers, Airbnb launched a campaign in 2015 asking people to perform random acts of kindness for strangers and document them on social media using the hashtag #OneLessStranger. The company gave about $10 each to 100,000 Airbnb users to help them perform the acts. As a result of the campaign, the company saw 91,000 new guests, 22,000 new hosts, and 1 million properties added to its website globally.

Figure 9.2 Virtual holiday. Send your Facebook profile to Cape Town.

9.7 Chapter exercises

1 *Evaluate a campaign*
   Critically analyze a social media campaign implemented by a major corporation, non-profit organization, or government entity over the past two years. Critically evaluate the campaign's content and explain whether the campaign was successful (include hard data). Describe the recommendations you would make if this organization were your client.

2 *Social media campaign*
   Develop a social media campaign for a company, non-profit organization, or government entity of your choosing. The completed assignment should consist of the following elements:
   (a) Description of the organization and the specific, measurable goal(s) of your social media campaign (for example: increase sales by a certain percentage)
   (b) Description of your social media strategy and the specific platforms you will utilize
   (c) Description of the content you will create

Chapter references

Airbnb. 2015. "Creating #OneLessStranger: Stories of Belonging." http://blog.airbnb.com/creating-onelessstranger-stories-belonging/
Alaimo, Kara. 2015. "Build Compelling Brand Identities: A Memo from the Social Media Strategies Summit." *The Public Relations Strategist*, July 20. https://www.prsa.org/Intelligence/TheStrategist/Articles/view/11129/1113/Build_Compelling_Brand_Identities_A_Memo_From_the#.Vb0qR_mAH6A
Alaimo, Kara. 2017. *Pitch, Tweet, or Engage on the Street: How to Practice Global Public Relations and Strategic Communication*. New York: Routledge.

Billboard. 2015. "YouTube Reportedly Still Unprofitable, Even with 1 Billion Monthly Users." February 26. http://www.billboard.com/articles/business/6487324/youtube-profit-1-billion-monthly-users-4-billion-revenue

Cohen, Heidi. 2013. "5 facts prove visual content is a guaranteed winner!" March 12, 2015. http://heidicohen.com/5-facts-prove-visual-content-is-a-guaranteed-winner/

ExactTarget. 2011. "The Social Breakup." http://www.exacttarget.com/resources/SFF8.pdf

Garcia, Helio Fred. 2012. *The Power of Communication: Skills to Build Trust, Inspire Loyalty, and Lead Effectively*. Upper Saddle River, NJ: Pearson Education.

Kerpen, Dave. 2011. *Likeable Social Media: How to Delight Your Customers, Create an Irresistible Brand, and Be Generally Amazing on Facebook (and Other Social Networks)*. New York: McGraw Hill.

Klamm, Dan. 2012. "How Ford Used Instagram to Promote the Fiesta's High-Tech Features." Mashable, February 2, 2015. http://mashable.com/2012/02/02/ford-fiesta-instagram/#.XT4pMOohsq1

Mander, Jason. 2014. "Tumblr and Instagram Have the Youngest Audiences." GlobalWebIndex, December 1, 2015. http://www.globalwebindex.net/blog/tumblr-instagram-audiences

Ogilvy & Mather South Africa. 2016. "Cape Town Tourism — Send Your Profile to Cape Town Case Study." http://oi.co.za/cape-town-tourism-send-your-facebook-profile-to-cape-town/ (accessed November 12, 2016)

Rybalko, Svetlana, and Trent Seltzer. 2010. "Dialogic Communication in 140 Characters or Less: How Fortune 500 Companies Engage Stakeholders Using Twitter." *Public Relations Review* 36: 336–341.

Signore, Scott. 2013. "3 Ways Video Helps with PR." *Ragan's PR Daily*, June 5. http://www.prdaily.com/Main/Articles/3_ways_video_helps_with_PR_14600.aspx

Sisco, Hilary Fussell, and Tina McCorkindale. 2013. "Communicating 'Pink': An Analysis of the Communication Strategies, Transparency, and Credibility of Breast Cancer Social Media Sites." *International Journal of Nonprofit and Voluntary Sector Marketing* 18: 287–301.

Statista. 2015. "Leading Social Networks Worldwide as of March 2015, Ranked by Number of Active Users (in Millions)." http://www.statista.com/statistics/272014/global-social-networks-ranked-by-number-of-users/ (accessed November 12, 2016).

Walter, Ekaterina, and Jessica Gioglio. 2014. *The Power of Visual Storytelling: How to Use Visuals, Videos, and Social Media to Market your Brand*. New York: McGraw Hill Education.

Index

.EPS 108, 110, 112, 119, 120
.PNG 112, 120
.TIF 81, 112, 120
"Bezier" Pen tool 110
"you" viewpoint 18, 27, 160

a

achromatic color schemes 75
activate verbs 17
Adobe Illustrator 54, 68, 108, 109, 117, 120, 133
Adobe InDesign 54, 61, 80, 104, 120, 168, 183
Adobe Photoshop 54, 58, 59, 101, 106, 107, 111, 116, 120, 121, 183
advertising 2, 3, 6, 9, 16, 18, 67, 145
alignment 49, 51, 130
alpha channels 111
analogous color schemes 75
animation 47, 99, 160
apostrophes 37
art director 46, 103
artists' color wheel 72

b

balance 49, 51
BANGPP 49, 50, 62
Barthes, Roland 1
baseline shift 56
Bernbach, Bill 18
bitmap image 67
black-plus color schemes 77
bleed 54, 132
Bly, Robert (Bob) 18, 23
body text 58
brainstorming 91
Burnett, Leo 18

c

central route 12
character attributes 55
chunking 27
client creative brief 84
color 71
comma 32
common writing mistakes to avoid 39
complimentary color schemes 75
concentric circle technique 20
conjunction 33
consistency 63
contrasting color schemes 75
convergent thinking 89
copywriting 17
corporate identity 18, 45, 118
creative directors 46

d

design ethnography 95
design managers 46
diary method 96
digital imaging 72, 79, 106
DiMarco 4, 19, 62
display type 58, 61
divergent thinking 89
drop cap 58
Dwiggin, W.A. 17

e

editing 30, 31
elaboration likelihood model 10
e-learning 104
em dash 35, 36
ethnography 95
explaining a process 15

Communications Writing and Design: The Integrated Manual for Marketing, Advertising, and Public Relations,
First Edition. John DiMarco.
© 2017 John DiMarco. Published 2017 by John Wiley & Sons, Ltd.

f

FAB   18, 138
fact checking and accuracy   23
faux type effects   57
features, advantages, and benefits (*see* FAB)
field notes   107, 108
five steps to find writing success   39
flowcharting   27
font   54, 55–59 (*see also* typography)
Foucault, Michel   4, 5

g

GACMIST   19, 41, 85, 86
Glaser, Milton   6, 148, 149
grayscale color   77
grids   49, 80
grouping   54
GROWN   39, 40

h

hanging indent   58
headlines   19, 29, 147
hierarchy   58
hyphenate   80

i

icon, index, and symbol   6
illustration   108
image proportions   79
imperative mood   17
indentation (typographic)   58
infographic   182
integrated sitemaps   100, 101
interviews   95
inverted pyramid   16, 24

j

journalism   22, 24, 164
justification   54, 66

k

kerning   56

l

layout   47
leading   56, 66
leads   24
legibility   61
letter spacing   66
Lewis, E. St. Elmo   18

linguistic value   3, 6
Lupton and Miller   3

m

marcom   9
market research   88, 89
marketing communications   9, 13, 45
mind mapping   94
monochromatic color schemes   74
motion graphics   69, 70
MS PowerPoint   104
MS Word   104

n

negative space   54
news quality   23
news writing   21, 42
non-fiction writing   9, 12, 16

o

opacity   111
Ogilvy, David   18
outline   27

p

Pantone color   77, 118
paragraph   58
paragraph attributes   57
parenthetic expressions   32
paths   111
perfect progressive tense   26
perfect tense   26
perimeter edge   54
peripheral route   12
persuasive copywriting   17, 41
photography   67
photojournalism   67
present tense   20, 26
presentations   104
product packaging   133
progressive disclosure   27
progressive tense   26
project scope   86
proximity (design)   54
proximity (news)   23

q

qualitative   88, 90
quantitative   3, 88

quotation marks   36
quotes and attribution   24

r
raster file   67
raw material   12
readability   60
reductionist   32
research   2
resolution   79, 118
rhetoric   10
rule of thirds   49

s
san serif   55
selections   111
semiotics   5
serif   66, 80
simple tense   26
six-color wheel   72
sketching   97
slogans   20
small multiples   27
space after paragraph   58
space before paragraph   58
storyboards   99
Strunk and White   31, 34
style sheets   62

t
technical communication   13
technical writing   13, 40
thumbnails   97
touchpoints   9
tracking   56
type and background   66
type posture   65
type size   65
type weight   65
typography   54

u
unobtrusive observation   95
use of order   16
USP   18

v
vector images   109
verb tense   26
visual research   89, 101
visual structure   27
visualizations   13, 17, 182

w
word-processing   104
word spacing   66